1-09

In Memory

of

Helen

Stadnyk

GARDENS

Gardens

An Essay on the Human Condition

Robert Pogue Harrison

THE UNIVERSITY OF CHICAGO PRESS

Chicago and London

ROBERT POGUE HARRISON
is the Rosina Pierotti Professor of Italian
Literature at Stanford University. He is the author
of *Forests* (1992) and *The Dominion of the Dead*
(2003), both published by the University
of Chicago Press.

The University of Chicago Press, Chicago 60637
The University of Chicago Press, Ltd., London
© 2008 by The University of Chicago
All rights reserved. Published 2008
Printed in the United States of America

17 16 15 14 13 12 11 10 09 08   2 3 4 5

ISBN-13: 978-0-226-31789-2 (cloth)
ISBN-10: 0-226-31789-7 (cloth)

Library of Congress Cataloging-in-Publication Data

Harrison, Robert Pogue.
Gardens : an essay on the human condition / Robert Pogue Harrison.
p. cm.
Includes bibliographical references and index.
ISBN-13: 978-0-226-31789-2 (alk. paper)
ISBN-10: 0-226-31789-7 (alk. paper)
1. Gardens–History. I. Title.
SB451.H37 2008
712–dc22
2007039946

∞ The paper used in this publication
meets the minimum requirements of
the American National Standard
for Information Sciences—Permanence
of Paper for Printed Library
Materials, ANSI Z39.48-1992.

To Eve and her daughters

CONTENTS

APPENDIXES

PREFACE

HUMAN BEINGS ARE NOT MADE TO LOOK TOO INTENTLY at the Medusa head of history—its rage, death, and endless suffering. This is not a shortcoming on our part; on the contrary, our reluctance to let history's realities petrify us underlies much of what makes human life bearable: our religious impulses, our poetic and utopian imagination, our moral ideals, our metaphysical projections, our storytelling, our aesthetic transfigurations of the real, our passion for games, our delight in nature. Albert Camus once remarked, "Poverty kept me from thinking all was well under the sun and in history; the sun taught me that history is not everything" (Camus, 7)—to which we could add that if ever history were to become everything, we would all succumb to madness.

For Camus it was the sun, but more often than not in Western culture it has been the garden, whether real or imaginary, that has provided sanctuary from the frenzy and tumult of history. As the reader of this book will discover, such gardens may be as far away as Gilgamesh's garden of the gods or the Greeks' Isles of the Blessed or Dante's Garden of Eden at the top of the mountain of Purgatory; or they may be on the margins of the earthly city, like Plato's Academy or the Garden School of Epicurus or the villas of Boccaccio's *Decameron*; they may even open up in the middle of the city, like the Jardin du Luxembourg in Paris or the Villa Borghese in Rome or the homeless gardens in New York City. Yet one way or another, in their very concept and their humanly created environments, gardens stand as a kind of haven, if not a kind of heaven.

Yet human gardens, however self-enclosed their world may be, invariably take their stand in history, if only as a counterforce to history's deleterious drives. When Voltaire ends *Candide* with the famous declaration "Il faut cultiver notre jardin," the garden in question must be viewed against the background of the wars, pestilence, and natural disasters evoked by the novel. The emphasis on cultivation is essential. It is *because* we are thrown into history that we must cultivate our garden. In an immortal Eden there is no need to cultivate, since all is pregiven there spontaneously. Our human gardens may appear to us like little openings onto paradise in the midst of the fallen world, yet the fact that we must create, maintain, and care for them is the mark of their postlapsarian provenance. History without gardens would be a wasteland. A garden severed from history would be superfluous.

The gardens that have graced this mortal Eden of ours are the best evidence of humanity's reason for being on Earth. Where history unleashes its destructive and annihilating forces, we must, if we are to preserve our sanity, to say nothing of our humanity, work against and in spite of them. We must seek out healing or redemptive forces and allow them to grow in us. That is what it means to tend our garden. The pronominal adjective used by Voltaire—*notre*—points to the world we share in common. This is the world of plurality that takes shapes through the power of human action. *Notre jardin* is never a garden of merely private concerns into which one escapes from the real; it is that plot of soil on the earth, within the self, or amid the social collective, where the cultural, ethical, and civic virtues that save reality from its own worst impulses are cultivated. Those virtues are always *ours*.

The reader who wanders around in this book will pass through many different kinds of gardens—real, mythical, historical, literary— yet all of the gardens under consideration here are, to one degree or another, part of the story of *notre jardin*. If history consists finally of the terrifying, ongoing, and endless conflict between the forces of destruction and the forces of cultivation, then this book weighs in on the side of the latter. In so doing it strives to participate in the gardener's vocation of care.

ACKNOWLEDGMENTS

WHILE THIS BOOK IS DEDICATED TO WOMANKIND IN GEN-
eral, I would like to thank in particular those *donne ch'avete intelletto
d'amore* who helped me bring it to fruition through their inspiration,
perceptive readings of early drafts, creative suggestions, and encour-
agement. They include Susan Stewart, Heather Webb, Andrea Nightingale, Weixing Su, Marjorie Perloff, and Shirley Hazzard. I would
also like to thank Christa for leading me into the garden of the sun
many years ago, and Molly for the garden on Gerona Road where all
my books have germinated and flowered.

As for "men of my own gender," as Woody Allen once called them,
I am grateful to Joshua Landy and Dan Edelstein for their readings
of, and comments on, the work in progress, and to David Lummus
for his invaluable help as my research assistant. Thanks also to Sepp
Gumbrecht for his stalwart friendship.

I was once told by John Freccero never to personalize the institution, yet I can't help thanking Stanford University for all it's done for
me over the years.

⁓ I ⁓

The Vocation of Care

FOR MILLENNIA AND THROUGHOUT WORLD CULTURES, our predecessors conceived of human happiness in its perfected state as a garden existence. It is impossible to say whether the first earthly paradises of the cultural imagination drew their inspiration from real, humanly cultivated gardens or whether they in fact inspired, at least in part, the art of gardening in its earliest aesthetic flourishes. Certainly there was no empirical precedent for the mineral "garden of the gods" in the *Epic of Gilgamesh*, described in these terms: "All round Gilgamesh stood bushes bearing gems . . . there was fruit of carnelian with the vine hanging from it, beautiful to look at; lapis lazuli leaves hung thick with fruit, sweet to see. For thorns and thistles there were haematite and rare stones, agate, and pearls from out of the sea" (*The Epic of Gilgamesh*, 100). In this oldest of literary works to have come down to us, there is not one but *two* fantastic gardens. Dilmun, or "the garden of the sun," lies beyond the great mountains and bodies of water that surround the world of mortals. Here Utnapishtim enjoys the fruits of his exceptional existence. To him alone among humans have the gods granted everlasting life, and with it repose, peace, and harmony with nature. Gilgamesh succeeds in reaching that garden after a trying and desperate journey, only to be forced to return to the tragedies and cares of Uruk, his earthly city, for immortality is denied him.

More precisely, immortal *life* is denied him. For immortality comes in several forms—fame, foundational acts, the enduring memorials of art and scripture—while unending life is the fabulous privilege of only a select few. Among the Greeks, Meneleus was granted this special exemption from death, with direct transport to the gardens of Elysium at the far end of the earth,

> where there is made the easiest life for mortals,
> for there is no snow, nor much winter there, nor is there ever
> rain, but always the stream of the Ocean sends up breezes
> of the West Wind blowing briskly for the refreshment of mortals.
> This, because Helen is yours and you [Meneleus] are son in law therefore
> to Zeus.
>
> (*Odyssey*, 4.565–69)

For all her unmatched beauty, it seems that this was what the great fuss over Helen was really all about: whoever possessed her was destined for the Isles of the Blest rather than the gloom of Hades. Men have gone to war for less compelling reasons.

By comparison to the ghostly condition of the shades in Hades, a full-bodied existence in Elysium is enviable, to be sure, if only because happiness outside of the body is very difficult for human beings to imagine and impossible for them to desire. (One can desire *deliverance* from the body, and desire it ardently, but that is another matter.) Even the beatified souls in Dante's Paradise anticipate with surplus of joy the resurrection of their flesh at the end of time. Their bliss is in fact imperfect until they recover in time what time has robbed them of: the bodily matter with which their personal identity and appearance were bound up. Until the restitution of their bodies at the end of time, the blessed in Dante's heaven cannot properly *recognize* one another, which they long to do with their loved ones (in *Paradiso* 14 [61–66], Dante writes of two groups of saints he meets: "So ready and eager to cry 'Amen' / did one chorus and the other seem to me / that clearly they showed their desire for their dead bodies, / not just for themselves but for their mothers, / and fathers, and the others who were dear to them / before they became sempiternal flames"). In that respect all of us on Earth, insofar as we are in our body, are more blessed than the saints in Dante's heaven. It is otherwise with the likes of Meneleus and Utnapishtim and Adam and Eve before the fall. The fantastic garden worlds of myth are places where the elect can possess the gift of their bodies without paying the price for the body's passions, can enjoy the fruits of the earth without being touched by the death and disease that afflicts all things earthly, can soak up the sunlight so sorely missed by their colleagues in Hades without being scorched by its excess and intensity. For a very long time, this endless prolongation of bodily life in a gardenlike environment, protected from the tribulations of pain and mortality, was the ultimate image of the good life.

Or was it? Certainly Meneleus is in no hurry to sail off to his islands in the stream. Telemachus finds him still reigning over his kingdom, a man among men. There is no doubt that Meneleus would opt for Elysium over Hades—any of us would—but would he gladly give up his worldly life prematurely for that garden existence? It seems not. Why? Because earthly paradises like Dilmun and Elysium offer ease and perpetual spring at the cost of an absolute isolation from the world of mortals—isolation from friends, family, city, and the ongoing story of human action and endeavor. Exile from both the private and public spheres of human interaction is a sorry condition, especially for a polis-loving people like the Greeks. It deprives one of both the cares and the consolations of mortal life, to which most of us are more attached than we may ever suspect. To go on living in such isolated gardens, human beings must either denature themselves like Utnapishtim, who is no longer fully human after so many centuries with no human companionship other than his wife, or else succumb to the melancholia that afflicts the inhabitants of Dante's Elysian Fields in Limbo, where, as Virgil tells the pilgrim, *sanza speme vivemo in disio*, we live in desire without hope. As Thoreau puts it in *Walden*, "Be it life or death, we crave only reality" (61). If Meneleus took that craving for reality with him to Elysium, his everlasting life there is a mixed blessing indeed.

But why are we posing hypothetical questions to Meneleus when we can consult Odysseus directly? Kalpyso's island, where Odysseus was marooned for several years, is in every respect a kind of Isle of the Blest in the far-flung reaches of the ocean: a flourishing green environment with fountains, vines, violets, and birds. Here is how Homer describes the scene, which is prototypical of many subsequent such idyllic scenes in Western literature:

> She was singing inside the cave with a sweet voice
> as she went up and down the loom and wove with a golden shuttle.
> There was a growth of grove around the cavern, flourishing,
> alder was there, and the black poplar, and fragrant cypress,
> and there were birds with spreading wings who made their nests
>   in it,
> little owls, and hawks, and birds of the sea with long beaks
> who are like ravens, but all their work is on the sea water;
> and right about the hollow cavern extended a flourishing
> growth of vine that ripened with grape clusters. Next to it
> there were four fountains, and each of them ran shining water,
> each next to each, but turned to run in sundry directions;
> and round about there were meadows growing soft with parsley
> and violets, and even a god who came into that place
> would have admired what he saw, his heart delighted within him.

(5.63–74)

This is the enchanted place that Kalpyso invites Odysseus to share with her permanently, with an offer of immortality included in the bargain. But we know the story: cold to her offer, Odysseus spends all his days on the desolate seashore with his back to the earthly paradise, sulking, weeping, yearning for his homecoming to harsh and craggy

Ithaca and his aging wife. Nothing can console him for his exile from "the land of his fathers" with its travails and responsibilities. Kalypso is incapable of stilling within his breast his desire to repossess the coordinates of his human identity, of which he is stripped on her garden island. Even the certainty that death awaits him after a few decades of life on Ithaca cannot persuade him to give up his desire to return to that very different, much more austere island.

What Odysseus longs for on Kalypso's island—what keeps him in a state of exile there—is a life of care. More precisely, he longs for the world in which human care finds its fulfillment; in his case, that is the world of family, homeland, and genealogy. Care, which is bound to worldliness, does not know what to do with itself in a worldless garden in the middle of the ocean. It is the alienated core of care in his human heart that sends Odysseus to the shore every morning and keeps him out of place in the unreal environment of Kalypso's island. "If you only knew in your own heart how many hardships / you were fated to undergo before getting back to your country, / you would stay here with me and be lord of this household and be an immortal" (5.206–9). But Kalypso is a goddess—a "shining goddess" at that—and she scarcely can understand the extent to which Odysseus, insofar as he is human, is *held fast* by care, despite or perhaps even because of the burdens that care imposes on him.

If Homer's Odysseus remains to this day an archetype of the mortal human, it is because of the way he is embraced by care in all its unyielding tenacity. An ancient parable has come down to us across the ages which speaks eloquently of the powerful hold that the goddess Cura has on human nature:

Once when Care was crossing a river, she saw some clay; she thoughtfully took up a piece and began to shape it. While she was meditating on what she had made, Jupiter came by. Care asked him to give it spirit, and this he gladly granted. But when she wanted her name to be bestowed upon it, he forbade this, and demanded that it be given his name instead. While Care and

Jupiter were disputing, Earth arose and desired that her own name be conferred on the creature, since she had furnished it with part of her body. They asked Saturn to be their arbiter, and he made the following decision, which seemed a just one: "Since you, Jupiter, have given its spirit, you shall receive that spirit at its death; and since you, Earth, have given its body, you shall receive its body. But since Care first shaped this creature, she shall possess it as long as it lives. And because there is now a dispute among you as to its name, let it be called *homo*, for it is made out of *humus* (earth)."

Until such time as Jupiter receives its spirit and Earth its body, the ensouled matter of *homo* belongs to Cura, who "holds" him for as long as he lives (*Cura teneat, quamdiu vixerit*). If Odysseus is a poetic character for Care's hold on humans, we can understand why he cannot lie easily in Kalypso's arms. Another less joyful goddess than Kalypso already has her claims on him, calling him back to a land plowed, cultivated, and cared for by his fathers and forefathers. Given that Cura formed *homo* out of humus, it is only "natural" that her creature should direct his care primarily toward the earth from which his living substance derives. Thus it is above all the *land* of his fathers—as Homer repeats on several occasions—that calls Odysseus back to Ithaca. We must understand the concept of land not merely geographically but materially, as the soil cultivated by his ancestors and the earth in which their dead bodies are buried.

Had Odysseus been forced to remain on Kalypso's island for the rest of his endless days, and had he not lost his humanity in the process, he most likely would have taken to gardening, no matter how redundant such an activity might have been in that environment. For human beings like Odysseus, who are held fast by care, have an irrepressible need to devote themselves to something. A garden that comes into being through one's own labor and tending efforts is very different from the fantastical gardens where things preexist spontaneously, offering themselves gratuitously for enjoyment. And if we could have seen Odysseus's patch of cultivated ground from the air, it would have appeared to us as a kind of oasis—an oasis of care—in the landscape of Kalypso's home world. For unlike earthly paradises, human-made gardens that are brought into and maintained in being by cultivation retain a signature of the human agency to which they owe their existence. Call it the mark of Cura.

While care is a constant, interminable condition for human beings, specific human cares represent dilemmas or intrigues that are resolved in due time, the way the plots of stories are resolved in due time. Odysseus experiences the endless delays that keep him from returning home as so much *wasted time*—for it is only with his return home that the temporal process of resolution can resume its proper course. His story cannot go forward in Kalypso's earthly paradise, for the latter is outside both world and time. Thus it represents a suspension of the action by which his present cares—which revolve around reclaiming his kingdom and household—work toward an outcome. No resolution is final, of course, and even death does not put an end to certain cares (as Odysseus learns when he talks to the shades of his dead companions in the land of the dead). Yet in general human beings experience time as the working out of one care after another.

Here too we find a correlation between care and gardens. A humanly created garden comes into being in and through time. It is planned by the gardener in advance, then it is seeded or cultivated accordingly, and in due time it yields its fruits or intended gratifications. Meanwhile the gardener is beset by new cares day in and day out. For like a story, a garden has its own developing plot, as it were, whose intrigues keep the caretaker under more or less constant pressure. The true gardener is always "the constant gardener."

The account of the creation of humankind in the Cura fable has certain affinities with, but also marked differences from, the account in Genesis, where the Maker of heaven and earth created a naive, slow-witted Adam and put him in the Garden of Eden, presumably so that Adam could "keep" the garden, but more likely (judging from the evidence) to shield him from the reality of the world, as parents are sometimes wont to do with their children. If he had wanted to make Adam and Eve keepers of the garden, God should have created them as caretakers; instead he created them as beneficiaries, deprived of the commitment that drives a gardener to keep his or her garden. It would seem that it was precisely this overprotection on God's part that caused Adam and Eve to find themselves completely defenseless when it came to the serpent's blandishments. Despite God's best intentions, it was a failure of foresight on his part (a failure of gardening, as it were) to think that Adam and Eve could become caretakers of Eden's privileged environment when he, God, went to such lengths to make sure that his creatures had not a care in the world.

Indeed, with what insouciance Adam and Eve performed the momentous act that gets them expelled from Eden! "And when the woman saw that the tree was good for food, and that it was pleasant to the eyes, and a tree to be desired to make one wise, she took of the fruit thereof, and did eat, and gave also unto her husband with her; and he did eat" (Genesis 3:6). It was not overbearing pride, nor irrepressible curiosity, nor rebellion against God, nor even the heady thrill of transgression which caused them to lose, in one mindless instant, their innocence. The act was committed without fear and trembling, without the dramas of temptation or fascination of the forbidden, in fact without any real motivation at all. *It was out of sheer carelessness* that they did it. And how could it have been otherwise, given that God had given them no occasion to acquire a sense of responsibility? The problem with Adam and Eve in the garden was not so much their will to disobedience as their casual, thoughtless, and childlike disposition. It was a disposition *without resistance*, as the serpent quickly discovered upon his first attempt to get Eve to eat the forbidden fruit.

It was only after the fall that Adam acquired a measure of resiliency and character. In Eden, Adam was unburdened by worries but incapable of devotion. Everything was there *for him* (including his wife). After his exile, *he* was there for all things, for it was only by dedicating himself that he could render humanly inhabitable an environment that did not exist for his pleasure and that exacted from him his daily labor.

Out of this extension of self into the world was born the love of something other than oneself (hence was born human culture as such). For all that it cost future humankind, the *felix culpa* of our mythic progenitors accomplished at least this much: it made life matter. For humans are fully human only when things matter. Nothing was at stake for Adam and Eve in the garden until suddenly, in one decisive moment of self-revelation, *everything* was at stake. Such were the garden's impossible alternatives: live in moral oblivion within its limits or gain a sense of reality at the cost of being thrown out.

But did we not pay a terrible price—toil, pain and death—for our humanization? That is exactly the wrong question to ask. The question rather is whether the gift of the Garden of Eden—for Eden was a gift—was wasted on us prior to the price we paid through our expulsion. As Yeats said of hearts: "Hearts are not had as gifts but hearts are earned / by those that are not entirely beautiful" ("Prayer for My Daughter," in *The Collected Poems of W. B. Yeats*, 188). In Eden, Adam and Eve were altogether too beautiful, hence also heartless. They had to earn their human hearts outside of the garden, if only in order to learn what beauty is, as well as what a gift it is. Through Adam and Eve we lost a gift but earned a heart, and in many ways we are still earning our heart, just as we are still learning that most of what the earth offers—despite its claims on our labor—has the character of something freely given rather than aggressively acquired.

Eden was a paradise for contemplation, but before Adam and Eve could know the quiet ecstasy of contemplation, they had to be thrown into the thick of the *vita activa*. The *vita activa*, if we adopt Hannah Arendt's concept of it, consists of labor, work, and action. Labor is the endless and inglorious toil by which we secure our biological survival, symbolized by the sweat of Adam's brow as he renders the earth fruitful, contending against blight, drought, and disaster. But biological survival alone does not make us human. What distinguishes us in our humanity is the fact that we inhabit relatively permanent worlds that precede our birth and outlast our death, binding the generations together in a historical continuum. These worlds, with their transgenerational things, houses, cities, institutions, and artworks, are brought into being by work. While labor secures our survival, work builds the worlds that make us historical. The historical world, in turn, serves as the stage for human action, the deeds and speech through which human beings realize their potential for freedom and affirm their dignity in the radiance of the public sphere. Without action, human work is meaningless and labor is fruitless. Action is the self-affirmation of the human before the witness of the gods and the judgment of one's fellow humans.

Whether one subscribes to Arendt's threefold schematization or not, it is clear that a life of action, pervaded through and through by care, is what has always rendered human life meaningful. Only in the context of such meaningfulness could the experience of life acquire a depth and density denied to our primal ancestors in the garden. To put it differently: only our expulsion from Eden, and the fall into the *vita activa* that ensued from it, could make us fit for and worthy of the gift of life, to say nothing of the gift of Eden. Adam and Eve were not ready—they lacked the maturity—to become keepers of the garden. To become keepers they first would have to become gardeners. It was only by leaving the Garden of Eden behind that they could realize their potential to become cultivators and givers, instead of mere consumers and receivers.

Regarding that potential, we must not forget that Adam, like *homo* in the Cura fable, was made out of clay, out of earth, out of humus. It's doubtful whether any creature made of such matter could ever, in his deeper nature, be at home in a garden where everything is provided. Someone of Adam's constitution cannot help but hear in the earth a call to self-realization through the activation of care. His need to engage the earth, to make it his place of habitation, if only by submitting himself to its laws—this need would explain why Adam's sojourn in Eden was at bottom a form of exile and why the expulsion was a form of repatriation.

Once Jupiter breathed spirit into the matter out of which *homo* was composed, it became a living human substance that was as spiritual in essence as it was material. In its humic unity it lent itself to cultivation, or more precisely to self-cultivation. That is why the human spirit, like the earth that gives *homo* his body, is a garden of sorts—not an Edenic garden handed over to us for our delectation but one that owes its fruits to the provisions of human care and solicitation. That is also why human culture in its manifold domestic, institutional, and poetic expressions owes its flowering to the seed of a fallen Adam. Immortal life with Kalypso or in Elysium or in the garden of the sun has its distinct appeal, to be sure, yet human beings hold nothing more dear than what they bring into being, or maintain in being, through their own cultivating efforts. This despite the fact that many among us still consider our expulsion from Eden a curse rather than a blessing.

When Dante reaches the Garden of Eden at the top of the mountain of Purgatory, he brings his full humanity with him into that recovered earthly paradise, having gained entrance to it by way of a laborious moral self-discipline that took him down through the circles of hell and up the reformatory terraces of Purgatory. Nor does his journey reach its endpoint in Eden, for it continues up through the celestial spheres toward some other more exalted garden: the great celestial rose of the heavenly Empyrium. Yet never once during his journey does the poet-pilgrim lose or forfeit the human care in his heart. Even in the upper reaches of Paradise, the fate of human history—what human beings make of it through their own devotion or dereliction—remains his paramount concern. In particular it is the fate of Italy, which Dante calls the "garden of the empire," which dominates the poet's concern throughout the poem. To speak of Italy as a garden that is being laid to waste through neglect and moral turpitude takes the garden out of Eden and puts it back onto a mortal earth, where gardens come into being through the tending of human care and where they are not immune from the ravages of winter, disease, decay, and death. If Dante is a quintessentially human poet, it is because the *giardino dello 'mperio* mattered more to him in the end than either Eden or the celestial Rose. If we are not able to keep our garden, if we are not able to take care of our mortal human world, heaven and salvation are vain.

To affirm that the fall was a repatriation and a blessing is not to deny that there is an element of curse in the human condition. Care burdens us with many indignities. The tragedies that befall us (or that we inflict upon ourselves) are undeniably beyond all natural proportion. We have a seemingly infinite capacity for misery. Yet if the human race is cursed, it is not so much because we have been thrown into suffering and mortality, nor because we have a deeper capacity for suffering than other creatures, but rather because we take suffering and mortality to be confirmations of the curse rather than the preconditions of human self-realization. At the same time, we have a tendency to associate this putative curse with the earth, to see the earth as the matrix of pain, death, corruption, and tragedy rather than the matrix of life, growth, appearance, and form. It is no doubt a curse that we do not properly value what has been freely given as long as we are its daily beneficiaries.

Achilles, who had a warrior's contempt for life while he lived, must die and enter Hades before coming to realize that a slave living under the sun is more blessed than any lord of the dead. When Odysseus attempts to console him during his visit to the underworld, Achilles will have none of it: "O shining Odysseus," he says, "never try to console me for dying. / I would rather follow the plow as thrall to another / man, one with no land allotted him and not much to live on, / than be a king over all the perished dead" (11.488–91). The slave is happier than the shade not because he is *laboring* under the sun but because he is *under the sun*, that is to say on the earth. To the dead Achilles, the former seems like a small price to pay for the latter ("I am no longer there under the light of the sun," he declares regretfully [498]). That such knowledge almost invariably comes too late is part of care's curse. Care engages and commits us, yet it also has a way of blinding us. Achilles' eyes are open for a moment, but even in death they close quickly again when his passions are enflamed. In no time at all, while speaking to Odysseus, he imagines himself back in the world of the living not as a slave but as his former formidable and destructive self, killing his enemies and perpetuating the cycle of reciprocal violence:

"[I] am not the man I used to be once, when in wide Troad / I killed the best of their people, fighting for the Argives. If only / for a little while I could come like that to the house of my father, / my force and invincible hands would terrify such men / as use force on him and keep him away from his rightful honors" (499–504). That our cares bind us so passionately to our living world, that they are so tenacious as to continue to torment us after death, and that they blind us to the everyday blessings we so sorely miss once we lose them—this suggests that there may be something incorrigible in our nature which no amount of self-cultivation will overcome or transfigure. It is impossible to know for sure, for the story of human care has not yet come to an end.

❧ 2 ❧

Eve

NOT ADAM BUT EVE IS THE PROGENITOR OF HUMANITY. It's thanks to her that there are progenitors at all; and if she must take the blame, she should also get the credit for the fall, which turned husband into father and wife into mother and gave the childlike couple a parental maturity they could never have achieved had they not found their way out of the cradle of Eden.

There was no fecundity of generations in Eden, for where there is no death there is no birth either. Hence the expulsion was not only a fall into mortality but also into what Hannah Arendt calls natality (initiation of new beginnings through human action). If Adam and Eve are in some mythic way Odysseus's primal ancestors, it is because ancestry, or the succession of generations, first became possible through their exile. By choosing mortality over immortality, Odysseus repeats the fateful choice of Eve and thereby proves himself an adult. Through that choice he reaffirms his place in the genealogical line that makes of mortal life a link in the chain of generations. It is in "the land of his fathers" that Odysseus finally reclaims his human identity as the son of Laertus and Antiklea, the husband of Penelope, and the father of Telemachus. Eve is the one who got boys to become men and who turned Adam into Odysseus.

Eve was created as a Stepford wife of sorts, with everything provided for her except the prospect of self-fulfillment. The same was true in a sense for Adam, yet, impressionistically speaking, Adam seems to have been less at odds with the mindless, ultimately feckless happiness the couple was expected to enjoy in their garden of ennui. This is evidenced by the intuition of several artists who have depicted the expulsion, among them Menabuoi, Masaccio, Michelangelo, and Dürer. It is invariably Eve who is moving toward the exit first, as if in eager anticipation of her new future, while Adam, looking forlorn, seems in dread of what's to come. Adam, no doubt, did not hear the call of natality as intensely as Eve. Indeed, it is doubtful that he ever would have taken the initiative when it came to the forbidden fruit. Eve's transgression was the first true instance of human action, properly understood. It was in itself already an act of motherhood, for through it she gave birth to the mortal human self, which realizes its potential in the unfolding of time, be it through work, procreation, art, or the contemplation of things divine. God should have foreseen that by endowing Eve with a potential for natality, he made it painful for her to endure the sterile mirror which the garden reflected back on her. One of Eve's daughters, the contemporary poet Eleanor Wilner, describes that mirror in her poem "A Moralized Nature Is like a Garden without Flowers":

> And nowhere
> in the shade of those *verboten* trees
> was there the feel of cool moss under-
> foot, never the veils of water, gravity-
> flung, over the edges of granite
> into the dark that pools below;
> no restless hours, no bug-eyed frog
> unfurling its tongue, no insect hum
> of propagation, no busy messengers
> of change; nowhere the silken bowers of
> desire into which the bees plunge, drunk
> on nectar and remembrance

of the larval honey-lust—
no flowers in Eden, not even one.

(*The Girl with Bees in Her Hair*, 46)

One is inclined to trust Wilner's ancestral memory of the place, for no one has a deeper reach into primal things than the author of *The Girl with Bees in Her Hair*, from which these verses come. That there was fruit without flowers in Eden suggests that a frozen, temporally suspended nature reigned there, a nature without beauty, for where things are unmarked by time, propagation, and death, they are devoid of beauty. Whatever else it may figure, beauty first and foremost figures mortality. But in Eden, as Wilner goes on to state,

> . . . beauty had no figure, no sacred
> symmetry, centripetal, slowly opening
> to a half-glimpsed nuclear core—
> hot enough to melt the arctic,
> icebound heart of God.
>
> One flower in Eden
> and they would have known
> beauty, and knowing that,
> would know how beauty fades.

> (Ibid.)

According to Diotima in Plato's *Symposium*, all our prospects of self-fulfillment, including motherhood, are linked to beauty: "All of us are pregnant, Socrates, both in body and in soul, and, as soon as we come to a certain age, we naturally desire to give birth. No one can possibly give birth in [the presence of] anything ugly; only in something beautiful" (*Symposium*, 53). The soul's pregnancy (from which come virtues, deeds, and ideas) is as much under the sway of finitude as is bodily pregnancy. All procreation is a response to, and in fact arises from, the imminence of death. "A promise of happiness" is how Stendhal defined beauty. Here we might revise the definition as follows: a promise of future. Yet knowing how beauty fades, we know that even the future will eventually fade into the past. We know this because, thanks to Eve, we have been handed over to both our mortal and natal selves, and through her we have all become pregnant, be it in body or in soul or in some other fashion. In other words, we have that in us that desires to become part of the world, to enter the flow of time, to achieve form and come into appearance. What is not finite cannot give birth, nor be filled with a promise of the future.

In Eden, Adam and Eve were in some sense blind to the world. In a single instant Eve changed that, and suddenly she became all eyes. It was as if Eve, in tasting the fruit, ate of the seed of mortal time, from which human vision was born. Here is how Wilner, in another poem titled "The Apple Was a Northern Invention," describes that moment when the human eye was opened:

> When she ate the pomegranate,
> it was as if every seed
> with its wet red shining coat
> of sweet flesh clinging to the dark core
> was one of nature's eyes. Afterward,
> it was nature that was blind,
> and she who was wild
> with vision, condemned
> to see what was before her, and behind.

(*The Girl with Bees in Her Hair*, 33)

Here too we should trust Wilner that the fruit was a pomegranate, not an apple. The pomegranate is the fruit of Persephone, who descends into the underworld for six months a year, during autumn and winter, like seeds that lie dormant in the earth until they blossom forth with new life in the spring, when Persephone rejoins her mother Demeter (goddess of agriculture) in the light. As time in its past and future recesses is opened up, the wonder of nature's appearances is disclosed to human eyes. Things appear in their immersion in time, their presence is now accented by the penumbra. A recessive background has entered the picture, allowing the phenomenon to appear all the more decisively and mysteriously as what it is. This shattering of immediacy—the fall away from complete absorption in things—was the first consequence of Eve's action. It is such shattering that gives appearances the penetrating depths in and out of which their forms, colors, and textures shine forth in their enigma.

The pomegranate, it seems, was not averse to lending its eyes to this woman. Who knows? Maybe it was the inner will of nature as a whole that operated through the serpent—its inner will to hand its beauty over to human testimony, to become visible in its phenomenal plenitude through a transfer of its eyes, that is to say its seed, to Eve's natal vision. In this scenario the serpent, tempting Eve to open her eyes, shed her blindness, and be reborn in a new visionary self, would figure as the ambassador of the world's desire to render its bounties manifest. Only something as bottomless and inexhaustible as human care could take proper custody of the wonders of the visible world. If Eve became "wild with vision" at the moment of her initiation, it's because it takes a wilderness of pain, travail, death, and suffering to give opacity and mood to appearances. Care is the price of an inexhaustible richness—the revelation of the visible world—and Eve did not bargain her way out of it. For that we owe her thanks, and more.

To Wilner's testament of beauty's evanescence we may add that of Wallace Stevens, a quintessential postlapsarian poet, whose poem "Sunday Morning" takes us inside the mind of a young woman who, in her earthly garden, meditates on matters of life and death, feeling the pathos of nature's beauty in her mortal yet seminal body. During her silent ruminations she asks herself:

Is there no change of death in paradise?
Does ripe fruit never fall? Or do the boughs
Hang always heavy in that perfect sky,
Unchanging, yet so like our perishing earth,
With rivers like our own that seek for seas
They never find, the same receding shores
That never touch with inarticulate pang?
Why set the pear upon those river-banks
Or spice the shores with odors of the plum?
Alas, that they should wear our colors there,
The silken weavings of our afternoons,
And pick the strings of our insipid lutes!
Death is the mother of beauty, mystical,
Within whose burning bosom we devise
Our earthly mothers waiting, sleeplessly.

(*The Collected Poems*, 69)

If one may attribute a deeper motive to Eve's tasting of the fruit, it was no doubt a burning desire to become an "earthly mother" of this sort. To make the fruit *real*—that was the underlying urge. If death is the price one pays for fruitfulness, so be it. But it is wrong to speak of death as the price of life's vitality. Death is rather its matrix. Stevens puts it even more peremptorily: "Death is the mother of beauty; hence from her, / Alone, shall come fulfillment to our dreams / And our desires." Death neither negates nor terminates life but gives birth to its intrinsic potentialities, especially its potentiality for appearance. Without death there is no fulfillment of potentiality nor any ever-changing moods of the phenomenal world. Death may "strew the leaves / Of sure obliteration on our paths," yet "she makes the willows shiver in the sun / For maidens who were wont to sit and gaze / Upon the grass." Death sets things into motion, including our desires. It is the generative source of nature's ceaseless movement into form:

Passions of rain, or moods in falling snow;
Grievings in loneliness, or unsubdued
Elations when the forest blooms; gusty
Emotions on wet roads on autumn nights;
All pleasures and all pains, remembering
The bough of summer and the winter branch,
These are the measures destined for her soul.

(Ibid., 67)

Appearances owe their poignancy—their almost unbearable beauty and power of evocation—to the time-boundedness that attunes us to the fleeting moods of nature. (In Stevens's poetry, the wind is the principal figure for this primordial movement of time in nature.) Such attunement was not possible in Eden. Since its environment was not mortalized, its garden was essentially moodless, precisely because care, which imbues nature with its pathos and passions, had no place there. Nature blossoms forth in a tapestry of soul-penetrating appearances only where human care pervades the picture, giving the visible world the power to intimate rather than merely indicate. Nature in its recessive presence intimates. Nature scenes along the walls of an airport terminal merely indicate. It is the difference between appearance and image. Where the phenomenon does not rise up from penumbral depths, there is no appearance as such but only a static and reified image. Nor are there any genuine moods that attune us to the rain or falling snow, the bough of summer and the winter branch. "These are the measures destined for her soul," writes Stevens. In Eden images never attained the status of appearances, not because the place itself was deficient but because Eve was not yet wild with vision. It took the pomegranate to give depth to her perception.

The woman in Stevens's poem, sitting in a "sunny chair" listening to "the green freedom of a cockatoo," is content to watch the spring unfold with its "wakened birds" that test "the reality of misty fields" before they move on elsewhere. She says to herself: "But in contentment I still feel the need of some imperishable bliss." Any descendant of Eve is bound to feel such a need, for we should not forget that, unlike Adam, Eve was created in Eden. She had a paradisiac origin, and through her we have all inherited a native nostalgia for some imperishable bliss. Yet if the latter were ever to be granted us, were we ever to experience it, we would lose at once both the bliss and the need for it. This is not to say that in our fallenness we have contentment instead of bliss. It is to say that the mortal earth's beauty contains a promise of imperishable bliss that is intimately familiar to us, even though its prospect is forever receding, leaving in its stead "comforts of the sun," "pungent fruit," "April's green," and other "things to be cherished like the thought of heaven."

When the seeds of the forbidden fruit of the pomegranate embedded themselves in her body, Eve became a seminal creature with natural affinities to the humic depths where plant life first takes root. This affinity in all probability made of Eve the first *human* gardener after the expulsion from Eden. She became a planter and cultivator of seeds even as she retained her Edenic nostalgias. In the Middle Ages it was believed that the seeds of all the plant species of the earth had, like Eve, their origins in Eden (Dante, *Purgatory* 28.109–20)—a hypothesis that every devoted human gardener, as well as every lover of nature's plant life, is inclined to believe. But unlike Eden, where there was no need for it, the mortal earth lends itself to cultivation through the act of delving into its soil. Pablo Neruda's "Oda a la jardinera," or "Ode to the Gardener," gives us a portrait of a latter-day Eve in her primordial role as gardener:

> Yes, I knew that your hands were
> a blossoming clove and the silver
> lily:
> you had something to do
> with the soil
> and the flowering of the earth;
> however,

when
I saw you delve and dig
to uncouple the cobble
and limber the roots,
I knew straight away,
my dear cultivator,
that
not only
your hands
but also your heart
were of the earth,
and that there
you were shaping
a thing
that was forever
your own,
touching
the humid
door
through which
swirl
the seeds . . .

Even so, love,
your hand
of water,
your heart of earth,
give
fertility
and power to my songs

Touching
my breast
while I sleep,
trees bloom

on my dream.
I waken and open my eyes,
and you have planted
inside of me
the darkening stars
that rise
in my song . . .

(Neruda, *Selected Poems*, 252–53)

In Genesis God puts Adam to sleep and extracts one of his ribs, from which he forges Eve (that she is made of bone already links her to the fecundity of death). In Milton's retelling of the story in *Paradise Lost* (8.452–90), Adam dreams of Eve during his slumber, and when he awakes, she stands before him in her full-bodied reality. That dream is the subtext of John Keats's reference to Adam in his famous letter on the imagination, which he wrote to Benjamin Bailey on November 22, 1817: "The Imagination may be compared to Adam's dream—he awoke and found it truth. . . . And yet such a fate can only befall those who delight in sensation rather than hunger as you do after Truth. Adam's dream will do here and seems to be a conviction that Imagination and its empyreal reflection is the same as human Life and its spiritual repetition" (*Selected Letters of John Keats*, 54). It is impossible to say for certain whether Neruda's "Ode to a Gardener" contains an allusion either to Milton's *Paradise Lost* or to Keats's letter, yet it is clear that what his *jardinera* shapes and plants with her hands has its "spiritual repetition" in the poet's song.

That Neruda's speaker is an Adam figure is clear, if only because of the allusion to the *jardinera* touching his breast while he sleeps. This act of hers casts her in the role of Creator—a terrestrial, as it were, and not divine Creator. The radical element in Neruda's poem is precisely the primordial creative power it accords to Eve's seminal activity, of which the poet's songs are but an outcrop or offshoot. Far from being a creature of the poet's imagination, the gardener here engenders and fosters that imagination. Trees bloom in his dream thanks to her having planted them there, just as it is she who plants in him the "darkening stars / that rise / in my songs." Her hands, not God's, do the primordial work of shaping, sowing, and fecundating. These same hands touch the doors between life and death, through which "swirl the seeds" of what grows both in the soil and in the soul.

Historically speaking, Neruda's "Ode to the Gardener" is exceptional in its sentiment, for Eve has hardly been loved enough by her descendants for planting the seeds of our humanity, of the human heart in its labors of love ("My heart labors at the roots," says the poet in the last verse of the poem). Which is to say she has not been loved enough with the terrestrial love she brought into the world ("So it is, my gardener: / our love / is / terrestrial"). What we lost through her act of transgression we never really possessed, for without a human heart in its midst, Eden was wasted on us. Yet the mortal earth into which we fell was not.

⁓ 3 ⁓

The Human Gardener

IN THE FABLE RECOUNTED IN CHAPTER I, CURA FIGURES as a personification of the hold that care has on human nature. Interestingly enough, she appears in the fable not only as a personification but also *as a personifier*—the very first of all personifiers at that—in that she shapes clay into a person. In the spirit of the fable, let us approach the creature of care (*homo*) not through its abstract concept, the way Heidegger does in *Being and Time*, but rather through one of its living personifications, namely the human gardener. For certainly no one embodies the care-dominated nature of human beings more than a gardener.

This is borne home with great natural verve by Karel Čapek in his short book *The Gardener's Year*, composed in 1929. Čapek, the luminous Czech author of the first half of the twentieth century, was a passionate amateur gardener, and he composed this book as a testament to the gardener's inextinguishable devotion to his plot of cultivated earth. Most of Čapek's commentators consider *The Gardener's Year* a minor work, but as Verlyn Klinkenborg remarks in the introduction to the Modern Library English edition of 2002, "most students of Čapek believe gardening is a subset of life, whereas gardeners, including Čapek, understand that life is a subset of gardening" (xii). Čapek's book articulates such an understanding in vividly embodied terms, and if I quote liberally from its pages in what follows, it is because, when it comes to showing how Cura reigns over the gardener's soul, this document—we might call it a confession—speaks more eloquently in its own voice than any summary or paraphrase could do.

The Gardener's Year is at once whimsical and earnest in its description of the gardener's obsessions. And every "real" gardener is by nature obsessive:

> I will now tell you how to recognize a real gardener. "You must come to see me," he says: "I will show you my garden." Then, when you go just to please him, you will find him with his rump sticking up somewhere among the perennials. "I will come in a moment," he shouts to you over his shoulder. "Just wait till I have planted this rose." "Please don't worry," you say kindly to him. After a while he must have planted it; for he gets up, makes your hand dirty, and beaming with hospitality he says: "Come and have a look; it's a small garden, but—Wait a moment," and he bends over a bed to weed some tiny grass. "Come along. I will show you Dianthus musalae; it will open your eyes. Great Scott, I forgot to loosen it here!" he says, and begins to poke in the soil. A quarter of an hour later he straightens up again. "Ah," he says, "I wanted to show you that bell flower, Campanula Wilsonae. That is the best campanula which—Wait a moment, I must tie up this delphinium." After he has tied it up he remembers: "Oh, I see, you have come to see the erodium. A moment," he murmurs, "I must just transplant this aster, it hasn't enough room here." After that you go away on tiptoe, leaving his behind sticking up among the perennials. (7–8)

Čapek's book follows the gardener's state of mind (which rarely strays far from his little plot) during the course of a year, beginning in the month of January. The gardener is a year-round cultivator. Even in winter months, when there is little he can do with his hands, he "cultivates the weather," fretting over too much snow, too little snow, the specter of black frosts, the winds, the bursts of sunlight that may cause the bushes to bud too soon. The weather is never right. "If it rains, he fears for his little Alpine flowers; if it is dry, he thinks with pain on his rhododendrons and andromedas" (10). In a humorous passage that reaffirms care's ecstatic self-extension into the world of nature and unto the God who has traditionally been imagined to hold sway over nature, Čapek writes:

> If it were of any use, every day the gardener would fall on his knees and pray somehow like this: "O Lord, grant that in some way it may rain every day, say from about midnight until three o'clock in the morning, but you see, it must be gentle and warm so that it can soak in, grant that at the same time it would not rain on campion, alyssum, helianthemum, lavender, and the others which you in your infinite wisdom know are drought-loving plants—I will write their names on a bit of paper if you like—and grant that the sun may shine the whole day long, but not everywhere (not, for instance, on spirea, or on gentian, plantain lily, and rhododendron), and not too much; that there may be plenty of dew and little wind, enough worms, no plant-lice and snails, no mildew, and that once a week thin liquid manure and guano may fall from heaven. Amen." For so it was in the garden of Eden, otherwise things would not have grown in it so well as they did, how could they? (58–59)

The gardener may obsess about the whims of the weather all he wants, but he knows that his will is a feckless agent when it comes to rain or shine, warm or cold ("If it were any use . . ." the passage just quoted begins). Care is accustomed to act, to take the initiative, to stake its claims, yet powerlessness and even helplessness are as intrinsic to the lived experience of care as the latter's irrepressible impulse to act, enable, nurse, and promote. The gardener cannot help but "cultivate the weather," as it were. Prayers, rain dances, implorations—perhaps even the concept of God himself—have their source in this inability of the gardener to remain impassive vis-à-vis the larger, uncontrollable forces that bear upon or determine the outcome of his efforts. So despite its active or motivated character, care is constantly being thrown back upon the limitations of its powers of action, is constantly reminded of its own inefficacy and essential passivity when it comes to phenomena like weather, blight, parasites, and rodents.

In Marcel Pagnol's novel *L'eau des collines* (*The Water of the Hills*), the hunchback farmer Jean de Florette appeals to God during a prolonged drought, as farmers are wont to do. One night as a storm gathers on the horizon and the sky begins to rumble, he rushes outdoors with his daughter in a state of wild expectation, only to realize that the clouds divide just above his farm, profusely discharging their load on the surrounding mountains but not on his dessicated fields. With his daughter sobbing at his side, he at first adopts an attitude of forbearance, but then he climbs on a rock and shouts to the sky: "Je suis BOSSU! Vous ne le savez pas, que JE SUIS BOSSU? Vous croyez que c'est facile?" ("I'm a HUNCHBACK! Do you know that I'm a HUNCHBACK? You think it's easy?" [*The Water of the Hills*, 165]). It is no easier to be hunchback than it is to discern a reason for the apparent indifference of God or nature to human plight. Care humbles its subject. The clay from which Cura fashioned *homo* is first and foremost the humus of human humility. The fall from Eden was as much a fall into the humility of impotence as it was into shame.

While nature (or God) can be ruthlessly cruel toward the solicitations of human care, as every farmer or gardener knows, its cruelty is in fact only a temporary suspension of its otherwise reliable generosity. (The ever-present threat of such suspension is what keeps human care both anxious and humble in its relations to nature.) Fortunately for the creatures of the earth, nature by and large tends to fulfill its obligations and promises. And fortunately for the gardener, there is enough of Eden in the mortal earth that despite the vagaries of the weather, the miracle of life erupts and blossoms year after year. Thus even in January, "without the gardener having suspected or having done anything, crocuses and snowdrops have pricked through the soil" (Čapek, *Gardener's Year*, 14).

Before one can become a "real" gardener, "a certain maturity, or let us say paternity, is necessary" (ibid., 8). When one is young, one is like Adam before the fall. One "eats the fruits of life which one has not produced oneself," and one believes a flower is "what one carries in a buttonhole, or presents a girl with" (7). For the gardener, by contrast, "a flower is something which hibernates, which is dug round and manured, watered and transplanted, divided and trimmed, tied up, freed from weeds, and cleaned of seeds, dead leaves, aphis and mildew" (6). The world of the gardener is not the world of the nongardener. Indeed, the gardener is an Adam who has reengaged with the element of which he is made ("for out of [the ground] wast thou taken" [Genesis 19]):

While I was only a remote and distracted onlooker of the accomplished work of gardens, I considered gardeners to be beings of a peculiarly poetic and gentle mind, who cultivate perfumes of flowers listening to the birds singing. Now when I look at the affair more closely, I find that a real gardener is not a man who cultivates flowers; he is a man who cultivates the soil. He is a creature who digs himself into the earth, and leaves the sight of what is on it to us gaping good-for-nothings. He lives buried in the ground. He builds his monument in a heap of compost. If he came into the Garden of Eden he would sniff excitedly and say: "Good Lord, what humus!" I think that he would forget to eat the fruit of the tree of knowledge of good and evil: he would rather look round to see how he could manage to take away from the Lord some barrow-loads of the paradisaic soil. Or he would discover that the tree of knowledge of good and evil has not round it a nice dishlike bed, and he would begin to mess about with the soil, innocent of what is hanging over his head. "Where are you, Adam?" the Lord would say. "In a moment," the gardener would shout over his shoulder; "I am busy now." And he would go on making his little bed. (23)

What Čapek calls paternity involves a shift of focus—away from the fruits of life to the soil in which they have their genesis. The gardener's relationship to soil begins with his own private plot, which he cultivates and comes to know in its proprieties, and from there it extends outward to the earth as a whole. Like Eve's eating of the pomegranate, gardening brings about a transformation of perception, a fundamental change in one's way of seeing the world, call it a phenomenological conversion. No longer does the eye stop at the surface of nature's living forms; it looks to the depths in which they stake their claims on life and from which they grow into the realm of presence and appearance. In this regrounding of the gardener's outlook, beauty takes on a genetic quality, call it a humic substrate, which it did not possess before. In Čapek's singular psychology of the gardener's disposition:

> In fact [when one is young] one does not care what one is treading on; one rushes somewhere like mad, and at most one notices what beautiful clouds there are, or what a beautiful horizon it is, or how beautifully blue the hills are; but one does not look under one's feet to note and praise the beautiful soil that is there. You must have a garden, though it be no bigger than a pocket-handkerchief; you must have one bed at least to know what you are treading on. Then, dear friend, you will see that not even clouds are so diverse, so beautiful, and terrible as the soil under your feet. You will know the soil as sour, tough, clayey, cold, stony, and rotten; you will recognize the mould puffy like pastry, warm, light, and good like bread, and you will say of this that it is beautiful, just as you say of women or of clouds. You will feel a strange and sensual pleasure if your stick runs a yard deep into the puffy and crumbling soil, or if you crush a clod in your fingers to taste its airy and tepid warmth. (87–88)

Gardening is an opening of worlds—of worlds within worlds—beginning with the world at one's feet. To become conscious of what one is treading on requires that one delve into the ground's organic underworld, so as to appreciate, in an engaged way, the soil's potential for fostering life. No one knows better than the gardener that in order to realize that potential, the soil needs an external agent, a husbandman, as it were, to undertake the labor of domestication and fertilization. Neruda's *jardinera* (chapter 2) showed us what it takes to maximize the soil's fitness for life as she delves and digs into the ground to uncouple the cobble and limber the roots, touching the humid door through which swirl the seeds. Soil is for the most part a battleground where the forces of life confront the merciless resistance of the lifeless and inanimate. "I tell you," writes Čapek, "to tame a couple of rods of soil is a great victory" (88). It is because gardening is fraught with so many risks of failure that its victories afford such a singular satisfaction. It is only by participating in the domestication process that one comes to realize what life is up against in its struggles to affirm its rights in the ground we tread upon, for the most part mindlessly. This ground is in places abundantly rich, but to relish that richness rather than merely take it for granted, one must know firsthand the poverty in which it all began:

And if you have no appreciation for this strange beauty, let fate bestow upon you a couple of rods of clay—clay like lead, squelching and primeval clay out of which coldness oozes; which yields under the spade like chewing-gum, which bakes in the sun and gets sour in the shade; ill-tempered, unmalleable, greasy, and sticky like plasters of Paris, slippery like a snake, and dry like a brick, impermeable like tin, and heavy like lead. And now smash it with a pick-axe, cut it with a spade, break it with a hammer, turn it over and labour, cursing aloud and lamenting.

Then you will understand the animosity and callousness of dead and sterile matter which ever did defend itself, and still does, against becoming a soil of life; and you will realize what a terrible fight life must have undergone, inch by inch, to take root in the soil of the earth, whether that life be called vegetation or man. (87–88)

If there is an "underlying" message in Čapek's book, it is that gardening is a form of education, a plunge into the depths of natural history, an immersion in the element where life first heroically established itself on Earth. To garden is to come to understand the efforts by which life forced a foothold for itself in a hostile and resistant clay. (By his own admission, everything to which Čapek devoted himself, including gardening, was part of an effort to understand: "To understand is my one mania; to express is another. Not to express myself, but to express things" [xi].)

Cultivating his garden plot somewhere in a corner of the city of Prague, Čapek came to understand intuitively what science now knows with theoretical certainty, namely that the first sparks of life—the first primitive cells with membranes containing RNA—occurred within common clay minerals, such as montmorillonite, which provided the basic platforms for the formation, growth, and division of some of the earliest living cells on Earth. In the beginning there was clay. It was the labor of living organisms, fighting every inch of the way, that turned it into humus. In the beginning was an Earth that aggressively resisted life's colonizing ventures. It took the tremendous self-affirming struggles of life itself to transform earth, sea, and air into elements hospitable to life. Life itself first brought about the conditions that favor life on the planet today. It was thanks to the relentless metabolism of primitive bacteria over untold millions of years that an atmosphere rich with oxygen and carbon dioxide slowly formed around Earth, which atmosphere made possible the process of photosynthesis, which in turn transformed the planet as a whole into a living organism. If over time Earth was turned into a thriving garden of sorts, primitive life was the original gardener that worked its soil and made it fit for growth. The human gardener with rump in the air is a latecoming participant in, as well as a beneficiary of, this chemistry of vitalization.

I do not mean to ascribe care, in the human sense, to primitive organisms. I would say rather that care, in its self-transcending character, is an expansive projection of the intrinsic ecstasy of life. What distinguishes life from the inanimate matter in which it has its origins is the continuous self-exceeding by which it bursts forth from the lifeless and ecstatically maintains itself in being through expenditures that increase rather than deplete the reserves of vitality. Life is an excess, call it the self-ecstasy of matter. Care in turn is a world-forming, ethically laden extension of the terra-forming forces that built, through an overload of vitality, what the late Stephen Jay Gould called the "full house" of our teeming biosphere. Through his devotion to the soil, Čapek's gardener is initiated into this mysterious law of surplus that makes of animate matter the overflow of its elemental constituency— a law that he is bound, insofar as he is human, to incorporate into his life in a fundamentally ethical way.

The Gardener's Year is anything but a moral allegory—it's a book about the gardener's love affair with the earth—yet if Čapek's experience as a gardener taught him a basic ethical principle that can be broadly universalized, it is the following: "you must give more to the soil than you take away" (88). The disproportion between giving and taking is first and foremost a principle of life—life exists where giving exceeds taking—yet it applies equally to human culture (it is not for nothing that the word *culture* has its roots in the soil). We should recall here once again that when Jupiter animated *homo*'s matter with spirit, his clay became an organic substance, at once spiritual and material in nature. Once it took shape and was given life, that substance lent itself to cultivation.

No one knew better than Čapek that the cultivation of soil and cultivation of spirit are connatural, and not merely analogical, activities. What holds true for the soil—that you must give it more than you take away—also holds true for nations, institutions, marriage, friendship, education, in short for human culture as a whole, which comes into being and maintains itself in time only as long as its cultivators overgive of themselves. Gardening for Čapek is an education in the self-imparting generosity on which life in all its basic forms depends (and human culture is but one of these forms, albeit an expansive one). Hence to conclude this excursion into Čapek's garden book, let us briefly look at how the author's personal commitments in two specific cultural domains—the literary and the political—reveal an essential affinity with his gardening ethic, if one may call it that.

To begin with the literary, we should note that the Czech language in which Čapek wrote was in every respect a husbanded entity. Čapek was keenly aware that a century or so before he was born, Czech was like crude rods of clay that needed to be "tamed" and rendered suitable for a national literature. Until the nineteenth century it had been spoken for the most part only in villages by the peasant classes (townspeople spoke mostly German; the aristocracy spoke French, German, and Italian; the clergy spoke German and Latin, see Klima). Over the course of the nineteenth century writers, poets, translators, and "national awakeners" devoted themselves to refining the resources of the language. They developed and expanded its expressive capacities, modernized its idiom, enlarged its vocabulary, gave it a new semantic and prosodic plasticity, and in general enabled Czech to express, as Ivan Klima puts it, "new kinds of experience, new human relationships, and a different way of regarding life" (Klima, introduction to Čapek's *R.U.R.*, viii). As a result of those efforts, during the nineteenth century "Czech literature passed through a course of development that had taken hundreds of years in other countries" (Klima, ibid.).

By the time Čapek joined the ranks of modern Czech authors in the early twentieth century, those efforts had already borne rich fruit, and as a writer he was their direct beneficiary. Like his predecessors, Čapek continued to cultivate the national language and broaden the range of its literary registers. His translations of modern French poetry into Czech laid the ground for Czech twentieth-century poetry. He explored, invented, or refined a wide variety of genres: plays, novels, short stories, pamphlets, political disquisitions, newspaper columns, and unclassifiable testaments such as *The Gardener's Year*. His engagement with the short story, for example, yielded a wondrous collection, the so-called *Pocket Tales*, in which he invented a unique kind of detective story, rich in psychology and enigma, liberalizing punctuation in the process and incorporating striking colloquialisms. As a novelist he explored a diversity of styles, plot devices, and idioms. *War with the Newts* is exuberantly humorous and stands as the forerunner of the great humoristic modes of later Czech writers like Bohumil Hrabal, Milan Kundera, Váklac Havel, Ivan Klima, and many others. Likewise, each of the novels that make up his remarkable trilogy *Three Novels* has a different and distinct narrative signature. Taken together, this novelistic production broke wide open the formal as well as thematic boundaries of storytelling, consolidating the foundation for future Czech prose. In sum, like his nineteenth-century predecessors, Čapek continued to nourish the soil of his mother tongue, assiduously. And like them, he gave that soil more than he took away.

The contemporary Czech writer Ivan Klima, who authored a fine book on Čapek's life and work, and whose introduction to the English edition of Čapek's play *R.U.R.* I have quoted from above, points out that Čapek's commitment to a national Czech literature was exceeded by, and in fact must be understood in the context of, his unconditional commitment to the Czechoslovak Republic that came into being after World War I. Čapek saw the republic, with its democratic institutions, as the only soil in which the literary, cultural, and political life of the nation could truly flourish. His allegiance to T. G. Masaryk, president of the Czechoslovak Republic, gave rise to *Talks with T. G. Masaryk*, a consequential book (consequential still today) that was both an encomium of Masaryk's life, deeds, and political ideas and an encomium of the principles of democracy to which both Masaryk and Čapek were passionately pledged. Čapek saw democracy—above all Czechoslovakian democracy—as a burgeoning yet vulnerable political entity that needed to be husbanded by its citizens (especially its intellectuals). As a citizen and not only a writer, he did far more than his fair share in this regard. Through his countless newspaper articles, political essays, commentaries, and feuilletons, Čapek waged an ongoing intellectual war during the 1920s and 1930s against what he saw as the greatest threats to Czechoslovakian democracy and to European humanism in general, namely totalitarianism. History subsequently bore out the truth of his unwavering conviction that German National Socialism on the one hand and Soviet Communism on the other threatened to destroy what had been so carefully nourished over the years within the framework of his nation's republican institutions.

Although he did not phrase it in exactly these words, it is clear from his political and journalistic writings that for Čapek the difference between democracy and totalitarianism is the difference between a garden and a swamp. (Čapek's essay "Why Am I Not a Communist?" is one of the most eloquent statements to this effect, summed up in the striking sentence "I cannot be a communist, because communism's morality is not a morality of help" [quoted in Klima, *Karel Čapek*, 131]). In a democracy citizens are caretakers of the state. In totalitarian societies, the state presumes to be the caretaker of its citizens. But a state that is not actively sustained by the care of its citizens—that does not grow through their participation in the maintenance and governance of its institutions—has neither the means nor the will to care for its citizens, except insofar as they serve the interests of the state.

It seems only fitting, symbolically speaking, that Čapek should have died on the eve of the Nazi invasion of Czechoslovakia (he died on Christmas Day, 1938, of a respiratory illness). It would have been altogether too much for his gardener's soul to witness the blight that was visited upon his nation first by Hitler and subsequently by the Soviets. Or perhaps the onset of that blight, in all its inevitability, conspired with his illness to end his life prematurely at the age of forty-eight.

Nazism and Soviet Communism took a toll on European humanity and culture which Čapek could not, even in his most pessimistic moments, have begun to conceive. Whether the third major danger that Čapek fretted over obsessively—modern technology—will bring about its own still-inconceivable forms of devastation remains to be seen. Čapek's play *R.U.R.* gives a parabolic idea of the deeper source of his concerns, namely that modern technology has none of the humility, devotion, and curatorial vocation of the gardener. It militates against the gardener's acceptance of the intrinsic limitation of his powers of action, his anxious but open passivity before the forces of nature, and his allegiance to the efforts by which life struggles to maintain its regime of vitality on Earth. When it comes to the soil—that is, the entirety of the natural resources locked away in the earth—the drive of modern technology is to extract, remove, and deplete rather than to cultivate, enhance, and foster. What Čapek feared most about its unbridled amassing of power was precisely the fact that technology takes away more than it gives back. In that respect, it is a not a good custodian of the future.

If life is indeed a subset of gardening, rather than the other way around, then there is every reason to believe that if humankind has to entrust its future to anyone, it should entrust it to the gardener, or to those who, like the gardener, invest themselves in a future of which they will in part be the authors, though they will not be around to witness its full unfolding:

> The gardener wants eleven hundred years to test, learn to know, and appreciate fully what is his. . . . We gardeners live somehow for the future; if roses are in flower, we think that next year they will flower better; and in some few years this little spruce will become a tree—if only those few years were behind me! I should like to see what these birches will be like in fifty years. The right, the best is in front of us. (117)

Even if history tells us that this is by no means always the case, the gardener must continue to believe that "the best is in front of us," for without such faith there would be no gardeners, and without gardeners there would be no future, for better or worse.

Jimmy's Garden. Photograph: Margaret Morton © 1991.
From *Transitory Gardens, Uprooted Lives*
(New Haven, CT: Yale University Press, 1993).

~ 4 ~

Homeless Gardens

HISTORY HAS NO MEMORY OF THE GREAT MAJORITY OF gardens that have graced the earth over the millennia—gardens being by nature impermanent creations that only rarely leave behind evidence of their existence—nor should it. Gardens are not memorials. They may, as long as they last, be places of memory or sites of recollection, but apart from a few lofty exceptions they do not exist to immortalize their makers or defy the ravages of time. If anything they exist to reenchant the present. That is why we should not think of them as works of art either. As Rainer Maria Rilke put it in a letter to Lou Salomé, the inner ambition of artworks is to transcend time and become everlasting: "the thing is definite; the art thing [*Kunst-Ding*] must be even more definite; removed from all accident, torn away from every uncertainty, lifted out of time and given to space, it has become enduring, capable of eternity" (*Rainer Maria Rilke and Lou Salomé*, August 8, 1903, 70). Gardens instead are plunged into time and uncertainty, openly contending with the vagaries of soil, weather, and elements. They have a way of slowing time down—allowing its flow to gather in placid ponds, as it were—but that is part of their power of enchantment, not their power of endurance.

Conventional wisdom has it that gardens first arose either as a by-product of agriculture or as a form of primitive agriculture. This is sheer speculation, however, and when it comes to speculations about origins we would do better to credit the intuition of poets rather than the conventional wisdom, if only because poetry's calling is as old as the world itself, while the conventional wisdom typically reflects the mentalities and creeds of a particular historical age. The poet W. S. Merwin, for example, believes that, if anything, agriculture arose as a consequence of gardening, not the other way around. There is no incontrovertible evidence available to us that could decide the matter one way or another, yet if gardens are to agriculture what poetry is to prose, then there are at least analogical reasons to trust Merwin that gardens came first.

The Italian scholar Pietro Laureano gives us other, more empirically based reasons to believe that well before the rise of agriculture our Paleolithic ancestors cultivated gardens. "The first timid experiments from which the techniques of domestication and cultivation were derived," he writes, "could not have had utilitarian goals." Why? Because "domestication, as well as the gathering and selection of species to obtain types with exploitable characteristics, are practices that come to fruition only after several generations, hence they cannot be explained by the need to procure alimentation or other immediate benefits" (*Giardini di pietra*, 37). From this premise Laureano deduces that the first gardens would have been created by hunter-gatherers for purposes that were "ritualistic, magical, or simply ludic and aesthetic, but not economic or productive" (ibid.). In sum, they would have had more to do with enchantment than with procurement—unless it was the procurement of opiates, spices, hallucinogens or healing agents. Humankind, after all, cannot bear very much reality. That it why the dictum of Thoreau cited earlier—"Be it life or death, we crave only reality"—is not the whole truth. There is an equally fundamental (and in no way antithetical) craving in human beings to transfigure reality, to adorn it with costume and illusion, and thereby to respiritualize our experience of it. Whatever forms they may have taken, whatever delights or drugs they may have yielded, the earliest human gardens must have been bound up at least in part with this imperative.

Earlier I suggested that the fall from Eden handed Adam and Eve over to a regime of care and the so-called *vita activa*. To recall

Arendt's tripartite division, the *vita activa* consists of labor, work, and action. Now if we ask where exactly gardens fit in this scheme, we are perplexed. They are not bound up with our biological survival, hence they are not subsumable under the concept of labor (agriculture is labor). Likewise, they are not exactly subsumable under the category of work. The epitome of work is art, according to Arendt, and it would seem that gardens do not share art's drive for permanence (see chapter 5 for further discussion of the relation between gardens and art). As for action, Arendt understands it as something that transpires strictly between human beings in their public worlds. Thus it would not seem that gardens fall under the rubric of action either. Or do they?

The fact that human being create such things as gardens is strange, for it means that there are aspects of our humanity which nature does not naturally accommodate, which we must *make room for* in nature's midst. This in turn means that gardens mark our separation from nature even as they draw us closer to it, that there is something distinctly human in us that is related to nature yet is not of the order of nature, in short, that gardens respond to a set of human needs that are not reducible to our animal needs. The latter claim seems to be confirmed by the fact that even in the most disenchanted of habitats, where the premium is on survival, gardens have a way of cropping up. In 1993 Diana Balmori and Margaret Morton published a book of photographs with commentary titled *Transitory Gardens, Uprooted Lives*. Dedicated "to the uprooted individuals who have tilled the streets of New York City in search of a home and, in the process, have laid bare the meaning of *garden*," the book offers a visual and written record of the makeshift gardens that homeless individuals, with painstaking effort and care, created for themselves in the slums of New York City. What do we have to learn from these creations? Chiefly this: that there is more to gardens, and to the affirmation of humanity that they entail, than we may have assumed.

The gardens in question are made of diverse, largely random materials: toys, stuffed animals, flags, found objects, milk cartons, recycled trash, piles of leaves, at times a simple row of flowers. We call them gardens because they are deliberately constructed, yet they as far removed as can be from the grand municipal gardens of our world capitals or the private gardens of the ruling class which traditional studies of garden art are most concerned and familiar with. In Balmori and Morton's words, the ghetto gardens of the homeless are *"compositions* made in open spaces . . . that have been constructed from a variety of elements and that, through their detachment from the usual conditions in which gardens are made, liberate the word *garden* from its cultural straightjacket" (4). This is certainly true, and well said, yet my primary interest here is not to liberate the semantics of the word *garden* but to ask about the deeper human urges that go into the creation of these so-called transitory gardens. What kinds of acts bring them into being? What motivates their authors, who lack the bare necessities of life, to invest so much of themselves in creations that do nothing to meet their survival needs? If we can better understand the human matrix from which such gardens arise, we can perhaps better understand what Arendt calls the human condition. And that is no academic matter.

Balmori and Morton remark, and their photographs confirm, that each of these transitory gardens (which may last a day, a week, or a month) has a unique personal signature or distinctive style, as it were. This leads the authors to speculate that the gardens arise from a basic human need in the individuals who made them: the need for creative expression. There is no doubt that the gardens evidence an irrepressible urge to create, express, fashion, and beautify and that self-expression is a basic human urge; yet when one looks at the photographs, it strikes one that for all their diversity of styles, the transitory gardens in question speak of various other fundamental urges, beyond that of embellishment and creative expression.

One of these urges has to do with creating a pocket of repose in the midst of turbulence, a "still point of the turning world," to borrow a phrase from T. S. Eliot. A sanctuary of repose, however contrived it may be, is a distinctly human need, as opposed to shelter, which is a distinctly animal need, so much so that where the latter is lacking, as it is for these unlikely gardeners, the former becomes all the more urgent. Repose is a state of mind made possible by the structuring of one's relation to one's environment. The gardens of the homeless, which are in effect homeless gardens, introduce *form* into an urban environment where it either didn't exist or was not discernible as such. In so doing they give composure to a segment of the inarticulate milieu in which they take their stand (almost defiantly). These gardens are in effect little precincts. It is in such well-defined precincts that human repose first becomes possible.

About gardens in general one could say that in their self-gathered forms they give human dimensions to an otherwise unbounded nature. Likewise the transitory gardens of New York City give human dimensions to an otherwise unbounded urban expanse. Through their compositional arrangements, they create an open enclosure (or enclosure within the open) that gives the amorphous circumambient environment a measure of human, and not just spatial, orientation (repose is a kind of orientation). One could say that these gardens visibly gather around themselves the spiritual, mental, and physical energies that their surroundings would otherwise dissipate, disperse, and dissolve. Their compositional formality, however loose or improvised, puts in place a measure of containment, or of delimitation, where before there was only an indifferent urban extension. By liberating the self-gathering and protective powers of form, they thus secure the limits necessary to human repose.

Another urge or need that these gardens appear to respond to, or to arise from, is so innate that we are barely ever conscious of its abiding claims on us. I mean our biophilia, as well as what I would call our chlorophilia. When we are deprived of green, of plants, of trees, most of us (though evidently not all of us) succumb to a demoralization of spirit which we usually blame on some psychological or neurochemical malady, until one day we find ourselves in a garden or park or countryside and feel the oppression vanish as if by magic. In most of the transitory gardens of New York City the actual cultivation of plants is unfeasible, yet even so (or perhaps even *more* so) the compositions often seem to represent attempts to conjure up the spirit of plant and animal life, if only symbolically, through a clumplike arrangement of materials, an introduction of colors, small pools of water, and a frequent presence of petals or leaves as well as of stuffed animals. On display here are various fantasy elements whose reference, at some basic level, seems to be the natural world. It is this implicit or explicit reference to nature that fully justifies the use of the word *garden*, albeit in a "liberated" sense," to describe these synthetic constructions. In them we can see biophilia—a yearning for contact with nonhuman life—assuming uncanny representational forms.

Certainly there is no mistaking the chlorophiliac urge on display in the various "community gardens" that have sprung up not only in New York but in inner cities all across America. These are most often vacant urban lots that have been transformed—by surrounding residents, homeless people, squatters, tenement dwellers, and others— into sanctuaries of dense vegetation. Here the premium is on green leafy things, vegetables, the verdant in its exuberant sprouting forms (grass lawns in fact are rare). Community gardens tend not to have the compositional character of transitory ghetto gardens; they seem rather like uninhibited, almost anarchic celebrations of chlorophilia within a confined urban space.

Entire neighborhoods have been transformed by the presence of these thriving gardens, many of which, as if by their power of enchantment, have created communities where none existed before. The following anecdote may serve as a real-life parable. A few years ago Karl Paige and Annette Smith happened to meet on the median of Quesada Avenue, near Newhall Street, in the Bayview District of San Francisco (a rough district, to say the least). Paige, a retired man who grew up on a farm in Mississippi, had come to the median with his saw to cut down a dying bush. Smith, a onetime farmer's daughter born in Alabama, had come to dig up worms as fishing bait for her brother. Engaging in conversation, they decided it would be worthwhile to try to plant a garden there on the median. After obtaining permission from the city, they began to clear the grounds of the beer cans, engine oil, old batteries, spark plugs, refrigerators, brake pads, mattresses, and fast-food flotsam that had come there to die. They plowed and fertilized the soil, sowed a generous variety of seeds, and, cordoning off the area with yellow tape, carefully nourished the marigolds, germanium, peanuts, basil, kale, snapdragons, and cactus that soon enough began to sprout. The wonder of such a garden in their midst brought out the surrounding residents, many of whom met each other for first time around the flowers, herbs, and vegetables.

Several other gardens have since cropped up in the neighborhood, and now, where addicts, pushers, and vagrants once urinated, trashed, and engaged in turf wars, there are different kinds of congregations. As one local resident declared to a reporter: "More and more over the last few months, people have been leaving their houses to gather in the center of the garden. Some people have met one another for the first time near the collard greens" (*San Francisco Chronicle*. September 2, 2004, A5). Demotic comments such as these confirm in a literal way what many classics of world literature and philosophy affirm in more figurative terms: a genetic, almost organic connection between gardens and forms of conviviality. In these ancient, medieval, and modern texts, gardens frequently appear as sites of conversation, dialogue, friendship, storytelling—in short, communalization. In the same way that the compositional gardens of the homeless represent a gathering of form, the community gardens of Bayview—and presumably all the other community gardens across America—bring about a gathering of people. This gathering power helps explains why gardens not only are topics and sites of conversation but are explicitly associated with the very ideal of conversation in many Western and non-Western texts alike.

Although no interlocutor seems to be present in them, the transitory gardens of New York also partake in this spirit of social intercourse. Insofar as they embody an affirmation, declare their human authorship, invite recognition, and call for a response, they represent speech acts, not in the banal sense of making "social statements" but in the sense of militating against and triumphing over a condition of speechlessness. They appear in their surrounding landscapes as so many "raids upon the inarticulate," to borrow once again from Eliot's *Four Quartets*. While there is certainly an element of creative expression at work in them, one senses that alongside or perhaps even beneath this will to expression lurks a more urgent need to break through barriers of aphasia and become loquacious, the way poems, for example, are loquacious. In effect these gardens amount to the beginning of a dialogue, and the interlocutor is whoever takes the time to notice and wonder at them. That is why the transitory gardens evoke even more starkly and more poignantly than do community gardens the distinctly human need that went into their making, namely the need to hold converse with one's fellow humans.

If speech belongs in essence to the public sphere, or to the *polis*, then both the compositional and community gardens under consideration here are first and foremost acts of political redemption. By overcoming the speechlessness to which their creators have been consigned by circumstance, they redeem the specifically human need to act, speak, and be heard, all of which are "political" in the most essential sense of the term. To that extent at least they do indeed belong to the sphere of human action, as Arendt conceives it. Their composition turns both deed and word outward, into or toward the public sphere where human beings acknowledge one another's humanity, in its essential dignity.

One thing that all nonimaginary gardens have in common is that they come into being through human agency. The fact that this is self-evident does not make it any less decisive. Whether they are situated at its center or at its margins, gardens have their proper locus in the polis, which for Arendt serves as the stage for human action (action always takes place in the "world that comes between men," says Arendt). This does not mean that gardens are a form of political action, as we ordinarily understand that concept, or that they perforce serve the political interests of those who created them. It means that however private or secluded they may be, they never exist independently of the world shaped by human action, even if they cannot be wholly contained or circumscribed by that world.

That is why we can go along with the German writer and philosopher Rudolf Borchardt, who, in his 1938 book *The Passionate Gardener* (composed during a self-imposed exile in Italy), writes: "whatever it is [a garden] is finally a human statement ... because a garden is always a notion of order. ... As a question of order it is also a question of example, education and redemption, since these are the things with which all notions of order are concerned" (32). Borchardt should have been more precise here, specifying that "these are the things with which all notions of *human* order are concerned." It is because the garden entails a notion of human order that Borchardt postulates a fundamental "tension" between the flower and the garden. Both flower and garden embody order, but of very different sorts: "The order within the flower is prehuman, and governs the flower itself. The garden speaks of human modes of order, where man is master, subduer, and transformer" (30). We have seen that where man is master, subduer, and transformer he is also slave, victim, and martyr, and that where he exercises his will most vigorously he also confronts the ultimate powerlessness of his will (chapter 3). Because "man" is in some sense trapped within his will-driven *vita activa*, and because he suffers from that entrapment, the flower fills him with yearning and nostalgia. "The human being connects with the flower by way of unreasoned longing: with the garden by way of will" (30). The flower confronts us with a beauty that exists independently of the human will—a beauty we cannot create but only cultivate in our gardens.

In addition to the tension between flower and garden and between unreasoned longing and will, there is another, correlative tension within human beings, according to Borchardt. "The human being embodies a tension between a nature which has since been lost and an unreachable Divine Creator," he writes, adding: "The garden stands at precisely the center of this tension" (33). The garden, in other words, stands at the center of a human mode of being that stretches between two impossibilities, or two irrevocable losses: nature and God. We may choose to understand the essence of this tension differently from Borchardt—as the tension, say, between a longing for closure and the open-endedness of human existence, or between our craving for reality and our craving for deliverance from reality—yet in the final analysis we must always remember that nature has its own order and that human gardens *do not*, as one hears so often, bring order to nature; rather, they give order to our relation to nature. It is our relation to nature that defines the tension at the center of which stands not only the garden but the human polis as such.

This embodied notion of human order—taking as it does many diverse forms—links the garden to the polis, that is to say to the realm of those interactions in and through which human beings, through their own initiatives, give form and articulation to their historical worlds. To say that the transitory gardens of New York are speech acts means that they speak, in a public if nonverbal mode, of the human need to make ourselves at home on an earth that does not necessarily make room for us.

Kingscote Gardens, Stanford University, 2007. Photograph: © 2007 by Godfrey DiGiorgi. All rights reserved.

ᨠ 5 ᨠ

"Mon jardin à moi"

"MAIS TON JARDIN À TOI, OÙ EST-T-IL?" THE QUESTION was posed to me one day by my friend Michel Serres after I had given him an account of the different kinds of gardens I intended to deal with in this book. Since I do not actually tend one of my own, I am tempted to say that *mon jardin à moi* is the form my reflections take in these pages. This is a manner of speech, to be sure, but it reaffirms my thesis that gardens are "figures" for many cultural activities that are not literally connected to gardening or garden making. Knowing Serres, however, I did not venture an answer of this sort, for he and I have in common the belief that just as spirit flowers out of matter, the figurative should blossom out of the real.

There is a "real" garden I would gladly call my own, even though I have no proprietary rights to it. It's called Kingscote and is located on the Stanford University campus, where I teach. I have sought out its recess on several occasions, hoping to gain greater clarity about what a garden is in essence, and I have indeed accessed thoughts and insights there that, had the place not existed, probably never would had seen the light of day, or the light of consciousness, if you prefer. If it is true, as Mallarmé once wrote, that "everything in the world exists to end up in a book," I'm more than happy to let Kingscote end up here, in this one.

For some reason it is almost always empty. Too small for recreational activities, with nowhere really to sit except on a low-lying limestone bench that is more ornamental than sedentary, it seems to have no purpose beyond its sheer self-affirmation as it lies there gathered within itself. It is neither ostentatious nor withdrawn, yet it has the aura of a secret. Few people, in fact, when you ask them about it, are aware of its existence, and in the various volumes about the history and architecture of Stanford in the university bookstore there is no mention of it. It is almost as if it didn't exist, yet once you step into it you get a sense that you are in the quietly palpitating heart of the university and that everything somehow radiates out from here.

A running hedge along one side and an array of lofty trees along the others define the garden's oval-shaped perimeter. The south side slopes upward toward an arboreal curtain that muffles the sound of car traffic on the adjacent street, and here, at an elevation of a few feet, a level terrace has been created that looks out over a pond, a grass lawn, and a sublime oak tree lording it over the north end of the enclosure. The only flora to speak of are two tulip trees, asymmetrically placed, that bloom voluptuously for a couple of weeks in March. Also, on the curved wall that rises up from the water on one end of the pond, a wild rose bush breaks through the overhanging evergreen foliage with extreme discretion once a year in spring. The entire space seems designed to showcase the Italianate, stone-bordered pond in the shape of an hourglass or figure 8, with its tiny footbridge, no more than three feet long, arching over its midpoint. The pond's diagonal is conspicuously out of alignment with the garden's main axis, and this off-center effect, I'm told, is typical of Japanese garden art.

It is what one might call a quintessentially lyrical garden. Unlike larger grounds that unfold in space and time as you wander around in them, here one gets a syncretic, unobstructed view of the whole. In *A Dream of Red Mansions*, a Chinese saga of the eighteenth century, a nobleman goes on a ceremonious tour of his newly designed garden, and lo and behold, "he had the gate opened then and they went in, only to find their view screened by a green hill. At this sight his secretaries cried out in approval. 'If not for this hill,' observed Chia Cheng, 'one would see the whole garden as soon as one entered, and how tame that would be' " (Tsao 97). By "tame" Chia Cheng means that there would be no developing intrigue, no itinerary of discovery for the viewer. Indeed, a tour of the nobleman's garden, which takes up several pages of narrative as the company proceeds along its pathways, reads like a story of enchanting marvels and surprises—an enclosed lagoon, a loggia, flowerbeds, lawns, poetic inscriptions—which reveal themselves to the company progressively, as if the garden, like the saga, followed a preconceived plot, which of course it does. In Kingscote there is no embedded plot as such, only a lyriclike crystallization of form, the whole of which is visible from any given angle.

Kingscote has no story to tell, yet in its lyric stasis it allows thinking to wander freely in and around the enigma of the phenomenon. For while the garden opens itself up to full view, it continues to hold something back, not in the mode of narrative deferral but in the mode of discretion. Certainly its appearance varies substantially depending on where you stand and on the time of day or year you come. It suffices to come here after nightfall and see the pond levitate in the moonlight like a dream image, or else during rainstorms, when the trees sway in a frenetic wind bred on the Pacific, to get a sense of how varied are the garden's guises, to say nothing of the effect one's mood and state of mind have on its self-manifestations. The garden's potential for appearance is never realized all at once, any more than a lyric's meaning and sentiment are exhausted by a single reading. "Slumbersong," for example, by Rainer Maria Rilke:

> Someday, when I lose you,
> will you be able to sleep without
> my whispering myself away
> like a linden's crown above you?
>
> Without my waking here and laying down
> words, almost like eyelids,

upon your breasts, upon your limbs,
upon your mouth?

Without my closing you and leaving
you alone with what is yours,
like a garden with a mass
of melissas and star-anise?

(*Translations*, 190)

If it is true that time, in its diurnal or seasonal unfolding, affects the garden's appearance, the opposite is also true. In Kingscote time has a different rhythm, a different quality of duration, a different confluence, than it does just beyond the confines. It is as if the aesthetically determined relations between things in the garden's precinct had the effect of slowing time down and, in so doing, intensifying or throwing into relief the sheer gift of things to perception. Whatever else they may be, gardens are first and foremost places where appearances draw attention to themselves, presenting themselves to us as freely given. This is true of gardens in general (with the inevitable exceptions), but it takes a lyrical garden like this one to accentuate the presence of something mysterious or impenetrable in the simple appearance of things. It does not dissimulate the mystery with an obstructing green hill or enfolded plot but agitates, albeit in a calm way, the strange and elusive depths from which the forms of the visible world arise. Appearances in the garden present themselves as freely given, and as fully given, yet they never exhaust their potential for self-manifestation in the punctual moment of presence. The self-same is never the same in Kingscote, and each new day, to echo the poet A. R. Ammons, is a new day when it comes to the appearance of what perdures in time.

In their self-gathered aspects, which bring the latent dimensions of appearance to presence, gardens like Kingscote seem like gateways to other worlds or other orders of being: not gateways for you to pass through but through which you may be called upon or visited, without moving from where you stand. This may explain in part why gardens in the human imagination often figure as the sites of visions and epiphanies, be they spiritual, erotic, or otherwise. Naussika appears to Odysseus in a garden; Beatrice's epiphany in *The Divine Comedy* takes place in the Garden of Eden. The palace garden is the site of the lover's conspicuous failure to appear in Rihaku's eleventh-century poem "The Jeweled Stair: A Grievance," wondrously translated from the Chinese by Ezra Pound:

> The jeweled steps are already quite white with dew,
> It is so late that the dew soaks my gauze stockings,
> And I let down the crystal curtain
> And watch the moon through the clear autumn.

> (Pound, *Selected Poems*, 131)

Likewise, the overbearing presence of a chestnut tree in the small *jardin public* of Bouville reveals the abyss of existential absurdity to Roquentin, the chlorophobic protagonist of Jean-Paul Sartre's *Nausea*. In sum, thanks to its intensification of appearances, you never know when you're in a garden what you may see that is not really there.

Dino Campana's poem "Autumnal Garden," which describes in vaguely surrealist terms a garden near a river (most likely the Arno), ends with the vision of a chimerical woman summoned by the hushed stillness of the scene:

> And from the distance silence like a chorus,
> tender and majestic,
> rises and breathes on high at my balcony;
> And in the odor of laurel,
> in the bitter, failing smell of laurel,
> from between the immortal statues in the sunset
> she appears to me, present.

> (Kay, 356)

The poet does not tell us whether she appears to him in the garden or in his mind, so interfused are the two, yet the poem leaves little doubt that it is the conjuring power of the garden that gives him access to the visionary depths from which the chimera comes forth. (Walking by Kingscote Garden one evening just after sunset, I stepped in for a moment, and in the hush of the hour it seemed as if a goddess or an angel would appear on the other side of the pond at any instant. I left in a hurry, to avoid any such visitation. For epiphanies usually come with the enjoinder "You must change your life," and evidently I was not ready to heed such a call.)

Artworks also stand before us as humanly created things whose principal purpose is self-exhibition; they too draw attention to appearance. Yet however much art may play a role in their design, gardens have a natural life of their own which exists independently of their formal determinations. Not matter, not idea, but *life* is the phenomenon that finds articulation in gardens. Our response to them is never "disinterested," is never merely aesthetic, if only because they appeal directly to our biophilia. In some cases, as in Zen rock gardens, they appeal more sublimely to our cosmophilia. In either case they remind us of our creaturely inclusion in the world of animate and cosmic matter. The experience of being in Kingscote is precisely that of being *in* it, alongside water spiders, birds at their ablutions, the lizard on the rock at the water's edge, the weeds, the boxwood, and all that thrives underground and in the air. Such inclusion makes you more—and less—than an aesthetic observer.

This feeling of inclusion derives in part from being in an enclosed space marked by borders. It is primarily a garden's perimeter that sets it apart, that gives shape and delineation to its living form (I call it a "living form" because, whatever else they may do, gardens conjugate life and form). Almost all the words for "garden" in world languages have etymons linked to the idea of fence or boundary. A garden is literally defined by its boundaries. However, while the latter provide demarcation and definition, they are for the most part relative. By that I mean they keep the garden intrinsically related to the world that they keep at a certain remove. Inside Kingscote one has a sense of being in a still spot of the surrounding whirl, yet the stillness is relative, dynamic, and unabstracted from the environment. Indeed, one could say that the stillness *draws its energy* from the whirl around its edges. For stillness is a form of energy. If there is something exemplary about Kingscote, it is the way its borders create a buffer against the bustle of university life at its margins, yet they do not exclude or shut out that bustle altogether. The commotion seeps in through the trees and makes itself heard in muffled accents, thus rendering the silence relational.

An essential tension is lost when gardens do not have porous, even promiscuous openings onto the world beyond their bounds. (Maybe this was the trouble with Eden—it did not have pressing in on its edges an outside world to define its limits, so our primal parents sought out the only limit that was available to them, to supply the place with a measure of reality.) The Campana poem, with its evocations of distance and urban surroundings, suggests that the inspirational power of gardens—or at least of certain kinds of gardens—owes as much to the permeability as to the consistency of their boundaries. Isolate them completely and you take away their havenlike character. Who would immure our great municipal gardens? What would the Jardin de Luxembourg be without the fence and open gateways that both distinguish it from and connect it to the Parisian swirl around it? When Thoreau went to Walden to cultivate his patch of ground, he placed himself strategically "a mile from any neighbor." Take away its relationship to the civic life around it and *Walden*—a still point of nineteenth-century American thought—would lose the tension that informs it. Gardens are vital to the degree that they open their enclosures in the midst of history, offering a measure of seclusion that is not occlusion.

As is the case with many other gardens, something about Kingscote makes room for what the bustling world tends to crowd out or stifle. It makes room for thought, vision, recollection, reverie, and the sort of deep time that is the natural element of such psychic phenomena. Yet even as it slows time down and draws attention to the appearances within its confines, the garden also courts the presence of the surrounding context. What the eye sees here is not confined to what appears within the enclosure. Or better, what appears here extends well beyond the garden's parameters, not so much because the eye can see through or beyond them as because the garden sends a message, embodies a statement, on behalf of its caretakers. Thanks to its location and setting, one never forgets—indeed, one is all the more intensely aware—that the surrounding university has woven its signature into the fabric of the garden's appearance.

Earlier I claimed that Kingscote is quintessentially lyrical, that it does not have the narrative emplotment of larger gardens that unfold their secrets and surprises along meandering pathways. While it is literally true that the whole is visible from any angle within the enclosure, it is also true that the garden's symbolic, institutional, and referential reach in fact overruns and transcends its relatively self-contained boundaries. As the lyric distillation of the university's gardenlike milieu as a whole, Kingscote's living form invites us to ask: Why has the academy, from the beginning of its institutional history, sought out, as its privileged setting, a gardenlike environment? What do gardens have to do with education? Do Kingscote and all the other gardens that grace the college campuses of North America and England have anything to do with the vocation of higher learning? If so, there is indeed a story lurking in this garden after all.

≈ 6 ≈

Academos

JUST A FEW MINUTES BY FOOT FROM KINGSCOTE GARDEN on the Stanford campus there is the so-called Quadrangle, a large geometric clearing along whose perimeter our humanities and sciences departments are clustered. Here various commencement ceremonies take place at the end of the school year. In the middle of this Quadrangle—hence at the very center of the university—there's a jacaranda tree that blossoms late in the spring semester, reaching the peak of its intensely blue bloom just around the time of graduation. I have to believe that it was planted there as a symbolic statement of sorts, to the effect that the graduating students, like the jacaranda, have thrived and flowered during their years in the university's well-tended garden.

This is not just a casual metaphor. Who among the throng of parents who descend on the campus during those scintillating days in June doesn't feel that he or she is in fact wandering the grounds of a beautifully kept garden complex, with its expansive lawns, fountains, groves, courtyards, and sports fields? You can see in the parents' faces the spell of their enchantment. You can also detect a trace of regret: most of them no doubt feel nostalgic for their own bygone college days, which were also spent in such a garden world on this or some other American campus. All of which leads us once again to ask: what does education have to do with gardens?

Institutions of higher learning in fact have a long history of association with the garden, be it the parks and groves of the famous Greek schools, the Roman villa, the bowers of Sainte-Geneviève in medieval Paris, the Italian garden academies of the Renaissance, the British "college garden," or the idyll of the traditional American campus. The question that interests us here is whether there is more to this association than just a matter of setting. Since it is obvious from the way I pose the question that I will be seeking an answer in the affirmative, let me go back to the beginning and consider the first major institution of higher education to be established in the West: Plato's Academy in Athens.

Or more precisely, just outside of Athens. As far as we know there were no gardens to speak of inside the walls of ancient Athens, beyond which Socrates rarely ventured. Socrates apparently could do without them when it came to engaging in philosophical discussion with his fellow citizens or "corrupting the youth of Athens" with his pedagogy. Socrates was a philosopher of the Agora, which was both an outdoor market and the location of many public buildings. The Agora for him was the proper and perhaps even only place to engage in "higher learning" and philosophical inquiry. Plato, who turned Socrates into the main character of his corpus of dialogues after his teacher's death by execution in 399 BC, defended and even championed Socrates' reluctance to stray from downtown Athens, yet when it came time to found his school, Plato chose as his location not the Agora but a gardenlike environment outside the city walls, in a grove sacred to the hero Academos. Why?

In *The Republic* Plato would write that a philosopher should "shield himself behind a wall," alluding no doubt to the Academy, as his school came to be known. In Plato's time the Academy was in fact a walled park, much like the immured hunting preserves of the Persian kings, from which comes the word *paradise* (*paradeisos* in Greek, from the Persian *pairideiza*, or "walled around"). Maybe it was the condemnation of Socrates by the Athenian courts that convinced Plato to seek out a measure of detachment from the polis when it came to setting up his school. Or maybe he came to believe that Socrates was finally too close to the radioactive center of things for his own good, or the good of philosophy. Or maybe there was nothing reasoned or deliberate about his choice at all. Whatever his deeper motivation or lack thereof, Plato's decision to plant his school in a park on the margins of Athens—removed enough to listen to the voice of reason, close enough to stay within earshot of the citizens—set a pattern for the future history of academia in the West.

Plato devoted his entire career not only to the task of educating but also to a sustained philosophical reflection on the nature of education. Therefore when it comes to the question of whether there is more than just a casual connection between gardens and pedagogy, we could hardly do better than to query Plato himself. It is singularly significant, for our purposes, that Socrates actually suggests a deeper analogical connection between the two in the only dialogue of Plato that places him (Socrates) in a verdant setting outside the walls of Athens. At the end of the *Phaedrus*, in one of the more famous passages of Plato's corpus, Socrates launches a polemic against the written word and the art of writing generally. A lot more has been made of Socrates' claims in this passage than has been made of the metaphors and similes that inform those claims, yet it is impossible to give an adequate account of the latter without doing justice to the former. Socrates declares: "The fact is, Phaedrus, that writing involves a similar disadvantage to painting. The productions of paintings look like living beings, but if you ask them a question they maintain a solemn silence. The same holds true for written words; you might suppose that they understand what they are saying, but if you ask them what they mean by anything they simply return the same answer over and over again" (*Phaedrus* 97).

The analogy here is with *life*. Nor is it only an analogy, for Socrates goes on to speak of a "living and animate speech" that comes forth from the soul of a person in real time. He claims that this animate speech, of which "written speech might fairly be called a kind of shadow," is "written on the soul of the hearer together with understanding." To write on the soul of a living person is altogether different from writing on papyrus. Genuine teaching does the former and is more like an act of planting than of inscribing. This becomes evident when Socrates declares that, unlike written speech, living speech "knows how to defend itself, and can distinguish between those it should address and those in whose presence it should remain silent" (98). This ability to discriminate between worthy and unworthy interlocutors is critical to the educator, as well as to the student, as the gardening analogy that Socrates now puts forth makes clear:

> Now tell me this. Would a sensible farmer take seed which he valued and wished to produce a crop, and sow it in sober earnest in gardens of Adonis at midsummer, and take pleasure in seeing it reach its full perfection in eight days? Isn't this something that he might do in a holiday mood by way of diversion, if he did it at all? But where he is serious he will follow the true principles of agriculture and sow his seed in soil that suits it, and be well satisfied if what he has sown comes to maturity in eight months. ... And are we to say that the man with real knowledge of right and beauty and good will treat what we may by analogy call his seed less intelligently than the farmer? ... Then when he is in earnest [and not merely in a holiday mood] he will not take a pen and write in water or sow his seed in the black fluid called ink, to produce discourses which cannot defend themselves viva voce or give any adequate account of their truth. ... It will simply be by way of pastime that he will use the medium of writing to sow what may be called gardens of literature, laying up for himself as well as for those who follow the same track aids to recollection against the time when the forgetfulness of old age may overtake him, and it will give him pleasure to see the growth of their tender shoots. (98–99)

What exactly were the "gardens of Adonis" that Socrates compares to writing? Adonis, we recall, was the lover of Aphrodite and died young; in celebration (or mourning) of his early death, the Greeks would throw potted plants out of the window on his festival day (the Adone). These "gardens" were in effect little bowls or boxes whose plants had just begun to sprout but had not yet produced seeds. The latter detail is crucial to Plato's analogy, for it means that unlike the fully grown plants whose seeds (*sperma*) the farmer sows judiciously, the gardens of Adonis are in effect sterile. By comparing written discourse to the seedless plants of the gardens of Adonis, Plato reiterates his fundamental claim that writing is not productive of truth, or that truth cannot fully blossom in written form.

This does not mean that writing is a deleterious or misguided activity. Creating "gardens of literature" (which presumably include the Platonic dialogues themselves, insofar as they are written down) is a "noble pastime," Socrates declares to Phaedrus, even if it is not much more that that: a pastime. The serious business of philosophy—and that means the business of education as well—entails sowing the seeds of truth in a different way from composing written discourses. That different way of sowing occurs when

> a man employs the art of dialectic, and, fastening upon a suitable soul, plants and sows in it truths accompanied by knowledge. Such truths can defend themselves as well as the man who planted them; they are not sterile, but contain a seed from which fresh truths spring up in other minds; in this way they secure immortality for it, and confer upon the man who possesses it the highest happiness which it is possible for a human being to enjoy. (99)

The difference between written texts and what transpires between teacher and student in live dialogue (or "dialectic") is the difference between sterility and fertility. While Socrates' argument works by analogy, the terms of his analogy—soil and soul—in fact share a natural affinity in that both are living substances. To the degree that life animates them both, soil and soul both lend themselves to cultivation, or to the gardener's caretaking activity. The soul is not only *like* soil, in other words, it is itself a kind of soil—call it an organic-spiritual substance—in which the teacher, like the gardener, can sow his most valuable seeds and nurture their growth to full maturity. (In the Cura fable, we recall, Jupiter breathes spirit into the clay out of which Cura creates humankind; and until death divides spirit from matter, the biospiritual nature of human beings remains in essence a humic, cultivatable substance.)

Knowledge, in Plato's conception, is rooted in life. The life of the mind is first and foremost that—life. It is the student's whole animate personhood that receives from the teacher the seeds of knowledge, providing them with the soil in which to grow. Thus the Platonic educator tends to launch his appeal dramatically and passionately directly to the student's *life*, for only where there is life is there a potential for growth. The passage from the *Phaedrus* quoted above contains Plato's most ardent declaration of faith in the mission of education. The "highest happiness" a human being can attain, he says through the voice of Socrates, comes from nourishing new life in the soul of a student. Plato would have known such happiness from both ends, for he was both a devoted educator and one of Socrates' most devoted students. Nor could he have become the former had he not begun as the latter. The teacher plants seeds in a student's soul which in turn will produce new seeds to be planted in other students' souls. By such transmission does education perpetuate its mission.

Plato declares that the fostering of new life in a student's psyche takes place through an extended conversation (*sunousia*) over time between teacher and student. Conversation in real time, through the medium of love and fellowship, is what makes fertile the receptive mind and allows for the transmission of philosophy's essential truths. In his famous Seventh Letter (if he indeed authored that letter—most scholars now believe he did), Plato elaborates on how such conversation comes about and what results it yields. To begin with Plato makes the astonishing assertion that the truths of his philosophy cannot be expressed in language, even less in written language, and that he, Plato, never committed his philosophy to writing: "No treatise by me concerning [knowledge of the matters with which I concern myself] exists or ever will exist. It is not something that can be put into words like other branches of knowledge; only after long partnership [*sunousia*] and in a common life devoted to this very thing does the truth flash upon the soul, like a flame kindled by a leaping spark, and once it is born there it nourishes itself hereafter" (*Phaedrus* 136).

These are among the most beautiful words in the history of philosophy, and most educators in matters of the spirit know what Plato means when he declares that certain types of knowledge are not assimilated by osmosis or communicated through speech but are born in a flash of insight somewhere deep inside the student's animate selfhood. That recess, where understanding is suddenly sparked into being after long interchange with a teacher, is not a place that words can reach, at least not directly or immediately. Words can communicate information and opinions (*doxa*), but they cannot, in and of themselves, reveal the truth of the matter of which they speak. They can at best help bring about the moment of insight. That is why written discourse is ineffective when it comes to an education in philosophy. It is deprived of the animating spirit that every now and then allows the inner meaning of words to spring to life in the student's mind. That animating spirit pervades the teacher's presence and ongoing conversation. Just as the gardener can cultivate life but not create it, so too the teacher cannot generate true knowledge but can only foster the process by which it's born in the student's mind.

Plato goes on to affirm that few souls are capable of understanding the real matter of philosophy and that knowledge of the good (which *is* the matter of philosophy) can take root only in a soul that is itself good. Where the soil is blanched and cursed, nothing will grow; and "where the soul is ill endowed . . . Lynceus himself could not make a man see" (*Phaedrus* 140). This is an expression of Plato's so-called elitism, founded upon the notion that the majority of humans simply are not endowed with a capacity to grasp "the matter itself" (*to pragma auto*), hence that "higher education" is only for the special few. Plato believed that only rarely does a committed teacher encounter a student who is suited for philosophy—that is, for the *life* of philosophy.

While his doctrine is no doubt elitist, there is as much humility in its creed as there is presumption, for it ends up placing such severe limitations on the efficacy of pedagogy as to preclude any triumphalist attitude on the part of the educator. The teacher is for the most part powerless to transmit knowledge. Only where the student is already fertile can education work its gardening magic. However devoted and democratic-minded he or she may be, however widely the seed may be scattered, the teacher will reach in a meaningful and lasting way only a tiny minority of his or her students.

The Platonic Academy, with its comparatively exacting "admission standards," was intended precisely for that minority. But to understand why Plato founded a school in the first place, one must take seriously the conviction expressed in the Seventh Letter that truth springs into being in the student's soul only after "long partnership and in a common life devoted to this very thing" (i.e., the matter of philosophy, or knowledge of the good). The Academy was the place where the student lived with "the matter itself" day in and day out, in the company of others who, like him, were "devoted to this very thing," and with whom the conversation of philosophy never fell silent. The conversation of philosophy thus meant more than verbal dialogue and formal discussion about philosophical problems; it meant a partnership, a shared devotion to philosophy. For philosophy to thrive it had to root itself in the life of its students, which in turn had to give itself over to philosophy. Before all else, philosophy was a way of life, and the Academy was where it was lived.

Those admitted into the Academy's sanctuary joined in effect a sect, a cult, a quasi-secret fraternity, as it were, with its own rituals, symposia, and festival days. "Symposia" here doesn't mean academic conferences but veritable feasts of food, drink, and conversation, which were an integral part of life at the Academy. We know little about what exactly went on in the Academy, yet it seems quite certain that in the general curriculum as much attention was given to the body (gymnastics and the regulation of diet) as to the mind (geometry, mathematics, dialectic) as well as to the soul (music and poetry). In sum, the goal of Platonic education was the cultivation of the *whole person*, for the truth toward which philosophy aspired was a total, not partial, truth. That is why philosophy's way of life was far more than simply a regime of studies and exercises; it was an attempt on the part of a preselected group of individuals to live in accord with the nature of the matter itself. In such a fraternity, founded on fellowship and conversation, everyone contributed to the life of philosophy, such that it was the community as a whole, and not just the aggregate of its individuals, that constituted the spiritual garden of the Academy.

It is undeniable that in some respects the Academy, located on the margins of Athens, was a self-enclosed *paradeisos* for the privileged few, detached from the tumult of life in the city. In other respects it was emphatically *not* a hermetic institution where knowledge was pursued for knowledge's sake, virtue for virtue's sake, and beauty for beauty's sake. Nor was the community of philosophers an end in itself. In effect, the Academy was, in conception as well as in fact, a nursery for future statesmen. Plato may have shunned the Agora and shielded himself behind a wall, yet this was merely a tactical, not ideological, decision. By that I mean that he was as fiercely pledged to the polis as his teacher Socrates had been and that his commitment to philosophy remained, until the bitter end, a commitment to politics, broadly understood. It is true that the sorry spectacle of Athenian politics had caused him to renounce his early ambition to become a statesman himself and led him to devote his life to reflection, yet Plato's turn to philosophy was anything but a renunciation of political engagement. On the contrary, that spectacle convinced Plato that there was no hope for the polis unless philosophers became rulers or rulers became philosophers. The Academy in effect had a well-defined political mission: to turn the future counselors of rulers, if not the future rulers themselves, into philosophers. Why this imperative? So that the main business of politics, the administration of justice, could be grounded upon the foundations of metaphysical truth. Any other grounding (such was Plato's exalted and naive faith in the calling of philosophy) would merely perpetuate the anarchy of the times and the nightmare of history.

However elitist or paternalistic his political ideology may have been—however hostile to democracy and promiscuous with despotism it in fact was—there is little doubt that Plato was at heart a "republican" in at least this respect: he considered himself first and foremost a citizen of Athens, and, like Socrates, he believed in the citizen's burden of responsibility for the welfare of the polis. If he felt called upon to educate the city's future leaders, it was because he held that the civic world is what its citizens make of it through their own acts and decisions, and that its fate is mostly in the hands of men, not the gods (for all he may have been wrong about, about this much he was right). A great deal depends on how we act, and how we act depends a great deal on knowing, or not knowing, what we are doing when we act. If human justice is to conform to the order of truth, it must be based on a comprehensive knowledge of the foundations of truth. It is because of this belief in the priority of foundational knowledge (naive though it may have been) that Plato fulfilled his duty as a citizen in the most radical way he could imagine: by devoting himself to educating the next generation of civic leaders, cultivating their potential to grasp the matter of philosophy. In the final analysis Athens was the garden that mattered most for Plato. Those who joined the Academy entered its heterotopia on the outskirts of the city to learn to become caretakers of the state.

While much of the emphasis at the Academy was on community, conversation, and the fellowship of philosophy, the ground in which higher education sowed its seed was the individual "soul" of the student. That soul, call it the student's selfhood, was receptive above all to the suasion of love. Plato learned from his teacher—learned not abstractly but in person, as it were—that the enabling element of the ongoing conversation of philosophy is love, *philia*, which could also take the form of *eros*, or sexual attraction. The essence of the pedagogical revolution that Socrates, and in his wake Plato, brought about was the introduction of love into the learning process—not just love of wisdom (*philosophia*) but also and above all love between student and teacher. The potential erotic component of such love makes us uneasy these days, yet despite our efforts to banish it from the equation, personal love between teacher and student—which is not carnal love per se but something very different in its essence—remains to this day the living core of a meaningful education in the realm of the spirit.

Unlike the professional sophists, who taught for wages, and despite Diotima's eloquent effusion in *The Symposium* about love's ascent from the particular to the universal, Socrates was committed to loving each one of his students personally. Or better, he loved that formative place in the student's soul where love of wisdom could take root and germinate. The personal is the ground in which the universal must sow its seed, and love is the main agent of the flowering of knowledge in its abstract, universal determinations. Plato was certainly one of the beneficiaries of the amorous pedagogical solicitude of Socrates, and if later in life he felt the need to found a school, it was in part to create an environment that was hospitable to love, an environment in which the life of philosophy could flourish as if under the care and supervision of a dedicated gardener. This patient, interpersonal, love-based education in its ideal concept finds its living figure in the full-bodied garden that, unlike the gardens of Adonis, comes into its own in due time.

If one considers the university in our time, its founding principles are different in many ways from those of Plato's Academy, yet one thing has not changed much. The university continues to serve as a site where the ongoing, interactive dialogue of education can take place in real time and physical space. The main justification for a university campus in an age of telecommunications and multimedia technology is the occasion it provides for conversation, personalization, and shared commitment, for the exchange of words among a community of learners and the free flow of love between teacher and student—a flow that passes through their bodies as much as through their minds. Studies have shown that children may watch and listen to many hours of television a day but if they don't actively engage in speech themselves, they never acquire language. Likewise, a virtual university that trafficks in what Socrates calls the "shadow" of animate speech may produce gardens of Adonis but not such gardens as those that come into being through the *sunousia* of learners and teachers.

Academic institutions have changed considerably, both in character and in self-conception, since Plato founded his Academy, yet in their highest humanistic calling they remain certifiably faithful to Plato's pedagogical revolution in its essential objectives: to give birth to knowledge rather than information, memory rather than mnemonics, and commitment rather than compliance. From Socrates Plato learned that certain kinds of pedagogy make their appeal to what is most personal in the student's selfhood—a recess in the self that is at once removed from and open to the world. If one conceives of that recess as a garden of sorts, as Plato did, then one can understand why he spoke of educators as gardeners of the soul, and why some of us, whether we consider ourselves his direct heirs or not, think of universities as among the most precious gardens in the world.

ᔚ 7 ᔚ

The Garden School of Epicurus

WHAT IS ONE TO DO IN SO-CALLED DARK TIMES, WHEN
the world that "comes between men" no longer gives them a meaningful stage for their speech and actions, when reasoned discourse loses
its suasion, when powerlessness rather than empowerment defines the
citizen's role in the public sphere? There are times when the thinker,
patriot, or individual has no choice but to withdraw to the sidelines,
as Plato did when he gave up the idea of becoming a statesman and
founded a school on the outskirts of Athens. In her book *Men in Dark
Times* Hannah Arendt writes: "Flight from the world in dark times
of impotence can always be justified as long as reality is not ignored,
but is acknowledged as the thing that must be escaped" (*Men in Dark
Times*, 22). The same could be said of the sanctuary that gardens have
traditionally offered people when their "human condition" is under
siege. A garden sanctuary can be either a blessing or a curse, depending on the degree of reality it preserves within its haven. Some gardens
become places of escape that try to shut out reality (like the garden of
the Finzi-Contini in Giorgio Bassani's novel, where a Jewish family
and their friends lose connection with reality after Mussolini institutes
the race laws in Italy). Other gardens, by contrast, become places of
rehumanization in the midst of, or in spite of, the forces of darkness.

In 306 BC—a time of ever greater darkening in the Greek world—
an avowed enemy of the Platonists took up residence in Athens and

began cultivating his garden, as it were. Thirty years of age, Athenian by birth but Ionian by upbringing and temperament, Epicurus purchased a house in the upscale Melite district as well as a small garden property just outside the Dipylon Gate, on the same road that led to Plato's Academy. We know that the garden cost him only eighty minas, which was twenty minas less than the sophist Gorgias typically charged his pupils for a year of instruction. That it was small in size is confirmed by various contemporary references to it as the "little garden" (*kepidion* or *hortulus*). Yet it was in this little garden that one of the greatest and most successful schools in history took root and spread out across the ancient world, flourishing among pagan and Christian nations alike for over seven hundred years.

The Garden School, as it came to be known, was the third of the permanent Greek schools, after Plato's Academy and the Lyceum founded by Aristotle on the northern margins of Athens. The three schools had similar infrastructures: a private house (for residence, libraries, and dining) and an extramural site (Academy, Lyceum, and Garden) for lectures and instruction. The main *legal* difference between the garden property of Epicurus and both the Academy and the Lyceum was that the title deeds of the former were registered in Epicurus's own name—in other words, it was private property—while both the Academy and the Lyceum contained gymnasiums that were located on public grounds. This proved a significant difference, for it meant that, unlike the Academy and Lyceum, the Garden School was not subject to the supervision of the city's gymnasiarchs; thus it was the first school to enjoy a measure of what we today call "academic freedom."

In its titular status as private property, the garden reflected one of the pillars of Epicurean philosophy: the affirmation of what Pericles had called "idiocy," by which he meant apoliticism, or keeping to oneself. Epicurus was in fact a militant idiot who thought of his garden as a haven from public life. He had no political ambitions nor any desire to engage in the affairs and squabbles of the polis. As a thinker, Epicurus distinguished himself from the mainstream of Greek thought by depoliticizing the concept of happiness and dissociating it from its traditional link to citizenship. Pythagoras, Protagoras, Plato, Aristotle, the sophists, and almost all other Greek thinkers prior to Epicurus, with the exception of the Cynics, believed that only as a member of the polis could a man fulfill his inner potential and become fully human and happy. "A cityless man is like a solitary piece of chess," Aristotle declared. This Greek article of faith, so dear to Arendt, was remarkably pervasive and persistent, even long after it had become clear to anyone with open eyes that leading a public life did little to promote happiness, and much to bring on disappointment and misery, in those who engaged in its endless polemics.

Epicurus's eyes were open. He saw that a political career meant a life of constant anxiety and, more often than not, an ignominious or violent end. He was present in Athens when the orator Hypereides and several others were executed, and when the noble Demosthenes avoided a similar fate by taking his own life. Epicurus observed new and ever more absurd installments of the same sorry spectacle of intrigue and folly that had disgusted Plato in his youth; yet unlike Plato, who believed that the polis had to be revolutionized by philosophy, Epicurus believed that the fracas and power struggles of the polis had to be resolutely shunned. Philosophy, or so he believed, should serve the interests of the *summmum* supreme *good bonum*, which is life, and not the interests of the city.

To understand how Epicurus's garden reflects and even embodies the core of his philosophy, we must keep in mind first of all that it was an actual kitchen garden tended by his disciples, who ate the fruits and vegetables they grew there. Yet it was not for the sake of fruits and vegetables alone that they assiduously cultivated the soil. Their gardening activity was also a form of education in the ways of nature: its cycles of growth and decay, its general equanimity, its balanced interplay of earth, water, air, and sunlight. Here, in the convergence of vital forces in the garden's microcosm, the cosmos manifested its greater harmonies; here the human soul rediscovered its essential connection to matter; here living things showed how fruitfully they respond to a gardener's solicitous care and supervision. Yet the most important pedagogical lesson that the Epicurean garden imparted to those who tended it was that life—in all its forms—is intrinsically mortal and that the human soul shares the fate of whatever grows and perishes on and in the earth. Thus the garden reinforced the fundamental Epicurean belief that the human soul is as amenable to moral, spiritual, and intellectual cultivation as the garden is to organic cultivation. Indeed, one could say that it was thanks above all to the garden that what Michel Foucault calls antiquity's *culture de soi* became the most essential element of Epicurean pedagogy. How so?

The ultimate objective of Epicurean education was not the attainment of wisdom or justice but the attainment of happiness. Epicurus understood happiness as a state of mind and believed that it consisted primarily in *ataraxia*, which we translate as "peace of mind" or "spiritual tranquillity" (in Greek it means literally the state of being unperturbed). Now *ataraxia* is not a spontaneous or "natural" state for human beings, who are typically afflicted by cares and a heightened awareness of death, which perturbs and unsettles the mortal soul. Human beings are not naturally given to serenity. Thus *ataraxia* is in fact a highly cultivated state of mind, one whose attainment requires systematic discipline, education, and unconditional devotion to the "true philosophy" of Epicureanism. Only a proper understanding of reality can free the soul from its death anxieties, which is why Epicurus called on his disciples to live day in and day out according to the established doctrines of Epicureanism, in which the life of philosophy and the philosophy of life were one and the same.

Since ataraxy is enabled by, or arises from, knowledge of the true nature of things, the student's first task was to gain a complete understanding of the axioms of the Epicurean doctrine. In the so-called Little Epitome—a brief, condensed text for beginners—Epicurus laid out his theory about atoms and the void, the mortality of the soul, and the absence of divine providence in human affairs. "Faith in the certainty of knowledge," he claimed, was the best antidote to human anxiety. Epicurus believed that human beings have a debilitating fear of death, not so much because they are afraid of dying but because they fear the unknown and thus are apprehensive about what happens to the soul after death. By holding fast to the certainty that the soul is composed of atoms, hence that no ghostly afterlife awaits it after death, the Epicurean may begin to shed anxieties about death and reinscribe its inevitability within the cosmic order of things. The cultivation of this certainty allows *ataraxia* to blossom in the soul over time.

How exactly does one cultivate such certainty? Whereas Platonism called for meditation on the immortality of the soul, Epicureanism called for meditation on mortality as the fate of both body and soul, which are born and die together ("we are born once and we cannot be born twice but to all eternity must be no more," quoted in De Witt, 218). Here too the garden played a crucial pedagogical role, for by revealing on a daily basis the interconnectedness of growth and decay, by revealing how death is the consummation and not merely the termination of life, it served to renaturalize human mortality in the minds of the disciples. The garden also served as a warning about the dangers threatening the state of *ataraxia*, which, once attained, calls for continued maintenance. *Ataraxia* is fraught with the same tension that pervades the self-gathered serenity of gardens, namely the tension between order and entropy. Epicureans who worked the *hortulus* knew that constant vigilance and intervention were necessary to keep the wilder forces of nature at bay, or under effective control. *Ataraxia* required a similar vigilance if it was not give way to deep-seated perturbations such as the fear of death or guilt before the gods. In other words, anxiety was not so much overcome as transfigured by the life of philosophy, the way gardens—when they are well conceived—transfigure rather than overcome nature. Indeed, a distinct tension pervades the state of *ataraxia*, albeit in a quiet and mastered form, much like the mastered tension that pervades the serene appearance of human gardens.

To fully appreciate how the activity of gardening was connaturally related to Epicureanism's *culture de soi*, we must understand the extent to which all Epicurean values and virtues were derived from the *summum bonum*—life—and the manner in which they were systematically cultivated for their power to enhance and promote the essential goodness of life, or what Epicurus called life's "pleasure" (in Greek, *hedone*, from *hedys*, sweet). Pleasure is the precious fruit of the Epicurean garden. Nothing is more misunderstood than the Epicurean notion of pleasure, which was in every respect a cultivated phenomenon. Pleasure, as Epicurus understood it, had little if anything to do with the gratification of appetites (Epicurus in fact repeatedly condemned lust, luxury, gluttony, and excessive indulgence of any sort). Instead it had everything to do with the Epicurean community's cultivation of personal and social virtues.

Chief among the Epicurean virtues is friendship. "Of all the preparations which wisdom makes for the blessedness of the complete life by far the most important is the acquisition of friendship" (quoted in De Witt, 308). Friendship is at once a good in itself—Epicurus held that it was more important to have someone to eat with than to have something to eat—and a pragmatic necessity. Friends come to each other's aid in times of need. The certainty that in moments of crisis one can turn to one's friends for protection and support fortifies spiritual tranquillity. Because they are a buffer against the unpredictable vicissitudes of life, friends help guarantee the relative security on which *ataraxia* depends for its constancy. Beyond the pragmatic considerations, however, friendship is indispensable to happiness in its own right, for nothing sweetens the flavor of life as much as good companionship. That is why the Epicurean must systematically cultivate the art of friendship, as if it were a living garden. Epicurus: "It is necessary, however, to prepare the way for [friendship] in advance—for we also sow seed in the ground" (ibid., 325). To acquire and preserve friendship demands foresight, deliberation, and self-improvement, for it requires developing qualities in yourself that will recommend you to your friend, make you attractive to your friend, and enhance the quality of your companionship.

Hence the importance of conversation. For Epicurus there is no greater instance of human pleasure, no higher form of mortal happiness, than intelligent, profitable, and pleasant conversation between friends who know how to listen, inspire, and enlighten. To become a worthy interlocutor it is necessary to gain a mastery of verbal skills, attain a degree of unaffected eloquence, and expand one's mind through a continuous engagement with philosophy. The best and most pleasurable conversations invariably involve an exchange of ideas and the probing of truth. The memory of such conversations affords happiness well into the future, becoming an inexhaustible reservoir of pleasure even in the direst moments of distress and pain. At the end of his life, Epicurus overcame the physical pains that afflicted him on a daily basis by recollecting with gratitude some of the conversations he had had with friends in years past.

It is in this same vein that Epicurus recommended the cultivation of "suavity" in one's demeanor and personality. Suavity was understood by Epicurus as a form of generosity to one's fellow human beings, especially to one's friends. One of the distinctive legacies of Epicureanism among the Romans was the cult of *suavitas*, which Cicero aptly defined as "a certain agreeableness of speech and manners" (ibid., 311). Suavity, which was radically opposed to the boorishness of the Cynics, the superciliousness of the Platonists, and the dourness of the Stoics, was a mode of comportment and quality of the voice that rendered one pleasing and attractive to others. It too was an acquired virtue, and throughout the ancient world a suave demeanor became a defining trait of the Epicureans.

Closely linked to suavity was *epiekeia*, or consideration for others. Epicurean *epiekeia*—the forerunner of Christian *caritas*—was not the formal courtesy of the "magnanimous man" or condescending noble but a genuine *philia* or love of humankind. It was shown to one's superiors, inferiors, and equals alike, taking the form of kindness, civility, graciousness, and respect. Consideration for others in no way meant sparing their feelings, however, when criticism or objection were called for. On the contrary, *parresia*, or honesty of speech, was a prime directive of the Epicurean. Against flattery and sycophancy, for which he had a particular loathing, Epicurus enjoined nonaggressive candor in all of one's dealing with others, no matter how humble or powerful they might be.

Personal or social virtues such as these, as well as the traditional moral virtues of temperance, prudence, courage, and justice, were all part of the Epicurean project of self-humanization. I would mention here a trio of others—patience, hope, and gratitude—which one might call existential dispositions toward the temporal ecstasies of past, present, and future. Contrary to popular opinion, nothing is more antithetical to Epicurean doctrine than the *carpe diem* attitude, with its eager grasping at the pleasures of the present. Living for the present moment dooms one to an endless anxiety about the present's inability to be arrested, its constant slipping away into nothingness. For the Epicurean, the proper attitude to be cultivated toward the present is rather *patience*, which entails a serene acceptance of both what is given and what is withheld by life in the present. Patience has nothing to do with renunciation. It means being prepared to endure privation without grievance and by the same token to receive blessings when they are granted. Integrally linked to patience is *hope*, which Epicurus defined as anticipation of the good to come. Hope is the proper disposition toward the future, just as *gratitude* is the proper disposition toward the past. Gratitude for the happiness of time past remains a source of happiness in the present and, by extension, a guarantor of happiness to come. Not even Zeus can take away the pleasures of the past (conversations with friends, for example), the memory of which exerts its blessings on the present and will continue to do so thereafter, whatever fate may have in store for the future.

Of these three virtues, gratitude is by far the most important. It is not only an effect or consequence of happiness but also a creator of happiness, for it allows the affirmation of life's intrinsic value to flourish and its pains and misfortunes to fall into oblivion. As the most essential ingredient of Epicurean happiness, gratitude falls wholly under the regime of *culture de soi*. In other words, it is an eminently cultivatable disposition: "it lies in our power to bury, as it were, unhappy memories in everlasting oblivion and to recall happy memories with sweet and agreeable recollection" (ibid., 322). The fool, by contrast, remembers only misfortunes and past errors. Those who cautioned against calling any man happy until the day he dies (in the famous dictum of Solon) Epicurus accused of ingratitude: "The adage which says, 'Look to the end of a long life,' bespeaks a lack of gratitude for past blessings" (ibid.). There is much that does not lie within our power—future misfortunes, for example—and many of our possessions, including health, friends, and wealth, can be taken away from us, yet nothing can take away our gratitude for past blessings.

For Epicurus, ingratitude was as common among men and women as it was corrosive of the human soul. Nothing much has changed—in fact societies have become ever more foolish and forward-looking—since Epicurus wrote: "The life of the fool is marked by ingratitude and apprehension; the drift of his thought is exclusively toward the future" (ibid., 326). Today we tend to believe that a forward-looking disposition keeps us young, but Epicurus held that the opposite is the case. The ungrateful man, absorbed by the future, turns prematurely old ("forgetting the good that has been, he becomes an old man this very day" [ibid.]), while the grateful Epicurean retains his hold on youth even in old age: "Both when young and old one should devote oneself to philosophy in order that while growing old he shall be young in blessings through gratitude for what has been" (ibid.). In a moment of true philosophical if not psychological insight, Epicurus even links ingratitude to gluttony: "It is the ungratefulness in the soul that renders the creature endlessly lickerish of embellishments in diet" (ibid., 327). Such gluttony, we might add, pertains also to those who would, if they could, go on living forever, never having had enough of life (and there are many such would-be immortalists among us today), whereas the Epicurean takes leave of life as after a feast, with a sense of fullness, contentedness, and satiation.

This brief review of the creeds and ethics of Epicureanism makes it clear that, in his drive to live a life free from the cares that tyrannized his fellow citizens, Epicurus in fact took his directives from a higher order of care than the one that governed the political agitations of the times. I mean his care for promoting the cause of human happiness as opposed to promoting the cause of this or that ideology or faction.

Epicurus believed that the purpose of philosophy was not to rule the city but to enhance a mortal life's potential for happiness, precisely by liberating happiness from its traditional connections to citizenship. Since the polis no longer promoted the cause of human happiness but, on the contrary, militated against it, it was necessary, or so Epicurus believed, to assume *personal* responsibility for one's happiness. Like the garden, personal happiness calls for self-cultivation and *culture de soi*. This was the essential lesson taught within the precinct of the Garden School.

Arendt writes: "It is essential [for those in flight from reality] to realize that the realness of this reality consists not in its deeply personal note, any more than it springs from privacy as such, but inheres in the world from which they have escaped" (*Men in Dark Times*, 22). That realization holds true for the Epicureans, for whom personal happiness was at bottom a demand made in the context of a world that either was politically indifferent to such a demand or held it in political contempt. Epicurus's retreat from the public realm was *not* a retreat into "privacy," as we understand that concept today. It may have been a retreat into idiocy, but not privacy. The garden was privately owned, to be sure, and this private ownership was an essential component of the school's marginal freedom from municipal authority, yet the intensely communal life of the Garden School belies any notion of privacy, as Arendt intends it. Epicurus did not retreat into a fortress of solitude; he retreated into a garden that, through the communal participation of all involved, blossomed into one of the most vital and most life-affirming schools of the ancient world.

Just as it was not a retreat into "privacy," neither was Epicureanism a retreat into what Arendt elsewhere calls "the life of the mind," focused on unworldly meditations and abstractions. Epicureans were not ascetics. They never vilified nor glorified the body. In addition to a contemplative life, they led an embodied life whose social, erotic, and sensual dimensions were embraced according to the measures dictated by doctrine. And while it could be said that Epicurus took strategic "flight from reality," he did not seek an "escape from reality." The difference is crucial. Epicurus sought out the asylum of his garden without ever ceasing to acknowledge the reality from which he was taking flight. Indeed, the garden for Epicurus was a place from which and in which reality itself could be reconceived, its possibilities reimagined. Or better, it was a place where the human and social virtues that were trampled on by the so-called real world could reflourish under carefully husbanded circumstances.

Friendship, conversation, gratitude, spiritual tranquility—these were not private pleasures of the isolated self, any more than the Epicurean garden was a place of solitude. They were virtues cultivated communally, or pluralistically as it were. One could call them social virtues, but perhaps it would be more precise to call them political virtues in exile. For political virtues have their foundation in social virtues. When the public sphere no longer allows them to thrive, it is all the more important for those social virtues to find asylum in special havens that are removed, but not detached, from the world.

Many philosophers both before and after him have worried the question of human happiness, and many have called for the cultivation of moral and social virtues, yet among the ancients Epicurus was one of the very few who called on his disciples to *cultivate mortality*. He did not call on them to heroically defy its limitations, nor to submit stoically to its necessity, but rather to cultivate mortality as the means as well as end of happiness. He looked at the human world in dark times and saw the absurdity of its dominant compulsions, its perverse drive to conspire against the condition of serenity, its tendencies to bring on sufferings that had little to do with the gods and everything to do with the human failure to humanize the world. Stoic resignation was not enough. Stoicism called for apathy, whereas Epicureanism called for self-responsibility, the pleasures of community, and a relationship to death that saw death as the proper fulfillment of life.

Arendt asks, "To what extent do we remain obligated to the world even when we have been expelled from it or have withdrawn from it?" (*Men in Dark Times*, 22). Epicurus instead asked: to what extent do we remain obligated to our humanity even after the world that comes between us has betrayed or disfigured it? To the end Epicurus's obligation was to the human, not to a world that had turned infernal. His Garden School did not presume to come to the world's rescue and save it from its own inferno. Its ambition was far more modest and finally far more efficacious: to make room for the human in the midst of the inferno by giving it soil in which to grow.

Are we Epicureans? One often hears these days that Western decadence has taken the form of an aggravated Epicureanism, but where is the garden? Where is the ataraxy? Certainly if one assumes the popular conception of Epicureanism as a crass philosophy of materialism that chases after the pleasures of the day, present-day societies in the West could be seen as Epicurean in their orientation. But in fact nothing could be further removed from the popular conception of Epicureanism than Epicureanism itself. By the same token, nothing could be further removed from Epicurean *ataraxia* than our compulsive frenzy, our emporium of desires, and our anxiety in the face of death. To that we must add that nothing could be more antithetical to the Epicurean ethic of cultivation than our ethic of consumption. Patience, hope, and gratitude? These are existential dispositions that we have all but exiled. We relate to the present in the mode of impatience, to the future in the mode of despair, and to the past with the fool's ingratitude. Where gratification takes the place of gratitude, as it does in our senile new world, gluttony becomes a destiny. This "ungratefulness in the soul that renders the creature endlessly lickerish of embellishments in diet" makes for a paltry and degenerate hedonism.

A genuine hedonism puts very different demands on us from the ones that guide our behavior today. It demands of us that as gardeners of human happiness, we turn the curse of mortality into the source of many blessings. Clearly we are far from being Epicureans.

⤞ 8 ⤝

Boccaccio's Garden Stories

HUMAN CULTURE HAS ITS ORIGIN IN STORIES, AND ITS ongoing history is one of endless storytelling. Where would we be without stories? without the art of recounting them? without their narrative organization of events and their structuring of time? If you ask me where I'm from, or what happened at the gathering last night, or why my friend is so distraught, I can hardly answer you without telling a little story. In its formal as well as informal modes, storytelling is one of the most basic forms of human interaction. The fabric of life itself is woven into and by stories, so much so that the quality of human conversation depends to a great extent on our mastery of the art of narrative. This art is something we either bring or fail to bring to bear, day in and day out, on our relations with others.

All good and well, you say, but what does storytelling have to do with gardens? That is a question we must put to the best storyteller in the Western canon, Giovanni Boccaccio, author of *The Decameron* and a host of so-called minor works that are anything but minor in stature.

Boccaccio's *Decameron* (1350) is one of the most elegant, if nondoctrinal, expressions of Epicureanism in its genuine latter-day form. Its introduction recounts how, during the height of the black death of 1348, seven young women and three men decide to leave the plague-ravaged city of Florence and retreat to a villa in the surrounding hills, where for two weeks they will engage in conversation, leisurely walks, dancing, storytelling, and merrymaking, taking care not to transgress the codes of proper conduct or compromise the *dignità* of the ladies. Nothing could contrast more vividly with the horrors of a pestilent Florence than the idyllic garden settings that await them in the countryside (garden settings in which most of the tales of the *Decameron* are told by the ten members of the *brigata*). In the city, civic order has degenerated into anarchy; love of one's neighbor has turned into dread of one's neighbor (who now represents the threat of contagion); the law of kinship has given way to every person for himself (many family members flee from their infected loved ones, leaving them to face their death agonies alone and without succor); and where there was once courtesy and decorum there is now crime and delirium.

During their two-week sojourn in well-manicured gardens and country villas, the young Florentines, in dire need of distraction from the desolation of death and of consolation for their family losses, set out to reestablish the bonds of community that in Florence have been all but shattered by the plague. While their escapade is indeed a "flight from reality," their self-conscious efforts to follow an almost ideal code of sociability during their stay in the hills of Fiesole are a direct response to the collapse of social order they leave behind. In that respect their sojourn is wholly "justified" by Hannah Arendt's standards invoked in the preceding chapter ("flight from the world in dark times of impotence can always be justified as long as reality is not ignored, but is acknowledged as the thing that must be escaped").

The *brigata*'s avowed objective is to maximize the *piacere*, or pleasure, afforded by their beautiful surroundings. We have already seen that Epicurean hedonism, far from being mere gratification of appetites or release from self-constraint, is a cultivated phenomenon that, like a garden, requires a certain structure within which to thrive. This is reaffirmed by the "queen" of Day One, Pampinea, who tells her cohort on their first day out: "A merry life should be our aim, since it was for no other reason that we were prompted to run away from the sorrows of the city. However, nothing will last for very long unless it possesses a definite form" (65). She goes on to correlate the words *order* and *pleasure* in her declaration to the effect that "our company will be able to live an ordered and agreeable existence for as long as we choose to remain together" (the Italian is more emphatic: *la nostra compagnia con ordine e con piacere e senza alcuna vergogna viva e duri quanto a grado ne fia*; literally, "with order and with pleasure and without any shame").

Following Pampinea's lead, the *brigata* gives its pleasurable activities a highly organized structure. Each member will take turns being "king" or "queen" for the day, thereby assuming responsibility for practical decisions regarding meals, siestas, walks, singing, observing the Sabbath, and so forth. Most important, the king or queen prescribes the theme for his or her day's stories. According to their plan, each member of the *brigata* tells one story a day, for a total of one hundred stories. Since the sojourn lasts exactly two weeks and there is no storytelling on two days of each week in observance of the Sabbath, there are ten days of storytelling in all (hence the book's title: *Decameron*). By giving their fourteen days such a "definite form," the members of the *brigata* not only secure the pleasure of their sojourn but also establish the order that underlies the architectonic of the *Decameron* itself.

Form giving is crucial to the *socialization* of pleasure, which in turn is crucial to its endurance and stability. Such socialization domesticates the wilder egotistical impulses of individuals, yet it has nothing to do with the repression or renunciation of appetites (most of the stories of the *Decameron* belie any such ethic of repression); instead, it has everything to do with turning the social order into the place where pleasure finds its ultimate fulfillment. In Boccaccio's world pleasure is unconditionally social, without in the least ceasing to be "natural." Nature and society are not antagonists; if anything, they are creative allies in the project of human happiness. Where pleasure keeps their respective claims in balance, it thrives like an Italian garden. That is one reason, among others, that the gardens of the *Decameron* appear as the ideal space for the *brigata*'s humanized *letizia* or "delight." The elegant way in which they conjugate nature and form make them "pleasure gardens" in more ways than one. Let us ponder for a moment this conjugation.

From Boccaccio's description, the *Decameron*'s gardens seem to have an aesthetic signature that relates them, if only by lineage or ancestry, to the Italian garden art of the Renaissance. This art, which came into its own in central and southern Italy during the sixteenth and seventeenth centuries, has been thoroughly studied and eloquently commented on by several excellent scholars over the past few centuries. I will not presume to add to their insights here but only remark that those scholars would definitely recognize in Boccaccio's gardens certain prototypical features of their object of study, namely a style of garden architecture in which art neither dominates nature (as in Versailles, for example) nor flatters nature (as in eighteenth-century English landscape gardens), but instead collaborates with nature to create a humanized space that is at once highly formal and perfectly "natural," in the sense that it puts nature's species and landscapes on informal display.

I will quote here from one especially perceptive commentator, Edith Wharton, whose book *Italian Villas and Their Gardens* is still one of the classics in this domain. In her introduction, titled "Italian Garden-Magic," Wharton writes that "one day" the Renaissance architect looked out from the terrace of his villa and discovered that the "enclosing landscape" was "naturally included" within his garden. "The two formed part of the same composition," she writes. If this discovery was the "first step" of the great Italian garden art, as Wharton claims, "the next was the architect's discovery of the means by which nature and art might be fused in his picture." She goes on:

> However much other factors may contribute to the total impression of charm, yet by eliminating them one after another, by *thinking away* the flowers, the sunlight, the rich tinting of time, one finds that, underlying all these, there is a deeper harmony of design which is independent of any adventitious effects. This does not imply that a plan of an Italian garden is as beautiful as the garden itself. The more permanent materials of which the

latter is made—the stonework, the evergreen foliage, the effects of rushing or motionless water, above all the lines of the natural scenery—all form a part of the artist's design. But these things are as beautiful at one season as at another; and even these are but the accessories of the fundamental plan. The inherent beauty of the garden lies in the grouping of its parts—in the converging lines of its long ilex-walks, the alternation of sunny open spaces with cool woodland shade, the proportion between terrace and bowling-green, or between the height of a wall and the width of a path. None of these details was negligible to the landscape architect of the Renaissance: he considered the distribution of shade and sunlight, of straight lines of masonry and rippled lines of foliage, as carefully as he weighed the relation of his whole composition to the scene about it. (8)

When one reads closely Boccaccio's description of the garden in the introduction to the Third Day (see appendix 1), one finds that it moves in two contrary directions. On the one hand, it introduces such a plenitude of flora, fauna, and fruits into the scene as to give the garden an Edenic character that is beyond any measure of realism. On the other hand, it exalts that "grouping of parts" and harmony of design that Wharton sees as the essence of "Italian garden-magic." As a result of this juxtaposition, the Edenic character of the garden comes across as illusory. The conspicuous emphasis on artifice accentuates the fact that this garden is a human creation, its enchantments are carefully engineered, and its environment remains subject to the laws of nature, hence vulnerable to the forces of decay, death, and disaster. Here too—here especially—the plague casts its long shadow over the walls that, like a temple, set this garden apart.

Even though it is walled in, the garden appears to the reader of Boccaccio's *Decameron* as the quintessence or distillation of its cultivated landscape and setting, where villas, loggias, gardens, meadows, lakes, and groves form a kind of super-garden ensemble that remains under the governance of human design (like much of the Tuscan landscape still today). And in case we had any doubt that a garden's walls are always permeable, the first story of the Third Day sends the uncouth Masetto into the immured grounds of a convent like a veritable force of nature, where, in the guise of a deaf and mute gardener, he will happily go about servicing the sexual desires of a coterie of nine nuns (see appendix 1, which includes this story). Walls, whether they are erected around the self or around a garden, do not keep nature out but at best submit nature to human regulation.

Masetto is a force of nature, to be sure, yet we must not (like the nuns) be fooled by his postures of uncultivated simpleton. While his sexual desires may be perfectly "natural" and unmediated, his behavior and tactics are anything but spontaneous. In fact one could say that he is in many ways the counterpart of the architect who designed the garden in whose setting this tale is narrated. By that I mean that he proceeds by design, plotting his course of action and executing it according to a plan that puts itself in the service of nature. In so doing he is also like the gardener who sows his seeds in advance and in due time reaps the fruits of his labor.

For all the changes that Masetto's presence introduces into the spiritual as well as erotic life of the convent, his intrusion does not result in anarchy and disorder. On the contrary, by the end of the story the libidinal energies of the convent assume a measured regulation and just distribution that enable them to flourish without undermining the foundations of the institutional order. The story is finally a celebration of the protagonists' resourcefulness when it comes to finding a way to give a "definite form" to pleasure. In this respect the Abbess, with whom he comes to an arrangement that is satisfactory to all, is no less heroic (according to Boccaccio's standards of heroism) than Masetto.

If in Christian symbolism a convent is where nuns celebrate their mystical marriage to Christ, Masetto's advent reterrestrializes its garden, as it were, by placing it back upon this earth and reopening it to the claims of nature. It is typical of Boccaccio's subtlety as a writer to introduce the Third Day—the most "pornographic" day of the *Decameron*—with allusions to Dante's *Purgatory* (*L'aurora già di vermiglia cominciava . . .*), which culminates in the Garden of Eden. The allusion to *Purgatory* is of course insidious, as the entire Third Day confirms, beginning with the Masetto tale's play on the number 9, which for Dante was the most holy of numbers (the Trinity times itself). When I say that Boccaccio reterrestrializes the garden, I do not mean simply that he turns it into a place of erotic delights à la *Romance of the Rose*, which figures as extended sexual allegory. I mean that he puts the convent's erotic economy under human governance. The convent's liberated yet regulated sex life now finds its proper figure in the thriving garden, under whose human governance nature's fruitfulness is allowed to thrive (the nuns give birth to many "nunlets and monklets"), albeit under carefully supervised and controlled circumstances.

Insofar as the garden in which the tale is told owes its existence to human design, it figures as more than just an appropriate setting for that tale. A deeper and more general analogy in fact binds together the garden and storytelling in the *Decameron*, for in general we could say that Boccaccio's narrative art is governed by aesthetic principles similar to those we find at work in the garden art of the Renaissance. I do not mean only the exquisite architecture of *The Decameron* as a whole, with its narrative frame, its integrated sequence of themes, its diversity of voices, and its sustained interplay of perspectives. I mean also the analogy between a story and a garden. A story, after all, is like a garden. It has its distinct shape, its articulated rhythm, its byways, its unfolding perspectives, its intrigues and surprises, its sinister undersides, its changing appearances, and its transitive relationship to the "real world" beyond its imaginary bounds. Most important for Boccaccio, if the story is well conceived and well told, it delights.

Take the Masetto tale. When one looks at the discreet artfulness that informs its straightforward style—I mean the orderly unfolding of the action, the extended allusions to Christian symbolism, the spoofing of courtly love (in particular the latter's proscription against the seduction of nuns), the humor that holds nothing back yet never stoops to vulgarity, the parody of Saint Augustine's doctrine that human speech has its source in unfulfilled desire (Masetto first speaks out because of oversatiation), the brilliant puns on the tropes of marriage and gardening—all this fuses literary artifice and naturalism in the way the Italian garden, if we believe Wharton and a host of other scholars, fuses nature and design. Indeed, Boccaccio's much-vaunted naturalism is not so much a doctrine of nature's sovereignty over human behavior and motivation as it is a particular style of storytelling. That uncontrived yet highly refined style for which Boccaccio is rightly famous—a style at once lucid and complex, bold and subtle, colloquial and learned—was the result of an extraordinary formalization of the art of narrative that served in effect to *naturalize* that art.

We can take the measure of his achievement by comparing Boccaccio with some of his more primitive sources. Consider the *Novellino*, a late-thirteenth-century collection of one hundred short vignettes which offers itself to the reader as a bouquet of beautiful flowers ("let us record here some flowers of speech, of elegant manners, elegant ripostes, elegant deeds, elegant generosity and elegant loves"). Story 89 of the *Novellino* is typical of its emphasis on punch line and repartee:

> A group of knights were dining one night in a great Florentine house, and there was a courtier present who was a great speaker. After they had finished eating, he began recounting a story that went on and on. A young man of the house who was serving, and who perhaps had not had his fill, called out to him by name and said: "Whoever told you this story did not tell you all of it."—And he answered: "And why not?"—And he answered: "Because he didn't tell you how it ends."

Boccaccio rewrites this vignette in the first novella of Day Six, which pays tribute to the *Novellino*'s celebration of wit and elegance in the prescribed theme for the day: to tell of "those who, on being provoked by some verbal pleasantry, have returned like for like, or who, by a prompt retort or shrewd manouevre, have avoided danger, discomfiture or ridicule." Here is Boccaccio's version:

As many of you will know, either through direct personal acquaintance or through hearsay, a little while ago there lived in our city a lady of silver tongue and gentle breeding, whose excellence was such that she deserves to be mentioned by name. She was called Madonna Oretta, and she was the wife of Messer Geri Spina. One day, finding herself in the countryside like ourselves, and proceeding from place to place, by way of recreation, with a party of knights and ladies whom she had entertained to a meal in her house earlier in the day, one of the knights turned to her, and, perhaps because they were having to travel a long way, on foot, to the place they all desired to reach, he said:

"Madonna Oretta, if you like I shall take you riding along a goodly stretch of our journey by telling you one of the finest tales in the world."

"Sire," replied the lady, "I beseech you most earnestly to do so, and I shall look upon it as a great favour."

Whereupon this worthy knight, whose swordplay was doubtless on a par with his storytelling, began to recite his tale, which in itself was indeed excellent. But by constantly repeating the same phrases, and recapitulating sections of the plot, and every so often declaring that he had "made a mess of that bit," and regularly confusing the names of the characters, he ruined it completely. Moreover, his mode of delivery was totally out of keeping with the characters and the incidents he was describing, so that it was painful for Madonna Oretta to listen to him. She began to perspire freely, and her heart missed several beats, as though she had fallen ill and was about to give up the ghost. And in the end, when she could endure it no longer, having perceived that the knight had tied himself inextricably in knots, she said to him, in affable tones:

"Sir, you have taken me riding on a horse that trots very jerkily. Pray be good enough to set me down."

The knight, who was apparently far more capable of taking a hint than of telling a tale, saw the joke and took it in the cheerfullest of spirits. Leaving aside the story he had begun and so ineptly handled, he turned his attention to telling her tales of quite another sort.

Where the *Novellino* tale offers the reader a single flower of wit, Boccaccio's version opens into a little garden, as it were. To begin with, it introduces a gender dynamic that gives a wholly different kind of punch to Madonna Oretta's repartee, which sparkles both in its elegance and its tact. The metaphor of horseback riding arises naturally from the scene (ladies and knights, a long and fatiguing walk in the country, etc.). The specifics of the knight's mangling of his tale are cataloged in what amounts to a kind of negative manifesto of narrative style, as the reader is directly drawn into the discomfiture and exasperation that the flailing performance induces in Madonna Oretta. The sexual connotations of horseback riding in the tale also serve to establish an overt parallel between the ineptitude of storytelling and the ineptitude of lovemaking. In sum, while it too culminates in repartee, there is a density to this reworking that involves far more than a punch line. It articulates an aesthetics of storytelling on the hand and (like all the stories of Day Six) a discreet social ethics on the other.

From one point of view, the analogy between horseback riding and storytelling is simply a clever figure of speech that gives Madonna Oretta the opportunity, through her "prompt retort," to extricate herself from an uncomfortable situation with an elegant metaphor, at the same time rescuing her interlocutor without offending him. But there is more to it than that, for horsemanship has a long traditional association with *virtù*—virtue understood as the mastery and control of recalcitrant forces —an association that can be traced all the way back to Plato's famous allegory in the *Phaedrus*, where the virtuous soul is compared to a charioteer who succeeds in keeping his horses, as they pull in different directions, on the straight path. By comparing the knight's bad narrative style to bad horsemanship, Boccaccio is in effect staking out an ethical, and not merely aesthetic, claim for good storytelling.

Nothing enhances human relations and the bonds of community more than mastery of the art of narrative. Stories provide a form of social pleasure, even when they are read (or nowadays seen) in the solitude of one's private chambers. Beyond their power to delight (or maybe this is part of their delight), they reaffirm in exemplary, dramatic, or allegorical modes the values that bind communities together. That Boccaccio viewed storytelling as part of an ethic of neighborly love is clear from his preface to the *Decameron*. There he declares that of all the moral virtues, the most important by far is gratitude (in this too he was a genuine Epicurean). He then goes on to present the *Decameron* to his reader as an act of gratitude for the generosity shown to him in the past by various friends in his time of need and distress (its one hundred stories are of course also set in a time of distress). He dedicates his book specifically to women, for they are the ones who are most in need of the kind of diversion and pleasure that literature can provide. Women, he says, are not as fortunate as men when it comes to finding relief for their sorrows or distraction from their ennui. Men have endless sources of distraction ("they can always walk abroad, see and hear many things, go fowling, hunting, fishing, riding and gambling, or attend to their business affairs"), while women are all too often "forced to follow the whims, fancies and dictates of their fathers, mothers, brothers and husbands, so that they spend most of their time cooped up within the narrow confines of their room" (46). In its dedication to such women, *The Decameron* presumes to offer them the temporary solace and pleasure that the *brigata* itself finds in the gardens of Fiesole. Stories do not alter reality any more than gardens do; yet by offering asylum from reality, both stories and gardens answer very real human needs, including the need to gain, from time to time, a distance from reality.

Day Six inscribes the art of storytelling within the larger context of the art of speaking well. Given that speech is the primary medium of social relations, here too there is an intrinsic ethical dimension to our linguistic comportment, our way of speaking, our mastery of the powers of expression, and our pursuit of eloquence. One could say that verbal virtuosity, in its many forms celebrated by Day Six, is at bottom a form of generosity toward others. (Generosity, along with its counterpart, gratitude, figures among the supreme human virtues for Boccaccio.) The art of speaking well may seem like a modest virtue in the larger scheme of human struggle and survival, yet Day Six reminds us that we meet our neighbor principally in the words we exchange, the converse we hold, the stories we tell, the manner of expression we adopt—it reminds us, in sum, that we come together in this garden of language, which, like all gardens, can thrive when properly cultivated. If there is a positive "morality" in the *Decameron*, it is to be found above all in Day Six's discreet *exempla* of style, and not in the hyperboles of moral virtue of Day Ten, whose *novelle* are for the most part lethally ironic.

Boccaccio was no moralist. He was not a reformer or would-be prophet. He was not especially preoccupied by human depravity or humanity's prospects for salvation. He did not harangue his reader from any self-erected pulpit of moral, political, or religious conviction. If the ethical claims for the *Decameron* which he lays out in his preface are finally extremely modest (the author hopes through his stories to offer diversion and consolation to those in need of them), it is because the human condition itself is a modest one. The plague demonstrates as much. To be human means to be vulnerable to misfortune and disaster. It means periodically to find oneself in need of help, comfort, distraction, or edification. Our condition is for the most part an affair of the everyday, not of the heroic, and our minimal ethical responsibility to our neighbor, according to Boccaccio's humanism, consists not in showing him or her the way to redemption but in helping him or her get through the day. This help takes many modest forms, not the least of which is rendering the sphere of social interaction more pleasurable through wit, decorum, storytelling, fellowship, conversation, courtesy, and sociability. To add to the pleasure rather than the misery of life: that is the *arché* or first principle of Boccaccio's humanism, which is not the triumphalist humanism of later eras (which saw self-reliant humankind as the glory of all creation) but the civil humanism of neighborly love. (It is not by chance that Boccaccio begins his preface with the word *umana*, or *human*: *Umana cosa è aver compassione degli afflitti* [It is human to have compassion for those in distress].)

It bears repeating that the *brigata*'s temporary escape from the demoralization of a plague-ridden Florence has no direct effect on the "reality" of things. After two weeks in their liminal garden environment, the ten storytellers return to the horrors they had left behind, yet meanwhile the stories of the *Decameron*, like the garden settings in which they are told, have intervened in reality after all, if only by testifying to the transfiguring power of form. By recasting reality in narrative modes, they allow what is otherwise hidden by reality's amorphous flow of moments to appear in formal relief, just as a garden draws attention to the aesthetically determined relations of things in its midst (chapter 5). That is the magic of both gardens and stories: they transfigure the real even as they leave it apparently untouched.

If Boccaccio's art of storytelling on the one hand and his humanist ethics on the other both find their correlate in the aesthetics of the Italian garden, his "politics" are no less related to that aesthetics. For all its emphasis on the virtues of form giving (be it applied to self, speech, human relations, or comportment), *The Decameron* contains withering denunciations of tyrants who would exercise absolute sovereignty over either nature or their subjects. Tancredi (Day Four, story 1) and Gualtieri (Day Ten, story 10) are the two most vivid incarnations of this tyrannical urge to total control. If the ideal garden is one where nature thrives under the governance of art, the tyrant is one who would subjugate and dominate nature through the imposition of an adventitious will. Politically speaking, this rejection of tyrannical power translates into Boccaccio's lifelong allegiance to Florence's republican institutions, which allowed *libertas* and civic order to coexist. It also accounts for his animus against those Italian city-states whose petty despots were quick to stifle civic freedom. Unlike his friend Petrarch, who courted the favor of presumptuous princes and frequently took up residence in their courts, Boccaccio consistently refused their blandishments and remained committed to the ideals of republican freedom. This commitment is evident everywhere in *The Decameron*, without ever becoming strident or drawing excessive attention to itself. Indeed, it is part and parcel of the *diletto* this book affords the reader on its every page.

Monastic, Republican, and Princely Gardens

SOME GARDENS LOOK INWARD, OTHERS LOOK OUTWARD, some unfold to the world, some shut themselves off from the world. The medieval cloister dreamed of Eden, in whose image it was conceived. There a world-shy spirituality found sanctuary from the tumult of earthly passions and, through prayer and silent contemplation, kept open the prospect of the soul's perpetual holiday in heaven. Within the walls of the monastic garden the mind could turn inward and, deep within its solitude, meditate upon the transcendent, unitary source of creation, who was present there by intimation only. Thus the garden embodied the promise of happiness more than happiness as such—the promise, that is, of an otherworldly *gaudium* beyond the bounds of mortal life. Although it too was made by humans, the monastic cloister turned the eye away from "what man has made of man" (Wordsworth) toward the Maker of humankind and the cosmos in which the human person, like a foundling, found himself immersed.

There are outward-looking gardens, by contrast, that open onto the scene of history in an expansive spirit of affirmation, drawing the eye to the civic setting into which they are nestled. For a case in point let us go back in time to the very beginning of the fifteenth century and take a stroll from the center of Florence across the Arno River to the villa of a Renaissance man of letters named Roberto Rossi. We set out with Leonardo Bruni, Coluccio Salutati, and Niccolò Niccoli, three lofty humanists who played important roles in the cultural and political life of Florence during the most vigorous period of the Florentine republic, when Florence successfully defended its freedom against the hostile tyrannies of rival Italian city-states, in particular Milan, whose despot, Gian Galeazzo Visconti, had the courtesy to fall ill and die during his siege of Florence in 1402. Bruni's *Dialogi ad Petrum Paulum Histrum*, composed around 1406, evokes these individuals' stroll through Florence on their way to Rossi's villa. Before entering the villa, they pass through a garden that delights Salutati: "How beautiful are the buildings of our city, and how magnificent!" he exclaims. "This was borne home to me while we were in the garden by these buildings we have before our eyes. . . . Look at the splendor of these edifices, observe the refinement and enchantment of them" (Bruni, 119).

Before proceeding further we should note that Salutati, Bruni, Niccoli, and Rossi (the principal interlocutors of Bruni's dialogue) were not particularly inward-looking men. They were major champions of Florentine "civic humanism," which, against the medieval ascetic ideal, advocated the primacy of the active over the contemplative life, shifted attention from salvation to liberty, and promoted an ideology of the citizen's civic responsibility and participation in the exercise of self-governance. Salutati served as chancellor of Florence from 1375 until his death in 1406. Bruni, who wrote a sparkling eulogy of Florence and its republican traditions, would succeed him in that capacity. Niccoli, an avid cultivator of classical antiquity, devoted much of his time to recovering ancient Latin texts from various parts of Italy and denouncing the "barbarism" of his medieval predecessors, who wrote bad Latin and shamefully failed to safeguard the cultural legacies of antiquity. Rossi was a Florentine humanist who devoted his life to learning as well as to the political life of his city.

The garden that delights Salutati is just enough removed from downtown Florence to offer a more panoramic view of the city than one could get while passing through the streets on the way there. Its main virtue for the civic humanist is that it opens onto the self-gathered splendor of Florence, the city of *libertas*, which Salutati goes on to extol in these terms: "Like Leonardo, I believe, in effect, that neither Rome, nor Athens nor Syracuse [was] ever so elegant and clean, but that in these respects our city surpasses them completely" (119–20). The friends join Salutati in his encomium of the virtues that elevate Florence over other cities, especially its staunch antagonism toward tyranny, and in no time at all their dialogue gravitates to the question of whether Caesar, with his imperial ambitions, was the "parricide of his country" (*patria sue fuerit parricida*). For these men of political passion, patriotism is everything, which is why for them Rossi's garden looks out first and foremost over a landscape of republicanism—a city, that is, where political sovereignty lies with the citizens, not with princes or prelates. What this garden reveals to them is a cleanliness and beauty whose curators are the city's free citizens. Indeed, from this vista it is Florence as a whole that appears as a garden well cultivated and well cared for by its citizens, artists, noble families, humanists, and poets.

To be more specific, from the civic humanistic perspective that Bruni's dialoguers bring to their view of it, Florence appears as the garden where classical culture, and especially preimperial Roman culture, is undergoing a flourishing rebirth. Punning on his city's name, Bruni states in his book's dedication to Pietro Paolo Istram: "In fact, this city is not only flowering [*florentissima est*] in the number of its inhabitants, the splendor of its buildings, the greatness of its enterprises, but it also preserves certain seeds of the most elevated arts and of culture in general, which for so long seemed extinct but instead are growing day by day" (78). Here the *umanitas* of the ancients, whose seeds had lain dormant for centuries, pushes outward into the realm of appearance and objectification. This "florencing" of antiquity figures as the first blossoming of what historians have traditionally called the Italian Renaissance, all of it made possible, according to Bruni and his friends, by the *cura* of those men of letters who made it their business to resurrect classical culture through their painstaking efforts to recover its lost works, emulate its examples, and recultivate its ideal of *umanitas* within themselves. It is surely with the resurrection of classical wisdom in mind that Bruni has his dialogue take place "on the occasion of those solemn feasts that celebrate the resurrection of Jesus Christ" (82).

The dialogue genre itself is one that Bruni presumed to revive from its classical, and above all Ciceronian, past. At the beginning of *Dialogi*, before the group settles down to discuss the book's main theme—namely, the state of culture in the present day—Salutati embarks upon a eulogy of dialogue. "Nothing is of greater use to your studies than discussion," he tells his younger companions, "in the course of which many eyes, so to speak, look at issues from different sides." Plurality of opinion, verbalization of thought, exchange of ideas—these are the virtues that Salutati promotes with an almost evangelical fervor, in implicit polemic against the monastic ideal of silent contemplation. Thought must flower in speech. The public sphere must blossom with discourse. "It is absurd to talk to oneself in the solitude of one's own room and then, in the company of others, to remain silent" (85). If culture is like soil, intercourse is what renders it fertile. Someone who gives himself over to intensive study but neglects to discuss with others what he has learned is like "the husbandman who, having the possibility of cultivating all of his land, sets out to plough only sterile zones of it and leaves the most fertile parts uncultivated" (89). That is not Salutati's shortcoming, for he avows, "I, who have always devoted all my time and energy to the activity of learning, have reaped from discussion and conversation such exalted fruits that most of what I have learned I believe I owe to intercourse with others" (89). Book learning alone does not cultivate the mind. Only productive conversation can do that.

Conversation is as essential to learning as it is to the life of the republic, for republicanism, as the civic humanists understood it, is all about a plurality of voices making themselves heard in an open forum. The exchange of opinion—even where the matter is not political in content, and even when it takes place in a private garden—is the best defense against unreasoned prejudice and blind ignorance, for it refers opinions to the claims of reason, which is the natural enemy of arbitrary tyranny. Discussion, debate, and deliberation are the means by which the citizens exercise their judicious wisdom in a republic. The injunction of monasteries and tyrannies to remain silent is an injunction against political responsibility.

Conversation fulfills another crucial purpose: the cultivation of the resources of rhetoric. Like most humanists of their generation, Salutati and Bruni were venerators of Cicero, in whom they saw a man of exceptional wisdom and learning who rose to the defense of the Roman republic against the imperialist factions. It was both through the power of the word and on behalf of the power of the word that Cicero challenged the republic's enemies. His dialogue *De oratore*, which the Florentine civic humanists took to heart, reminds its readers that the "flowers" of rhetoric, to use a classical topos, blossom above all under those forms of government where speech matters, where consensus is achieved by reasoned persuasion rather than by autocratic decree, and where political decisions are submitted to the crucible of argument and counter-argument in the public forum. It is not by chance that *De oratore* is set in a garden (Crassus's Tusculum villa), nor that its setting explicitly recalls the extramural *locus ameonus* of Plato's *Phaedrus*, which also deals with the art of rhetoric. Yet unlike Plato, who was as wary of the political powers of rhetoric as he was of democracy, Cicero believed in and championed the republican alliance of eloquence and wisdom. *De oratore*, which is everywhere in the background of Bruni's *Dialogi*, is in fact as much a defense of republicanism as an encomium of the art of rhetoric.

As they look out over Florence from Rossi's villa in 1406, the humanists in Bruni's *Dialogi* see the revival of liberty, learning, eloquence, and wisdom—virtues whose seeds had been sown by those Roman ancestors who had founded Florence as a Roman colony. Whether they saw things "realistically" or through the lens of their republican idealism is not of primary concern here (the Florentine republic, even in its heyday, was far from an ideal entity; it was largely oligarchic in character, with only its leading citizens exercising real political power). What matters is that they saw themselves as the curators of this renascent garden. In a republic all citizens are gardeners. Believing as they did in the efficacy of a citizen's words and actions, the civic humanists had no doubts that it was their dedication to their cause, their commitment to the wisdom of the ancients, and their crusade against the ignorance of their medieval forefathers that brought about this renaissance. Even more important, they believed that the open freedom of the public sphere was the very soil in which the revival was able to take root. It is this freedom that Salutati presumes to see from the open garden of Rossi's villa.

With the decline of the Florentine republic and the rise of the Medici in the second half of the fifteenth century, the Italian Renaissance took on a very different character under the sponsorship of popes and autocratic princes. While it preserved many of the earlier humanism's cultural values (eloquence, learning, veneration of classical antiquity, etc.), it divorced the cultivation of those values from the phenomenon of political citizenship. As the citizen gave way to the subject, the "garden" now belonged to the prince alone, and its various embellishments served mostly to reflect his glory. The symbolism of the garden of the Medici palace in Florence is revealing in this regard. It was an enclosed garden, much like a cloister, with Edenic motifs intended to exalt the power of the prince more than the power of God (in that sense its sympathy with the medieval cloister were more aesthetic than theological). Likewise the garden of the ducal palace of Urbino, which was patterned on the Medici model, was also an enclosed garden, where the duke would periodically hold audience with his subjects in his godlike role of judge and dispenser of justice. The fact that this garden was designed to be seen from the windows high above it marks it as a princely garden par excellence.

To gauge the nature of this monopolization of power by the prince, pope, or duke, we have only to compare Bruni's *Dialogi* with one the great dialogues of the Italian High Renaissance, *The Book of the*

Courtier by Balthasar Castiglione. Over four nights in the ducal palace of Urbino, the dialogue's discussants—an august group of nobles and men of letters—set out to define the qualities an ideal courtier should possess: elegance, grace, agility in arms, accomplishments in arts and letters, a pleasing manner in speech, bearing, and conduct. *The Courtier* is a formidable treatise on self-cultivation, to be sure, promoting the notion that the courtier and palace lady should act with a studied artfulness under a veneer of natural grace and nonchalance, much as the Italian Renaissance garden brought nature under the governance of art in a way that enhanced rather than overpowered the appearance of nature. However, what Bruni and Salutati would have found distressing about Castiglione's book, had they been able to read it a century earlier, is the way it internalizes and sycophantically embraces the political reality of the times, namely the monopolization of power by a single ruler rather than its distribution among a plurality of free citizens. Almost all the personal qualities whose acquisition Castiglione recommends to his courtier have as their ultimate objective neither the courtier's self-realization nor his or her contribution to the flourishing of the city but rather the refinement of his or her ability to please the prince and gain his favor.

The art of speaking well, for example, is divorced from its political vocation (i.e., to persuade in an open forum) and is recommended for its power to render conversation in court more gracious and lively and ultimately more pleasing to the prince (a too fervent insistence on one's own opinions, for example, is a courtly vice annoying to the prince and hence to be avoided at all costs). Wit, gravity, learning, manliness—all such qualities serve finally to ingratiate. *The Book of the Courtier* could have as its subtitle *Subordination with Elegance*, if such candor did not go directly against the book's ethic of camouflage, pretense, and dissimulation.

The incommensurability of the political worlds of the two dialogues is best reflected by their settings. Bruni's *Dialogi* is set outdoors in daytime, with the protagonists moving through the streets of Florence and viewing the city from an elevated open vista. In *The*

Courtier the setting is insular, sequestered, and nocturnal. The dialogues take place over four nights in the same room inside the ducal palace of Urbino. Neither the Bruni dialogues nor the Castiglione dialogues literally take place in a garden (in the *Dialogi* they take place on the second day in a portico, in *The Courtier* they take place in an elegant chamber), yet one could say that, emblematically speaking, the difference between the open garden of Roberto Rossi's villa and the self-enclosed garden of the ducal palace of Urbino tells us all we need to know about the difference between the political contexts from which these texts arise and to which they respond. With Bruni, the self-fashioning of the humanist is above all a form of political activism; with Castiglione, the self-fashioning of the courtier is above all a form of political subservience. With Bruni, the external world beckons; with Castiglione, the world beyond the court is muffled and shut out. With Bruni, the republic itself is the garden; with Castiglione, the garden is a trope for cultivation of manners.

In the fourth book of *The Courtier* one of the speakers, Pietro Bembo, embarks on a long, exalted soliloquy that shifts the focus away from the court to the realm of ideal, disembodied beauty. The otherworldly thrust of his Neoplatonic speech seems to go directly against the book's prevailing concerns with worldly personal attributes that have their proper place in the court of the prince, not in the court of heavenly beauty, so much so that Bembo has to be called back down to earth with a discreet tug at his tunic by one of the palace ladies seated next to him. This tension, if not downright contradiction, between Bembo's mystical flight on the wings of divine love and the courtly context of his speech is not as substantial as it might seem at first glance. To begin with, the speakers in Castiglione's dialogue set out to paint a portrait of the perfect courtier, and this gives the book a certain idealizing Platonic strain. More important, Renaissance Platonism first flourished in Florence during the consolidation of power by the Medici. Under the patronage of Cosimo de Medici, Marsilio Ficino founded his Platonic Academy in 1462 at Villa Careggi, outside Florence, and during the reign of Lorenzo il Magnifico (d. 1492) many of the leading intellectuals and humanists of Florence were lured into its garden, where they turned their attention to things beautiful and divine, poetic and mythic, and left the business of governing to the prince. The de facto derepublicanization of Florence that took place under the Medici had something to do with the enhanced appeal of Platonism, without doubt. What with its speculative drive and dreams of a transcendent order of ideal beauty, Platonism was at once a distraction, a consolation, and a form of spiritual intoxication. This, coupled with Ficino's brilliant efforts to reconcile Platonism with Christianity, made the courts of Italy particularly hospitable toward the new philosophy.

Ficino saw his Academy as the veritable rebirth of Plato's Academy in Athens—the *academia platonica redeviva*—yet in truth they were two very different kinds of institutions. The Academy at Careggi emphasized the passionate spiritual transcendence of Platonism far more than Plato's Academy did. What Ficino believed was reborn at Careggi was the "garden of the Muses"—the Muses to whom Plato's Academy, according to tradition, was dedicated. These were the Muses who, in Ficino's mind, gave Plato his divine poetic powers and inspired the lofty myths and fables that pervade his works. The Careggi Academy's garden had summoned within its walls not only the Muses but a whole congregation of gods, goddesses, and heavenly nymphs whose inspirational powers were generously showered on the great Plato. Jupiter, Saturn, Minerva, Apollo, Venus, Mercury—all played an engendering role in the birth of Platonic philosophy, according to Ficino. That is why that philosophy was endowed with the powers of divine prophecy: "For occasionally he [Plato] rages and wanders, as does a prophet, and he does not serve the human order, but the prophetic and divine order; nor does he act so much as a teacher as a priest and prophet . . . precipitating at times into divine furor" (Ficino, 1129). So writes Ficino to Lorenzo il Magnifico in the proem to his translations of Plato.

With this heavy emphasis on the oracular aspects of Plato's corpus, there was a concomitant deemphasizing of Plato's political concerns in Ficino's Platonism. The Academy at Careggi emphatically did *not* presume to be a training ground for future statesmen. It had no purpose beyond what took place within its own walls: "In the gardens of the Academy poets will hear Apollo singing beneath the laurels. In the vestibule of the Academy orators will watch Mercury declaim. And in the portico and courtyard, lawyers and governors of cities will hear Jove himself as he sanctions the laws, dictates justice and governs the empire. Likewise in the inner chambers, philosophers will come to know their Saturn, contemplator of the secrets of the heavens" (1129–30). With such passionate rhetoric Ficino portrays his Academy as the place where the gods are called back to earth so that they may commune again with mortals through the medium of Platonic wisdom. Ficino makes it clear that philosophy, personified as Sophia, has no business venturing into the city of man, that her true homeland is in the Academy's garden, which suffices unto itself. Every time she strays beyond the garden's walls she loses her way and gets defiled. Here is how he expresses it in the proem:

> Plato girded Sophia's temples with a headband and put a robe on her, befitting of the august daughter of Minerva. He anointed her head, hands and feet with sweet smelling oil . . . sprinkled and decorated [her] with various flowers. Thus it was, and still is, with the goddess who walks within the walls of the Academy, so ornate. But whenever she wanders outside of the gardens of the Academy, she not only always loses her perfumes and flowers, but (how dreadful!) she fall in with mercenaries; and, stripped of the robes of her priesthood, she wanders about denuded of her dignity, like a deformed and profane woman, no longer pleasing to her cousins Phoebus or Mercury; nor is she esteemed by her grandfather Jove or by her mother Minerva. But as soon as she returns to the walls and gardens at the advice of her mother she regains her old decorum, and there she rests freely as in her own homeland. (1129)

We will not find in Plato anything close to this Botticelli-like image of Sophia adorned with flowers, perfumes, and headbands. Even more than her beauty, it is Sophia's vulnerability that Ficino allegorizes here. Philosophy needs enclosed walls, in essence it needs *protection*, if it is to preserve its intrinsic dignity. Such protection begins with the prince, who sponsors the Academy and grants its members the privilege of dwelling with Sophia in her native garden. Ficino spares no praise, nor does he shrink from adulation, when it comes to expressing his gratitude to both Cosimo and Lorenzo for their patronage of philosophy. ("My parents gave me birth," he writes, "but through Cosimo I was reborn unto the divine Plato.") His gratitude was certainly genuine, for he believed that only the prince had the means (the wealth, authority, and power) to secure the garden of philosophy against the hostile forces of world—including the forces of political ambition and conniving. Without the prince's benefaction, Sophia wanders the sublunary world in a daze, stripped of her adornments and exposed to the vulgarities of the street.

The safe haven of Villa Careggi brought together a vibrant community of scholars, poets, artists, and philosophers bound together by their devotion to the ideals of Platonic wisdom. If civic humanism dreamed of self-determination, the Platonic Academy dreamed of an altogether more extravagant humanism that bypassed the political sphere altogether. To reconjoin the human with the divine in the enchanted garden of philosophy—this was the guiding idea of the Platonic Academy. This reconjoining was to be achieved by pursuing various disciplines—jurisprudence, rhetoric, ethics, music, metaphysics, and the like—through systematic and rigorous study. Yet even more important than the *negotium* of study was the leisurely *otium* of celebration. The Academy promoted above all fellowship, discussion, feast, and "joy in the present." The injunction to rejoice in the present—*laetus in praesens*—was inscribed on the wall of the Academy garden as a reminder that *here* is where the spiritual harmonization of the human and the divine takes place, and *now* is its occasion. *Laetitia*—a word with Epicurean associations that Boccaccio invokes repeatedly to describe the *brigata*'s sojourn in the gardens of Fiesole—is the garden's second name, for the gods are not grave, nor anxious, nor remorseful. They are festive, hence the spirit of the Academy should be one of divine playfulness, as befits a true pleasure garden ("here young men, with ease and joy, grasp moral precepts in the midst of jokes and the art of disputing in the midst of play," writes Ficino to Lorenzo). As Lorenzo himself wrote in a poem ("Canzone di Bacco," or "Song of Bacchus"): "Let us keep perpetual holiday."

The difference between the monastic cloister's silent contemplation of God and the "perpetual holiday" of Ficino's Academy was the difference between striving to elevate the human toward the divine and seeking to call the gods down to earth. Yet it was within the confines of the garden walls that each was to take place. In both cases those walls shut out the civic domain, where persons deal with one another as human beings and not gods. As for princely gardens like the one at the ducal palace at Urbino, they did not so much shut out the civic domain as symbolically incorporate it under the unitary rule of the despot. Yet here too the parallel between cloister gardens and princely gardens was more than the fact of their enclosure. Both were spaces with one central organizing principle that the perimeter rotated around—God in one case, the ruler in the other. In what I have called open gardens, the organizing principle is fundamentally different. The open garden is not lorded over. It does not have a single, unitary focal point but numerous points of focus, and within it one may meander freely, as Salutati and his friends do in Bruni's dialogue, unconfined by its perimeters. With the rise of absolute monarchies, the open gardens of Europe were destined to retreat into the shadows.

⫷ 10 ⫸

A Note on Versailles

IT WAS MY INTENTION TO AVOID DISCUSSING THE GARDENS of Versailles in this book, if only out of modesty. The voluminous and mostly excellent scholarship that has been devoted to the place over the centuries calls for nothing less, yet beyond that, modesty seems like the only proper response to a work of art whose intrinsic immodesty achieves a degree of astonishing beauty. Earlier I expressly claimed that gardens—despite the artfulness that goes into their design and creation—are both more and less than artworks (thanks in part to the biophiliac responses they provoke in us). The gardens of Versailles are clearly an exception, for this is as close as one can get to subjugating the natural world to pure form and bringing the potentially anarchic forces of life under such control as to extinguish them altogether. I once spent two consecutive days in Versailles. On the first I was left breathless by the sheer radiance of what the eye is hardly able to take in and assimilate. By the end of the second, I found myself longing for an hour in the provincial *jardin public* of Bouville, where the excessively organic presence of a chestnut tree nauseates Roquentin, the chlorophobe in Sartre's *Nausea*. Modesty is something of a self-protective reaction to the self-glorification of the Sun King that is on display in Versailles.

And then there is the palpable evidence everywhere of what Saint-Simon called *ce plaisir superbe de forcer la nature* (this proud desire to dominate nature). Here was no Italian Renaissance architect who "one day discovered that the enclosing landscape was naturally included within his garden, and that the two formed part of the same composition," to recall Wharton's comments on Italian garden-magic. Far from securing "the means by which nature and art might be fused in his picture," the architect of Versailles (André Le Nôtre) seems to have first sent in an army of human bulldozers to clear away whatever grew here, reducing the grounds to a flat, empty plane on which to project the master design. One cannot help but feel a tremor of anxiety, if not dread, before this complete domination of nature.

That is of course exactly the kind of reaction the gardens are designed to provoke—an almost cowering sense of trepidation in the face of the power that imposed this form on them. Everything about the gardens insistently reminds one of their monarchic creator. There are intersecting vectors of reference everywhere, all of which lead back to the palace, which is to say to the king in his unconditional sovereignty. It is impossible not to fall into line here, so heavy-handed is the *Gleichschaltung*, or coordination, demanded of the viewer by the iron laws of symmetry that govern the gardens' perspectives. The fact that Louis XIV has been long dead, or that the French Revolution decapitated the institution on which the authority of his kingship rested, does nothing to relax the intense referential pressures of the grounds. As long as these gardens stand, Louis XIV lives on as their focal point of convergence. *Le roi est mort, vive le roi.*

It's not so much the *subordinate* character of the gardens that makes one feel nervous and wretched after a day and a half at Versailles—the fact that on the one hand they remorselessly subordinate nature and on the other subordinate themselves to the king's glory—it's rather their representational character that oppresses you. Representational gardens make demands on the viewer that are coercive and constricting. I should probably personalize that statement and say that I respond most expansively to gardens that bring the "lethic" or hidden dimensions of nature, form, and thought to presence. Where gardens become representational—where what the eye sees cannot be properly viewed except by reference to a preestablished order of meaning—they stifle if not abolish the freedom to wander that more liberal types of gardens make room for. Versailles, where even wandering is centrally controlled, is a masterpiece of representational garden art, and the more it succeeds in its ambitions (to synthesize all its art under the unitary symbolism of *le Roi Soleil*), the more it ends up oppressing a sensibility like mine, which favors clarity pervaded by opacity over representational transparency.

These are some of the personal reasons I wanted to leave Versailles out of this essay. The reason I decided to include a few abbreviated remarks after all is because Versailles provides an opportunity to mention an aspect of my theme that deserves some attention, if only in passing. So far I have talked a great deal about gardens and the cultivation of virtues. But vices are every bit as cultivatable as virtues, and what we see in the gardens of Versailles—not representationally but transubstantially, as it were—are vices that have assumed exquisitely cultivated forms. For some aesthetic sensibilities, a highly refined vice is far more beautiful than any earnest virtue. Vices in fact are more susceptible to the transfigurations of form than are virtues, which is one of the reasons the former thrive so well in highly formal court settings, like Versailles. The cultivation of envy, spite, pride, or greed does not transform those vices into virtues; on the contrary, by submitting them to extremely regimented rules and protocols, it gives them a style that renders them sublime while leaving their vicious essence intact. The gardens of Versailles accomplish something along exactly such lines.

I mentioned how an early visitor to Versailles spoke of *ce plaisir superbe de forcer la nature*. In the seventeenth century, the adjective *superbe* still had a dark Christian connotation of pride, or *superbia*. Certainly there is in the Versailles gardens an aesthetic drive to tame, and even humiliate, nature into submission. But even more pertinently, one could say that the garden project had its very genesis in the vice (or capital sin) of *superbia*. We know that the idea for the Versailles gardens came to Louis XIV on August 17, 1661, when his finance minister, Nicolas Fouquet, unveiled the magnificent gardens he had built for himself at Vaux-le-Vicomte. So sublime and awesome were those gardens that Louis XIV stormed out of Vaux-le-Vicomte in a rage. Shortly thereafter he had his minister arrested and cast into a dungeon, where Fouquet languished for the rest of his life, never to be pardoned by the king, despite many earnest appeals from various quarters. No doubt the sumptuousness of Vaux-le-Vicomte suggested that only a corrupt minister could afford such luxury. But in Louis's mind Fouquet's offense was graver than that. The gardens were a gesture of pride vis-à-vis the king himself, for the splendor of Vaux-le-Vicomte was beyond all proper measure. Only the king was entitled to such grandeur. Just as Lucifer in his pride overreached his station and sought to be the equal of God, so too Fouquet had arrogated for himself the king's regality. And just as God cast Lucifer into the depths of hell, so too Louis threw Fouquet into a dungeon.

Louis was outraged by Vaux-le-Vicomte, to be sure, yet at the heart of his indignation—lurking within his sense of affronted solar sovereignty—there was also a good deal of envy. So envious and jealous was the king of what he saw at Vaux-le-Vicomte that, after punishing his minister, he promptly hired Fouquet's team of architects, gardeners, and engineers and initiated the project of building the gardens of Versailles. Le Nôtre, who had designed Vaux-le-Vicomte, was put in charge of the project, and much of what had gone into the Vaux gardens by way of conception, design, and narrative technique was directly translated to Versailles. In that sense what we see in Versailles is a magnificence born of envy, jealousy, rivalry, and profane imitation, to say nothing of an absolutist presumption of power.

And what of pride, *superbia*? If pride is defined by insubordination and overreaching, can a king be prideful? He can be so only with respect to God, for on Earth there is nothing more exalted than his personhood, according to the royalist thinking that Louis XIV helped render peremptory. In his arrogation of the powers and stature of God on Earth the absolute monarch remains the living incarnation of *superbia*. Never had the Christian sin of pride institutionalized itself to such an extent as it did under the absolute monarchy of Louis XIV. To the degree that the gardens of Versailles were designed with one overriding purpose in mind, namely to exalt the Sun King and reaffirm his analogical kinship with God, they put pridefulness on open display and gave it one of the most sublime forms it would ever take, without in the least extenuating its vice.

Yet the superb architecture of the gardens of Versailles embodies a pride that goes well beyond the now obsolete presumptions of absolute monarchy. I mean the fiercely humanistic pride that began in the so-called age of reason and that triumphalistically proclaimed humankind the "master and possessor of nature" (Descartes, *Discourse on Method*, 1637), calling on men to pursue that mastery and possession through a scientifically enhanced exercise of power and will, or will-to-power for short. The militant humanism of the age is also on full display at Versailles. While we long ago ceased to credit doctrines regarding the divine right of kings, and while few among us believe we are living in an age of enlightenment, we still have not sufficiently dismantled the doctrine of humanity's divine right, which in many ways still reigns supreme in contemporary Western societies, in practice if not in theory. For all its perverse beauty and wondrous transfiguration of pride, Versailles will not be of much help to us when it comes to finding a less presumptuous relationship to nature than the one bestowed upon us by that era.

On the Lost Art of Seeing

IN CHAPTER 5 I REMARKED THAT A GARDEN IS A PLACE where appearances draw attention to themselves, but that doesn't mean they necessarily get noticed, no matter how much they may radiate or beckon the eye. Where appearances recede into the depths of space and time even as they come forward to stake their claim in the phenomenal realm, they make special demands on our powers of observation. That is bad news for gardens, for nothing is less cultivated these days in Western societies than the art of seeing. It is fair to say that there exists in our era a tragic discrepancy between the staggering richness of the visible world and the extreme poverty of our capacity to perceive it. Thus even though there are plenty of gardens in the world, we live in an essentially gardenless era.

I don't know how to phrase this without sounding curmudgeonly, so I will simply assert as a matter of fact that among the young people I encounter on a daily basis—and I encounter quite a few, given my profession—most are much more at home in their computers, or in the fictions and skits that reach them on a screen, than they are in the three-dimensional world. In fact I have the impression that a great many of them no longer see the visible world at all, except peripherally and crudely. On our university campus, for example, they invariably walk through a dramatic Papua New Guinea sculpture garden with their heads down, as if afraid even to glance at the sublime towering forms that call out to be scrutinized and wondered at. I have seen student after student pass under a tree in late afternoon with an owl hooting lustily just overhead and never raise their eyes. I have queried several students over the years and have confirmed that the majority of them are oblivious of the existence of most of what makes the Stanford campus one of the most articulated, diversified, and embedded of American campuses. It's astonishing how small a proportion of the university grounds enters the typical student's purview after three or four years of residence here. Most of the groves, courtyards, gardens, fountains, artworks, open spaces, and architectural complexes have disappeared behind a cloaking device, it would seem. These are not students who lack curiosity. In fact if you take the time to draw their attention to a particular enclave and point out some of its subtler features, as I do on occasion, they are invariably impressed and even wondrous, as if seeing the site for the first time. In fact many of them *are* seeing it for the first time, no matter how often they have walked right by or through the place.

Almost a century ago Rainer Maria Rilke poetically hypothesized in his *Duino Elegies* that it was the earth's destiny to become invisible, that a process of transmutation of the visible into the invisible had begun to take place. Maybe this wholesale desertion of the visible world by the young is part of that fateful story. It's not that the world is any less visible than it was in the past; rather its plenitude registers with us less and less. It is *in us* that the transmutation takes place. Thus it is not a question of generational deficiency but of epochal transformations in the framework in and through which the world reveals itself. The basic inability to see a garden in its full-bodied presence is the consequence of a historical metamorphosis of our mode of vision, which is bound up with our mode of being. For as our mode of being changes, so too does our way of seeing. The faculty of human vision is not neutral. It is as subject to the laws of historicity as are our life-worlds, our institutions, and our mentality. In that regard human vision is fundamentally different from animal eyesight, however much the latter may remain the organic substrate of the former. In human beings the loss of eyesight does not necessarily entail a loss of vision. Vision sees cognitively and synthetically; it apprehends things in organized dispositions and meaningful totalities. This is another way of saying that human vision is above all a *way* of seeing, one that is inextricably bound up with the "regimes of presence," as Reiner Schurmann called them, that inform the history of our being in the world. What our vision sees (and just as important, what it doesn't see) is determined by historically unfolding frameworks that preorganize or predispose the empirical reach of our perception.

We live in an age, then, whose dominant perceptual framework makes it increasingly difficult to see what is right in front of us, leaving a great portion of the visible world out of the picture, as it were, even as it draws the eye to a plethora of pulsing images. Italo Calvino gives an insightful depiction of the age in his book *Mr. Palomar*, which is all about Palomar's repeated failures to render his life more meaningful by looking at the world with heightened attention and intensified focus. Palomar, introduced in the book's opening pages as "a nervous man who lives in a frenzied and congested world," is particularly challenged on a visit to one of Japan's most famous monuments, the Ryoanji Zen garden in Kyoto (see "The Sand Garden" in appendix 2). The leaflet passed out to tourists reads: "If our inner gaze remains absorbed in the viewing of this garden, we will feel divested of the relativity of our individual ego, whereas the sense of the absolute *I* will fill us with serene wonder purifying our minds" (83). But what Palomar experiences is precisely the difficulty of aligning the inner gaze with his view of the garden, for the "neurasthenic" world to which he belongs gets in the way. It militates against any attempt to "concentrate on looking." Although that world puts everything on visual display, overcapitalizing sites and images, it in effect conducts a war on vision—the kind of thoughtful vision, that is, that harmonizes inner gaze and external object. The array of lenses and movie cameras that "frame the rocks and sand from every angle" do nothing to come to the rescue of such vision but on the contrary conspire with the framing strategies that petrify it. As for the more "earnest" tourists who check everything they see against what is signaled in their guidebooks, and vice versa, they are the ones whose vision is most obscured of all.

The established tourist itinerary has deprived the Zen garden of the "so much space and so much time around it" without which it simply cannot reveal its depths to human vision, at least not in the modes it was designed to. "We can view the garden as a group of mountainous islands in a great ocean, or as mountain tops rising above a sea of clouds," says the pamphlet—but in fact we *cannot* view it as such, nor can we "see it as a picture framed by the ancient mud walls." Least of all can we "forget the frame as we sense the truth of this sea stretching out boundlessly." Again, the world gets in the way, flattening the horizon of space and time. Thus Palomar has no choice but to "look at [the garden] in the only situation in which it can be looked at today, craning his neck among other necks," and what he sees, predictably enough, is a reflection or projection of the world he lives in and to which he belongs. In the sand he sees "the human race in the era of great numbers," and in the boulders he sees a "nature indifferent to the fate of mankind." Despite the tentative suggestion of a "possible harmony" between these "non-homogeneous harmonies," the two orders of being are anything but fused in Palomar's mind after his heroic effort at concentrated looking. They remain insuperably isolated one from the other. In the final analysis what he ends up seeing in the Zen garden is the impossibility of accessing its spiritual transcendence. All because the garden does not have enough space and time around it in which to unfold its appearances.

Space and time have both a subjective and an objective extension. The world to which we belong determines or frames both dimensions (subjective and objective), as well as the mutual interpenetration of the two. What Calvino describes in his Zen garden vignette is to a certain degree true of all thoughtfully designed gardens. For gardens to become fully visible in space, they require a temporal horizon that the age makes less and less room for. Time in its subjective and objective correlates is the invisible element in which gardens come to bloom.

Certainly gardens require seasonal time to grow into their cultivated forms. In Goethe's *Elective Affinities*, for example, the elderly master gardener points out some trees that his father had planted when the son was a young boy and that are just now reaching their maturity. And as Čapek wrote in a passage quoted earlier: "The gardener wants eleven hundred years to test, learn to know, and appreciate fully what is his. . . . I should like to see what these birches will be like in fifty years."

By the same token, once they have come into their living forms, gardens require time to be seen by the viewer. Gardens like Stowe and Stourhead in England receive many thousands of visitors a year, many of them arriving in tour groups that spend a few hours on the premises before moving on to the next site. It is difficult, if not impossible, under such fleeting circumstances to experience thoughtful gardens like Stowe and Stourhead the way they were meant to be experienced, that is as places of self-discovery, of spiritual cultivation, of personal transformation. Long gone are the days when most of us had the time or the will, let alone the attention span, for that. As a consequence, these gardens no longer show themselves to the majority of us (they may show themselves to their caretakers, who spend hours a day on their grounds, but not to the casual visitor). They may offer us images of themselves, but what is lacking in the images is the radiance of the phenomenon as such, which reveals itself only in deep time, the kind of time our age no longer has time for. In sum, we are more or less blind to the phenomenon.

If we wanted to speak formulaically, we could say that human vision in the present age sees primarily images rather than appearances. Earlier I remarked that the difference between appearance and image is that the former intimates while the latter merely indicates: where the phenomenon does not rise up from penumbral depths, there is no appearance as such but only a static and reified image (chapter 2). A garden is nothing if not phenomenon, and the penumbral depths in question belong as much to the garden as to the mind or soul of the beholder. Where these two dimensions of depth encounter and flow into one another, the phenomenon makes its appearance. Where one or both dimensions are absent, the phenomenon falls short of its "ostensive" potential, that is to say its potential for showing itself as what it is.

It suffices to read Andrew Marvell's poem "The Garden" to get a sense of just how expansive the phenomenon can be under circumstances different from the ones described by Calvino. Here the speaker descends into the garden's recesses, which are indistinguishable from the psychic depths that the garden opens up in its visitor (see appendix 3). The spiritual, mental, and imaginative movement that takes place in the latter's mind never loses touch with what the eye perceives in the appearances that surround it. Indeed, it is in and through the appearances that the movement takes place, culminating in a Zen-like vision of other, more boundless worlds than the one perceived by the ocular organ:

> The mind, that ocean where each kind
> Does straight its own resemblance find;
> Yet it creates, transcending these,
> Far other worlds, and other seas;
> Annihilating all that's made
> To a green thought in a green shade.

The *itinerarium mentis* that takes place during the course of the poem, sending the mind on its way to "other worlds, and other seas," never takes flight from the garden that enables and hosts the journey. Rather the journey gets under way only as the speaker *lingers* in the garden. Sometimes the most intense journeys—the most visionary journeys—take place while one stays put, in moments of stillness unscorched by "passion's heat."

Japanese gardens in general, and Zen gardens in particular, are designed to maximize the phenomenon's disclosive wonder, its opening up of the recessive depths where space and time flow into one another. Having never been to Japan myself, I will not presume to pontificate upon the subtle nature of Zen gardens; instead let me quote Shonin, a master Japanese gardener in Michel Tournier's novel *Gemini*, who says the following about the underdetermined composition of the Zen garden: "A Zen garden is to be read like a poem of which only a few half lines are written and it is up to the sagacity of the reader to fill in the blanks" (Tournier, 380). The austere minimalism of the Zen garden combines sand and rocks in arrangements that are to be viewed from "one predetermined point, usually the veranda of a house." While the viewpoint is fixed, the eye is free to wander, and with it the "inner gaze" of the mind. For it is the mind, "where only ideas meet and embrace," which does the seeing here, not independently of the eye but in and through the eye. Because the garden is charged with latency, it opens itself to a proliferation of independent views. Thus "the samurai praises its fiery, brutal simplicity. The philosopher its exquisite subtlety. The lover shows what intoxicating consolation it affords" (380). Nothing is seen that is not there; rather what *is* there reveals itself in any number of appearances and guises.

Shonin declares that the concentrated energy of the Zen garden revolves around the contrast between wet and dry. "Nothing is apparently drier than that expanse of white sand with one, two or three rocks arranged upon it. Yet in reality, nothing is wetter. Because the skillful undulations imprinted in the sand by the monk's fifteen-toothed steel rake are none other than waves, wavelets, and ripples of an infinite sea" (ibid.). The stones on the pathway are "boisterous eddies of water" or "a dry waterfall, petrified and immobilized in an instant." There is nothing representational about the sand and the rocks. They do not symbolize concepts or "stand for" something else. Seen in its phenomenological plenitude, the sand itself is a boundless sea in the mind of the viewer, just as the rock is a mountain for the one who sees it as such. The transfiguring powers of vision arise from the penumbral depths of the phenomenon. Or in Shonin's words, referring to the beholder: "These niggardly materials [sand, rocks, shrub and wall] are merely a mould into which to pour his mood of the moment and make it serene. In its bareness, the Zen garden contains potentially all the seasons of the year, all the countless countries of the world and all states of soul" (380). The crucial word here is *contains*. The garden contains all that exceeds what literally meets the eye. This way of seeing—call it "depth perception" in the radical sense—is made possible by the way the garden discloses the presence of what doesn't show itself to the eye, or by the way the garden calls forth into the realm of appearance all that remains latent in the phenomenon.

Nothing embodies the phenomenon more forcefully than the Japanese garden stone. The stone is a central element not only of the Zen garden but also of the Japanese house and tea garden. It shows a face to the world while its underside remains concealed from view, sinking into the earth like the roots of a plant. "The stones should never be simply laid upon the ground," says Shonin. "They must always be partly buried" (375). Why? Because "a stone has a head, a tail, and a back, and its belly needs the warm darkness of the earth." A stone possesses special powers—the power to transmit energy or "spirits" along its axis, for example, or to channel invisible cosmic forces—but only as long as it remains partially buried in the earth. The fact that it is partially buried does not mean that it shows only a partial view of itself. It in fact offers a full view of itself as something that draws from the earth the energy or luminosity of its radiance. An unburied stone would have no such radiance. It would not appear, it would only exhibit. Only where the visible recedes into the invisible does it manifest itself as phenomenon. Shonin:

> The stones in a garden are classed in three degrees of importance: the principal stones, the additional stones and the *Oku* stone. The additional stones escort the principal stone. They form a line behind the reclining stone, they are grouped about the base of the standing stone, they gather like support below the inclined stone. The *Oku* stone is not visible. The final, intimate, secret touch which animates the whole composition, it can fulfill its mission while remaining unperceived, like the soul of a violin. (375)

The *Oku* stone is another name for the "lethic" or nonapparent dimension in which the garden's partially buried stones are buried. Where the *Oku* stone's "secret touch" does not animate the phenomenon, vision is emptied of its depth perception. Or better, where vision is no longer capable of depth perception, the hidden presence of the *Oku* stone no longer "animates the whole composition." In that sense the *Oku* stone is not a stone at all but the underside of appearance as such. It is that which comes to appearance without necessarily becoming wholly visible or accessible, precisely like a stone that remains partially buried.

It takes particularly acute depth perception to perceive a latent form in a block of marble. According to Michelangelo's famous theory of extraction, he did not give form to stone when he sculpted a statue; rather, he drew out the form that already lay hidden within by removing the "excess matter" surrounding it. But Shonin asks: "Why carve with a hammer, a chisel or a saw? Why torment the stone and make its soul despair? The artist is a beholder. The artist carves with his eyes" (Tournier, 372). Shonin's very different concept of sculpture shifts the emphasis from making to seeing, thus collapsing the (very Western) distinction between artist and viewer. "The sculptor who is a poet is not a breaker of stones. He is a collector of stones." Japan has more than one thousand islands and more than 750,000 mountains, all of them teeming with pebbles, stones, and boulders. "The beauty is there," declares Shonin, "but just as much buried and concealed as that of the statue which your sculptor draws with taps of his mallet out of the block of marble. To create this beauty, one has only to know how to look" (372–73). Knowing how to look is the poet-sculptor's art. It is not only its precondition but also the form and substance of that art. Looking is as creative as making, provided it is possessed of the art of seeing. Yet even in Japan, if we believe Shonin, the art of seeing is bound to history, and eventually (like all things precious) it gets lost across the ages:

> You will see in tenth-century gardens stones selected at that period by collectors of genius. The style of those stones is

incomparable, inimitable. Of course, the Nipponese beaches and mountains have not changed in nine centuries. The same fragments of rock and the same pebbles are still strewn on them. But the tool for collecting them has been lost forever: the collector's eye. Stones like these will never be found again. And the same is true of every inspired garden. The stones with which it is filled are the work of an eye which, while leaving behind the evidence of its genius, has carried away the secret of it forever. (373)

Whether Shonin's reflections in Tournier's novel offer genuine insights into the essence of Japanese gardens or whether they are finally the adventitious musings of a Westerner in the voice of a Japanese master, they give further articulation to my general claim that eyesight does not equate vision, that vision's "inner gaze" correlates with the latency of the phenomenon, and that vision's perception of the visible world is both determined and altered by the historical unfolding of the ages. If gardens are microcosms animated by the "secret touch" of the *Oku* stone, as it were, then it is fair to say, once again, that they have become largely invisible to us—not because the *Oku* stone is missing from the gardens but because it is missing from the age to which we belong. Ours is an age of stones that are not partially buried in the earth; or alternatively, it is an age without any "green shade." If there is no green thought without green shade, then there is no real thinking in the age at all; for like the Japanese garden stone, thought must be partially buried if it hopes to gain access to what is not already self-evident. If there is much that we are no longer able to see today in the visible world, it is because the inner gaze needed to apprehend it is either obscured or directed elsewhere. Our vision these days is attuned to the virtual rather than the visible, to images rather than appearances, and to representations rather than phenomena.

This does not bode well for gardens, whose living forms recede into lethic depths that are accessible to our inner gaze but not necessarily to our eyesight. For the rocks in a Zen garden to appear as mountainous islands, or for a recess of the Villa Cimbrone in Ravello, with a half-veiled statue of Venus at the center of its enclosure, to appear as the site where love has returned to earth to recast her spell on mortals, or for a lane in Stourhead to appear as the pathway to self-discovery, what is required at the very least is a willingness to linger and a readiness for thought that our present frenzy finds abhorrent. There is not enough serenity in the age for gardens to become fully visible to us. That is why one could say that we live in a gardenless age, despite the fact that there are plenty of gardens in our midst.

What are we to do with these gardens that nevertheless continue to grace the visible world? Shonin says that the tenth-century Japanese gardens contain stones that "are the work of an eye which, while leaving behind the evidence of its genius, has carried away the secret of it forever." The same could be said of the many gardens in the West that have survived from prior times and been restored, embellished, or maintained by heroic curators. These gardens have left behind evidence of their genius, but perhaps their secret has not been carried away forever. One has to believe that the secret endures in the phenomenon itself. Perhaps these gardens are exactly where we need to turn to in order to relearn the art of seeing and reaccess the deep time folded within their forms. The visible world, after all, has not vanished. It has merely become temporarily invisible. There is every reason to believe that gardens can help us rescue its visibility, provided we give them ample space and time to show themselves. It would not be the first time that gardens have come to our aid in a time of need.

ᗒ 12 ᗕ

Sympathetic Miracles

ARISTOTLE ONCE WONDERED: "HOW IS IT THAT RHYTHMS and melodies, although only sound, resemble states of the soul?" (*Problemata*, c. 19). In the same vein one could ask: how can a garden made of plants, water, and stone resemble a state of the soul? I would not even use the word *resemble*. Kingscote Garden does not resemble my *ataraxia*, nor do I bring that state of mind with me into the garden; rather, I find it there. If Kingscote were to disappear one day, so would the special inner tranquillity it provides access to. There are no states of the soul that do not have their proper place in the world; and if there were no places in the world, there would be no soul in it either.

In one of his earliest essays, titled "Love of Life," Albert Camus speaks of walking into a cloister garden in San Francisco and "melt[ing] into this smell of silence, becoming nothing more than . . . the flight of birds whose shadows I could see on the still sunlit portions of the wall" (Camus, 55). For a moment—and Camus's affirmation of life is all about moments of intensity, rather than the continuum of experience—the fusion between state of mind and garden is so complete that the former upholds and keeps in being the latter:

In the sharp sound of wingbeats as the pigeons flew away, the sudden, snug silence in the middle of the garden, in the lonely squeaking of the chain on its well, I found a new and yet familiar flavor. I was lucid and smiling before this unique play of appearances. A single gesture, I felt, would be enough to shatter this crystal in which the world's face was smiling. Something would come undone—the flight of pigeons would die and each would slowly tumble on its outstretched wings. Only my silence and immobility lent plausibility to what looked like an illusion. (ibid.)

It is difficult when reading this passage not to think of the critical noonday moment of utter stillness and immobility when Meursault kills the Arab on the beach in Camus's *The Stranger*. *The Stranger* has long been standard reading in French high schools, and when students are asked the inevitable question "Pourquoi Meursault tue-t-il l'Arabe?" the inevitable response is "A cause du soleil." It may seem like a pseudo-answer, yet it is far more exact finally to say that Meursault killed the Arab because of the sun than to suggest that the overwhelming brilliance of the sun is somehow the "objective correlative" of Meursault's state of mind. T. S. Eliot spoke of the "objective correlative" in art as "a set of objects, a situation, a chain of events which shall be the formula of that particular emotion," i.e., the emotion or inward state of mind that the artist seeks to convey. But *The Stranger*, like the cloister passage cited above, suggests that in some cases a state of mind is consubstantial with an external element or place, rather than merely correlated with it according to rules of analogy or representation. This is especially true of gardens, which conjugate life and form, or soul and sense, in ways that transcend the formula of objective correlation.

In Shirley Hazzard's novel *The Evening of the Holiday*, Sophie, a young English woman, falls in love with Tancredi on an extended summer holiday in Italy, where she is visiting her Italian aunt Luisa. Tancredi is married but separated, and his wife never makes an appearance in the novel. When Sophie moves into Tancredi's house, they sleep in a bed that lies in the midst of a garden:

They slept in a room upon whose high, high ceiling the painted branches were obligingly abundant with an equal variety of fruits and flowers. The white walls had at one time borne panels of a similar decoration, but these had to a large extent been worn away and even, around doors and windows, painted over. . . . The bed was mounted on a low step between two windows. Its four corner posts, spirally carved, had been intended to support a canopy, which had long since disintegrated, leaving unobscured overhead the view of ripe oranges and full-blown roses." (Hazzard, 81)

It is not clear whether this is Tancredi's matrimonial bedroom (Hazzard is a master of the unsaid), but we know that its painted garden is adjacent to the outdoor garden where every morning the couple take their breakfast. This garden world is not the image or natural analogy of their flowering, colorful, and ultimately illicit romance. Their romance, with all its enchantments and unresolved tensions, belongs to, and has its abode in, this garden world. There is no other place where the romance could take root, no other place in which it could transplant itself.

That garden world includes the country villa of Sophie's aunt Luisa as well. One day while the lovers are lunching at Luisa's villa, the garden just beyond the dining hall takes a terrible pounding during a violent thunderstorm, which frays everyone's nerves. As the storm rages, "they came to the end of the fruit and sat on around the table without speaking" (75). It was "the end of the fruit" in more ways than one. During the silence that ensues, Luisa (not Sophie) wonders to herself why "love so often makes for trouble, for such a fuss? Tancredi had a wife and children. And in Italy there is no divorce. It could only end badly for everyone" (ibid.). During the entire scene Hazzard allows her free indirect discourse to enter Luisa's thoughts while leaving Sophie's unvoiced. Sophie's muteness gives an ominous resonance to the blasts of thunder bursting both inside and outside her mind. "Sophie suddenly exclaimed: 'But this is awful!' Their minds [Luisa's and Sophie's?] were running so much in two directions that she herself added: 'This storm.' " "This" is richly ambiguous, pointing at once to the storm that assails the garden "with a violence that seemed almost intentional" and to whatever is taking place in Sophie's psychic world at the time. From this moment on, though this does not become evident until later on, Sophie's relationship to Tancredi begins to undergo a transformation, for reasons that are never fully disclosed. She slowly begins to disengage from him, even as the passion between them grows more critical and intense. A few weeks later Sophie will return to England, without ever explaining her deeper motives to a bewildered Tancredi.

We are not in the realm of objective correlatives here, à la *King Lear*, where the violent thunderstorm provides a "formula" for the psychic upheaval and mental breakdown that Lear undergoes in act 3 of the play. Again, Sophie's state of mind is not "reflected" in or correlated with the suffering garden; rather, the two infuse one another. The storm that fells the garden's flowers and levels its plants does not simply figure, in an analogical way, the potential disaster that awaits the love between Sophie and Tancredi should they remain under the sway of their present passion. It is the disaster itself, one that comes in the form of a revelation, the exact content of which remains undisclosed to the reader even as it openly manifests its effects in the wounds inflicted on the garden. While we cannot be sure exactly what goes on in Sophie's mind, there is no doubt that she suffers these same wounds within herself during the storm. By the same token, while we do not know finally whether she realizes, in a lightning flash of insight, that her affair with Tancredi is wreaking havoc on the world into which she has intruded and where she does not by rights belong, we do know that her voluntary self-expulsion from the garden spells the end of a romance that had its proper—or perhaps improper—place there.

The Japanese master gardener in Michel Tournier's novel *Gemini* declares: "Garden, house, and man are a living organism which it is wrong to break up. The man must be there. The plants will only grow well under his loving eye. If the man quits his home for any reason at all, the garden withers and the house falls into ruins" (Tournier,

374). The truth of Shonin's statement has been borne out earlier in the book by the death of Deborah, an American expatriot. She and her husband Ralph had built a house on the island of Djerba, off the coast of Tunisia. On "an arid soil producing nothing but alfalfa, prickly pears and aloes," Deborah brought into being a great garden thriving with all kinds of unlikely flora, trees, and water plants. It was a veritable "riot of vegetation in the midst of the desert," says the narrator, Jean, adding: "It was more than her work, her child, it was an extension of herself." This "sympathetic miracle," as Jean calls it, was the result of a forty-year struggle "in which every day had seen the arrival at the harbor of Houmt Souk of packets of seeds, bundles of bulbs, sacking-shrouded shrubs and, above all, bags of chemical fertilizer and humus" (337). Jean describes Deborah's relation to her garden as "a *continuous* process of creation, by which I mean one that renewed every day and every hour, just as God, having created the world, did not sit back but continues to keep it going, to breathe life into it, without which all would return to nothingness in an instant" (ibid.).

The depth of this sympathy and self-extension into the garden becomes evident when Deborah falls seriously ill on a trip away from Djerba. In her feverish state she can talk of nothing but her garden, "as though she had committed a crime" by abandoning it. "She was afraid for her oleanders because their next flowering season would suffer if no one had deadheaded them. She worried about whether the azaleas had been pruned, whether the lily and amaryllis bulbs had been lifted and divided, whether the pools had been cleared of the duckweed and frog spawn that infested them" (ibid.). Her husband and Jean rush her back to Djerba, arriving on the eve of a cataclysmic rainstorm that, during a night of protracted agony, at once devastates the garden and puts an end to Deborah's life. It is not clear whether the garden's destruction provokes Deborah's death or whether her illness and absence from Djerba leave the garden vulnerable to the ravages of the storm.

Precisely because our gardens infuse, and are infused by, our states of mind, they are also pervaded by a palpable sense of vulnerability.

However mastered it may be, an underlying tension haunts their appearances, if only because gardens stand apart from and in contrast to, yet always in the midst of, the rambunctious world beyond their confines. Insofar as they are sheltered domestic creations, gardens are by nature precarious in their status, however artificial they may be in their style. There is always a danger of the proverbial snake in the grass. Likewise the states of mind for which gardens serve as domiciles are precarious. As Eugenio Montale puts it in a poem about a rustic garden full of lemon trees, "Here by a miracle is hushed / the war of the diverted passions," only to add: "But the illusion wanes and time returns us / to our clamorous cities" ("The Lemon Trees," Montale, 3).

In the fusion of place and soul, the soul is as much of a container of place as place is a container of soul, and both are susceptible to the same forces of destruction. This is borne out in a poem by the Irish poet Desmond O'Grady, "Pillow Talk," which juxtaposes the world of "daily struggle" to the garden of matrimonial love, figured here in the famous immovable tree-bed of Odysseus and Penelope. In a reversal of the traditional symbolic values of light and shadow, the world of struggle belongs to the light, in all its agony, while the world of matrimonial sanctuary belongs to the shade of "glad white arms" and shadowed shoulders:

> And, out of the light's agony,
> leaving behind all past destruction,
> let's lie us down again on that old bed
> steadfast under the bamboo and seaweed ceiling,
> opening glad white arms to one another.
>
> Then let me tell you all that story
> That's the skill of survival in the daily struggle:
> the blows given, the beatings taken,
> of wandering for years and of wins and losses
> in the search not to end a destroyer.

> While I watch over you, let down your long hair
> to shadow your shoulders before sleep,
> for all this place shall break
> and fall apart should you go absent.

(O'Grady, 416)

The word *all* occurs in each of the poem's three stanzas. In the last instance it refers to the house, its outlying garden, and the domestic shelter of love. That "all this place" could fall apart should the wife go absent is testimony of a conjugation that remains irreducible to the logic of objective correlatives. The place can break even if its walls remain intact. The question left open at the end of the poem is whether the garden of marriage can be protected from "all past destruction" and, conversely, whether the garden itself can provide that protection.

After one has wrecked one's youth, brutalized one's soul, and numbed one's mind, can a garden come to the rescue and bring one back to life again? This is a question for Patrick Lane, one of Canada's leading poets, who at the turn of the century, at sixty years of age, from one day to the next, gave up the alcohol and drugs that had kept him in their thrall since the age of fifteen. His remarkable autobiography, *What the Stones Remember: A Life Rediscovered*, published in 2005, tells the story of how he entrusted a shattered state of mind and a battered body to the healing powers of his half-acre garden on Vancouver Island, hardly ever leaving it during the first year or more of his abstinence. The book has twelve chapters, one for every month of the first year he spent trying to get a handle on himself in the haven of his garden. Here is the poet's voice in early January 2000:

> I am withdrawing from the scourge of forty-five years of drinking. Two months ago I stumbled into a treatment center for alcohol and drug addiction. Now, I am barely detoxed. Standing here among the sword ferns my senses seem to be thin glass, so acute at their edges I am afraid I will cut myself simply by touching the silicon edge of a bamboo leaf.

The flicker's blade of beak as it slices into the apple makes me wince. My hands are pale animals. The smallest sounds, a junco flitting between the viburnum leaves, a drop of water falling on the cedar deck, make me cringe. I can smell the bitter iron in the mosses on the apple tree's branches. My flesh at times is in agony, and I feel as if I have come from some shadowed place into light for the first time. I feel, for the first time in years, alive. (Lane, 4)

The newly born are fragile and vulnerable to an extreme, but those who are newly born after nearly half a century of aggravated self-abuse are even more so. Day in and day out the poet draws strength from the vitality of the garden, whose plant, animal, and insect life reveals itself to him as if for the first time. Surrendering himself to the garden's plot of life, Lane declares: "The garden begins with my body. I am this place, though I feel it at the most attenuated level imaginable" (ibid.). It is truly a case of handing one's state of mind over to a place: "I am not thinking of what I will do, I am just trying to feel where I am. . . . My presence here is that new" (6–7).

In his garden Lane sometimes discovers empty or full bottles of vodka from former days. "The whole garden seemed like a drinker's minefield, a place of terror" (122). Endurance and patience—lessons learned from the garden—are what enable him to pour the contents of an unearthed bottle into the kitchen sink: "The bamboo stand for endurance. . . . They give way to the forces around them, but after the wind they lift back straight again. Having this kind of flexible strength is to have a *bamboo mind*" (77). Likewise: "Patience, I say, be like the koi in deep water. There is a time for everything. The gardener knows his hours, just like the fish do. All things in this garden wait for the sun to climb higher" (21).

Chuang Tzu once dreamt that he was a butterfly and wondered whether it was he who dreamed he was a butterfly or a butterfly that dreamed it was him. Likewise for Lane, "the garden and I dream each other and everything here is one harmony" (98). In this harmony, the present recovers its bonds with the past. When Lane recalls the past, "it is alive and it is as if it is dreaming me. Without the past I can't learn to live in the unfolding present" (98). We live in an age that wants to forget, that wants to render the present discrete and discontinuous, "but forgetting means having to repeat everything that came before. . . . The clear moments of memory must be understood. It is only then they can be let go" (ibid.). The garden is where this retrieval of time past takes place. It is by dreaming himself into the garden that he reanimates the limbs of time, be it personal, historical, or geological time, for all these dimensions of the past come together in this half-acre of land, which is his extended body. Marcel Proust declared that "the true paradises are the paradises we have lost," but Lane's garden-dream leads him to a different conclusion: "Nothing is lost. The ancient paradise of metaphor and myth grows under my living feet" (136).

Lane also discovers during his healing process that "two people occupy this garden's rooms": he and his companion Lorna (135). Some of the stones and objects in the garden were placed there by her, and during their twenty years of cohabitation the two of them had planted and cultivated many of the garden's species. Lorna "has suffered my addiction for years," and now "her small arms around me in these new nights are another kind of garden" (20). While digging in his garden, Lane discovers the presence of all those who over the millennia worked the earth with their hands, including his dead mother, who taught him the ways of gardening when he was a young boy. Slowly but surely the garden on Vancouver Island becomes a veritable *world*—one that includes Lorna, people from his past, ancient predecessors, and of course his immediate neighbors among the plant, animal, and insect life of the garden.

Lane's book is about one man's tenuous hold on life under extreme circumstances, yet the aggregate of vital forces that comes together in his garden belongs to the planet's cosmic life as a whole. Stone, sky, water, air, plant, bird—these are what the poet understands his soul in its human worldliness to be made of, to be the manifestation of, finally.

The reason one can call a garden a state of the soul is that garden and soul are composed of the same essential ingredients, which splinter into an array of wondrous forms that, however diverse, preserve their kinship with one another. If soul and garden did not share a common substance, how could the latter reanimate the former and fill it with new life? How could it give the soul back its past as well as its future? How could one dream the other, and vice versa? It's only our stupor that prevents us from recognizing that the force that through the green fuse drives the flower drives my green age, the force that blasts the roots of trees is my destroyer. And if Lane is right, nothing rouses us from such a stupor as much as a living garden.

ஜ 13 ஜ

The Paradise Divide:
Islam and Christianity

IT IS WORTHWHILE TO CITE ONE MORE PASSAGE FROM Tournier's novel *Gemini*, where one of the narrators, pondering the wisdom of Japanese gardens, contrasts the Eastern cult of serenity with our Western courting of stress, tumult, and danger. Here is what he says:

The balance which the Japanese had created between human and cosmic space, these gardens situated at their point of contact, constituted a wiser, more ordered undertaking in which failures were fewer—theoretically even impossible. This balance—which is called serenity when it wears a human face—seems to me, in fact, to be the fundamental value of Eastern religion and philosophy. It is extraordinary that this idea of serenity should have so small a place in the Christian world. The story of Jesus is full of crying, weeping and sudden dramas. The religions that have sprung from it have wrapped themselves in a dramatic atmosphere which makes serenity look lukewarm, like indifference or even stupidity. The failure and discrediting of Madame Guyon's quietism in the seventeenth century provides a good illustration of Western contempt for all values that do not relate to action, energy and emotional tension. . . . The forty-five-foot-high bronze figure [of the Buddha statue in Kamakura], standing in the middle of a wonderful park, radiates gentleness, protective power and lucid intelligence. . . . Children laugh and play in the Founder's shadow. Whole families have themselves photographed in front of him. Who would ever think of having his picture taken in front of Christ crucified? (Tournier, 379–80)

For the cultural historian, Tournier's remarks are astonishingly perceptive. Peace and quietude have never been dominant ideals in Western culture, whether in ancient times, Christian times, or modern times. The only notable exception to the long tradition of Western contempt for serenity is Epicureanism, although one could say that even Epicureanism was at bottom a polemical rather than a peaceful philosophy (much of its energies went into denouncing the Platonists, for example, and vying with rival philosophies). Where does it come from, this hypertension of the West—this inability of ours to sit still, as if stillness were a prelude to death rather than beatitude?

Modernity has no doubt exasperated our disquiet, has even rendered it pathological, but the roots of this condition lie deep in the premodern past. No one will deny that there is a strong monastic strain in Christian spirituality, with its silent cloisters of contemplation, yet Tournier is onto something essential when he points to the tumultuous *drama* of the Christian narrative. If Christianity is part of the history and etiology of Western restlessness, as I believe it is, it is because of its "unquiet heart," as Saint Augustine called it, which finds no repose until it reaches some impossible place outside of space and time where God, in a way that is never fully explained, finally puts an end to its otherwise endless yearnings. No matter how post-Christian we may have become in the West, the unquiet heart of the Christian past still agitates inside us.

Our spiritual restlessness marks one the great divides not only between Eastern and Western philosophies, as Tournier claims, but between Christianity and Islam as well. This is not to suggest that Islam and Buddhism, for example, are on one side of the divide and Christianity on the other. The divide between the former two religions is no doubt as great as the one between Islam and Christianity, yet in this chapter my intention is to focus exclusively on the latter, and to do so from a very specific point of view: the two religions' visions of paradise. I believe that by comparing and contrasting these respective visions, one can reveal the true depth and extent of the divide that separates the two traditions. While one could of course stress the elements held in common by Islam and Christianity, what interests me here the most are the differences.

For someone acquainted with the Hebrew and Christian scriptures, there is much in the Qur'an that is familiar, to be sure, yet a striking aspect of the Qur'an that distinguishes it from its predecessors is its abundant references to the afterlife, as well as its vivid descriptions of the delights and rewards that the righteous may expect in paradise. Astonishingly enough, there are no explicit mentions of paradise in the Hebrew Bible. In the New Testament—and this despite an obsession with the afterlife in Christian theology, poetry, and iconography—there are extremely few, mostly fragmentary, references to paradise. Where the Hebrew Bible remains largely silent on the topic and the Christian Bible remains vague and reticent, the Qur'an does not shrink from evoking time and again both the agonies of hell and the pleasures of paradise.

Another significant difference between Islam and Christianity is the fact that Islam boldly identifies paradise with the Garden of Eden. Indeed, in Islam the two poles of the afterlife are hell and the earthly paradise. In the Christian afterlife, by contrast, Eden is a kind of half-way place between hell and heaven, insofar as the Christian abode of the blessed is not an earthly but a heavenly paradise. Much is at stake in this distinction, not only theologically but culturally, and in the pages that follow I will try to show that a religion that points to a celestial paradise is far more restless in its soul than one that envisions Eden as the ultimate dwelling place of the blessed.

If Islam is indeed a "religion of peace," as its defenders keep insisting, it's not so much because it rejects war (the history of the Islamic world belies any such proposition, as does the history of Christendom) but because its paradise is a place of repose, where the righteous "shall be lodged in peace together amidst gardens and fountains." It is to this preexisting Eden of serenity, abundance, and harmony with the cosmic order that the faithful shall come after death: "They shall enter the gardens of Eden, together with the righteous among their fathers, their wives, and their descendants. From every gate the angels will come to them, saying: 'Peace be to you for all that you have steadfastly endured. Blessed is the reward of Paradise'" (13:21–24). It is difficult for us in the West to understand how the religion in whose name so much violence is unleashed these days can have peace as its highest ideal. Even more challenging is to fathom how *the demand for peacefulness* in Islam might be behind the great upheavals. One of the major challenges we face in this regard is the fact that in the West we are driven by desires very different from the desire for peace. That difficulty is compounded by our naive assumption that the desires that drive us are universally shared, whereas they are in fact anything but universal in nature. One day we will hopefully overcome this limitation and realize that it is not so much our modern Western values (freedom, democracy, gender equality, etc.) but rather the unconstrained frenzy of the West—our relentless demand for action, change, innovation, intervention, and a systematic transgression of limits—that offends the very core of Islam in the eyes of the extremists. Where paradise is imagined as a garden of perfect tranquillity, our incurable Western agitation takes on a diabolical quality.

One of the problems that confront a non-Muslim reader of the Qur'an (I do not presume to speak for Islam's adherents) is how to interpret its beautifully sensuous descriptions of Eden. In the book's first evocation of the earthly paradise, it seems that Eden is indeed a place of inward grace and spiritual peace: "Theirs shall be gardens watered by running streams, where they shall dwell forever: spouses of perfect chastity, and grace from God" (3:16–17). Yet in the vast majority of subsequent passages about the earthly paradise, it is difficult if not impossible to read the language of fruits, fountains, virgins, and silk as merely symbolic or figurative, if only because the endless repetition of the same motifs places a heavy emphasis on the literal referent as the true substance of God's gift to the faithful. Here are some examples:

> As for the righteous, they shall be lodged in peace together amidst gardens and fountains, arrayed in rich silks and fine brocade. Yes, and we shall wed them to dark-eyed houris. Secure against all ills, they shall call for every kind of fruit; and, having died once, they shall die no more. (44:45–57)
>
> They shall recline on jeweled couches face to face, and there shall wait on them immortal youths with bowls and ewers and a cup of purest wine (that will neither pain their heads nor take away their reason); with fruits of their own choice and flesh of fowls that they relish. And theirs shall be the dark-eyed houris, chaste as hidden pearls: a guerdon for their deeds.
>
> There they shall hear no idle talk, no sinful speech, but only the greeting, "Peace! Peace!" (56:19–26)
>
> But the true servants of God shall be well provided for, feasting on fruits, and honored in the gardens of delight. Reclining face to face upon soft couches, they shall be served with a goblet filled at a gushing fountain, white, and delicious to those who drink it. It will neither dull their senses nor befuddle them. They shall sit with bashful, dark-eyed virgins, as chaste as the sheltered eggs of ostriches. (37:46–49)
>
> Theirs shall be gardens and vineyards, and high-bosomed maidens for companions: a truly overflowing cup. (78:31)
>
> God will deliver them from the evil of that day, and make their faces shine with joy. He will reward them for their steadfastness with Paradise and robes of silk. Reclining there upon soft couches, they shall feel neither the scorching heat nor the biting cold. Trees will spread their shade around them, and fruits will hang in clusters over them. (76:10–14)

Even in translation these passages, taken from different sections of the Qur'an, convey the incantatory effect of the Qur'an's descriptions of paradise. Time and again the book evokes the rewards that await the faithful in reiterative verses whose exquisite musicality gives the reader a foretaste, as it were, of the sensuous enchantments of Eden. The effect is mesmerizing. We in the rain-abundant modern West may fail to appreciate the meaning of fountains in a waterless place, the meaning of green in a desert, the meaning of rich clothing and physical comfort under the intense sun of the Middle East. And certainly this paradise seems made for men rather than women: it seems to represent a particular male fantasy of satisfied appetites, where the houris are of the same ontological order as fruits and ostrich eggs. The Westerner who knows little about Islam is immediately inclined to wonder where Islamic women go after death—what sorts of rewards await *them*? A fruitless speculation, no doubt, but an irresistible one nonetheless. The Qur'an calls on the believer to trust God's infinite wisdom, even when—or especially when—it leaves certain questions unanswered.

Certainly such passages as those cited above confirm the *terrestrial* quality of the Islamic paradise. The garden is a place where no material or sensuous pleasure is denied. Fruits, soft couches, dark-eyed virgins, and gushing fountains are ready at hand, immediately available, ready for endless consumption. In short, Islam is not about the denial, repression, or sublimation of desire, as some believe; it is all about pleasure's postponement to the afterlife. Earthly life calls not so much for self-overcoming or the struggles of moral reformation; it calls rather for patience. Eden is where abeyance will give way to gratification, where waiting will give way to having, where the desert will give way to the garden. If death is a welcomed prospect for so many would-be Islamic jihadists, it is because death marks the end of deferral and the beginning of delectation. Or so they believe.

The verses cited above suggest, if not confirm, that the Islamic paradise is a place where enjoyment and repose reinforce one another rather than work against one another. An apt figure or image of this synergy between enjoyment and repose is the Edenic tree whose fruits hang in clusters over the blessed, who recline in its shade. In the West, by contrast, a veritable *gaudium* is almost antithetical to any homeostatic state of repose, as we will see shortly.

I have raised the question whether the language in which the Qur'an articulates its vision of the afterlife is to be understood literally or in some other more figurative or spiritual way. My comments so far—which are those of a lay reader—favor a literalistic interpretation of the text's figures of speech (fruits, rivers, virgins, reclining couches, etc.). I tend in this literal direction not because I wish to exclude a figurative interpretation, à la Sufism, but because I believe the Qur'an explicitly warns its readers not to doubt the veracity of its letter. Unlike the inscrutable and often unreliable God of both the Hebrew and Christian scriptures, the God of the Qur'an is absolutely trustworthy. He does not play games with his servants. He does not promise one thing and deliver another. He does not remain silent or absent at the most critical moments (Jesus on the cross, for example). He is a lucid, fair, and unwhimsical God. This is especially the case when it comes to the promises he makes to the faithful about the rewards they may look forward to in paradise. At least that how I interpret the insistent reiteration of the phrase "Which of your Lord's blessings would you deny?" in the following passage:

> But for those that fear the majesty of their Lord there are two gardens (which of your Lord's blessings would you deny?) planted with shady trees. Which of your Lord's blessings would you deny?
>
> Each is watered by a flowing spring. Which of your Lord's blessings would you deny?
>
> Each bears every kind of fruit in pairs. Which of your Lord's blessings would you deny?
>
> They shall recline on couches lined with thick brocade, and within reach will hang the fruits of both gardens. Which of your Lord's blessings would you deny?
>
> Therein are bashful virgins whom neither man nor jinnee will have touched before. Which of your Lord's blessings would you deny?

Virgins as fair as corals and rubies. Which of your Lord's blessings would you deny?

Shall the reward of goodness be anything but good? Which of your Lord's blessings would you deny?

And beside these there shall be two other gardens (which of your Lord's blessings would you deny?) of darkest green. Which of your Lord's blessings would you deny?

A gushing fountain shall flow in each. Which of your Lord's blessings would you deny?

Each planted with fruit trees, the palm and the pomegranate. Which of your Lord's blessings would you deny?

In each there shall be virgins chaste and fair. Which of your Lord's blessings would you deny?

Dark-eyed virgins sheltered in their tents (which of your Lord's blessings would you deny?) whom neither man nor jinnee will have touched before. Which of your Lord's blessings would you deny?

They shall recline on green cushions and fine carpets. Which of your Lord's blessings would you deny? (55:49-70)

Who would deny that these are literal promises and not just sensuous images of abstract, disembodied blessings? Would God dare to say to the faithful, upon their entry into the afterlife, "That is not what I meant, that is not what I meant at all"? In the final analysis, the very real yet abstract gardens of Islamic art seem far more chaste in their symbolic spirituality than the imaginary carnal plenitude of the Qur'an's earthly paradise (see appendix 4).

By the same token, there is no denying the *basso continuo* of chastity, sobriety, and spiritual peace in these same passages. Those who say that the rewards promised by the Qur'an have *only* a literal referent are probably as mistaken as those who would see them as purely figurative. This fault line between the sensual and the spiritual, between the literal and the metaphorical, between the sign and its referent runs straight through the gardens of paradise described by the Qur'an. Or perhaps it is not a fault line at all but rather a harmonization of possible contradictions. Gardens after all are never either merely literal or figurative but always both one and the other.

Certainly the same ambiguity (between the literal and figurative) pervades the whole concept of jihad, about which so much is made today. Does it mean a literal holy war against the enemies of Islam, or does it mean rather the inward moral struggle of the soul to attain self-mastery? Perhaps every great religion draws its energy from the tension it creates between the literal and metaphorical poles of its proclamation. If Islam has given us some of the most beautiful, formal, and serene gardens in the world, it is no doubt thanks to the way their designers brought that tension into sublime harmony—the harmony between spiritual abstraction on the one hand and radiant sensuality on the other, or between the beauty of form and its contemplative content. Perhaps that fusion is what gives those gardens their foretaste of things to come, or not to come, as the case may be (see appendix 4).

It is difficult to compare the Islamic vision of paradise with the Christian vision, for as I mentioned earlier, the Christian scriptures, unlike the Qur'an, offer only scant allusions to, and even fewer images of, the kingdom of God. Beatitude in the Christian scheme of things is an altogether enigmatic, elusive, almost unimaginable state, precisely because the Christian heaven is not an earthly but a celestial paradise that by definition defies representation. But even calling it a "celestial paradise" is saying too much, for it is not clear whether the kingdom of God is located in the celestial heavens at all, except by analogy. It could be all around us, or it could be beyond the universe of space and time altogether. It could be in one's inward and invisible heart or it could be in one's resurrected body. To dwell in the presence of the Lord in heaven—how does one describe something as vague as that except through generic evocations of radiant luminosity and musical harmonies?

In the Christian tradition there is only one person who dared undertake an extended representation of the Christian paradise, and that person was Dante. Dante's *Paradiso* is the most heroic work of literature ever written—heroic because the poet from the start is fully aware of the impossibility of his task, yet he undertakes it nonetheless, without ever shrinking from the challenges of representing the unrepresentable, saying the unsayable, imagining the unimaginable. Thus it is to that exceptional yet quintessentially Christian canticle of the *Divine Comedy* that we will now turn our attention, in order to gauge just how much is at stake in the difference between a religion that envisions paradise as an earthly garden and one that envisions it as a transterrestrial heaven.

When one considers the "plot" of the *Divine Comedy*, the journey undertaken by Dante's pilgrim should, by all narrative rights, end in the Garden of Eden at the top of the mountain of Purgatory. The journey begins in a state of sin (the dark wood of canto 1). The pilgrim descends through the nine circles of Hell (in so doing he sees the consequences of sin). He then climbs the seven terraces of Purgatory (in so doing he understands the causes of sin, namely misdirected love). By the time he passes through the ring of fire and enters Eden, he is poised to shed his human guilt and recover his original innocence. As Virgil tells him, his once fallible will (the seat of sin) is now *libero, dritto e sano*, free, straight, and sound. All that was lost through the fall has now been regained. End of story. But we know that the story does not end there. Eden is not a destination but only a temporary stop on the way to Paradise. "Qui tu sarai con me poco tempo silvano" (Here you will be a forester for a little while with me), says Beatrice to Dante in Eden. After spending only a few hours in Eden, Dante ascends to the celestial spheres with Beatrice, leaving the garden behind. Why?

Because it seems that Dante's will, even after its complete reformation, is not really at home in the everlasting peace of the earthly paradise. There is a desire in that Christian will of his which remains unrequited. It is a desire for ecstasy, not serenity; for self-transcendence, not self-possession; for heaven, not Eden. As Dante depicts it, beatitude is not a homeostatic state of reconciliation but a dynamic, intoxicating process of self-surpassing. Where the will demands ecstasy, the self-contained happiness of Eden cannot satisfy it. In Eden the "new wine" dies on the vine. Indeed, the realm of Paradise in Dante's *Divine Comedy* is so beyond the human and the earthly, so indescribable in its bliss, that its beatitude can be understood only as rapture. Dante in fact tells his reader in the first canto of *Paradiso* that the region he is now entering is altogether ecstatic in nature—that is, it stands outside the poem's capacity to represent it in word, image, or concept. If Dante nonetheless proceeds to "write paradise," he does so in a highly charged language of fervor, ardor, inebriation, and self-transcending desire. Anyone who has read *Paradiso* can attest to the fact that its narrative register is altogether preorgasmic and that there is intensification of the rhetoric of ecstasy as the journey proceeds through the celestial spheres.

The Qur'an may speak of virgins "fair as corals and rubies" and "chaste as hidden pearls" or "the sheltered eggs of ostriches," but the *mood* of Eden in the Qur'an is altogether reposeful, free from the violent compulsion of desire, while in Dante's *Paradiso* the mood is one of heightened sexual excitation. Consider, for example, the erotic intensity of the imagery and language in the following verses—especially in the words uttered by Beatrice to her pilgrim lover in the last tercet. The two of them are gazing at a swarm of angels who, like bees in a flower bed, enter and exit the great river of light in *Paradiso* 30:

> E vidi lume in forma di rivera
> fulvida di fulgore, intra due rive
> dipinte di mirabil primavera.
>   Di tal fiumana uscian faville vive,
> e d'ogni parte si mettien ne' fiori,
> quasi rubin che oro circumscrive;
>   poi, come inebriati da li odori,
> riprofondava sé nel miro gurge,
> e s'una intrava, un'altra n'uscia fori.

"L'alto disio che mo t'infiamma e urge,
d'aver notizia di ciò che tu vei,
tanto mi piace più quanto turge . . ."

(*Paradiso* 30.61–72)

And I saw light that took a river's form—
light flashing, reddish-gold, between two banks
painted with wonderful spring flowerings.
    Out of that stream there issued living sparks,
which settled on the flowers on all sides,
like rubies set in gold; and then, as if
    intoxicated with the odors, they
again plunged into the amazing flood:
as one spark sank, another spark emerged.
    "The high desire that now inflames and incites
you to grasp mentally the things you see,
pleases me more as it swells more . . ."

No English translation can properly convey the erectile ardor of the original, where visionary ecstasy before the river of light takes on an explicitly tumescent character in the verbs *urge* and *turge*. In Dante's paradise, *all* of the saints (and not only the pilgrim) find their joy in a breathless transport. Their gaze is forever directed toward an ever-higher principle of transcendence; they yearn for things to come (the resurrection of their bodies, for instance, or Christ's appearance within their midst). While Dante looks into Beatrice's eyes, her eyes always look into the beyond. In this paradise the saints are projected beyond themselves, in anticipation of something imminent but still out of reach. Not so in the earthly paradise of the Qur'an, where the righteous recline on couches face to face and where fruits hang overhead, ready for the picking. If Islam's paradise is a place of contentment, Dante's is a place of desire's intensified expectation.

The rapture of Dante's heaven is as removed as can be from the placid tranquillity of Eden, either as Dante describes it at the end of *Purgatory* 27 or as the Qur'an describes it in the passages quoted earlier. The *Paradiso*'s "dramatic atmosphere" indeed seems to share in that "western contempt for all values that do not relate to action, energy and emotional tension," to recall the words of Tournier quoted at the beginning of this chapter. There is no question that the *Paradiso*'s atmosphere is thoroughly dramatic. The pilgrim's experience in celestial spheres consists of a continuous series of excesses, blackouts, sensorial overloads, and orgasmic releases, all culminating in the great fulmination of the last canto's face-to-face vision of God. The pilgrim's "doors of perception" are constantly being cleansed, expanding ever wider with each new planetary sphere, until they are blown open altogether by the infinite. Meanwhile the poet whose task it is to describe this ecstatic experience continues to struggle against impossible odds. From start to finish, *Paradiso* totters on the brink of disaster. As the poem reaches higher and higher, the possibility of failure—failure to describe the indescribable—becomes more and more imminent. This extremely high risk of failure gives the canticle an almost unbearable tension and drama, of the sort we in the West have come to expect from our greatest poets. Nor would anything less satisfy us.

I am not suggesting that the antagonism between Islamic extremism and Western modernity can be traced back to the fact that in the Christian imaginary Eden lies somewhere between the turmoil of history and the rapture of heaven, while in Islam paradise *is* envisioned as Eden. Yet one could say that there is at least something *symptomatic* about Dante's impatience with Eden, just as there is something symptomatic about the televangelist's intoxication with the kingdom of God on Sunday mornings. It reveals the existence of a craving in the Western soul that cannot be fulfilled by the ideal of serenity or the self-contained contentment of Eden.

In the West we tend to speak of "Islamic extremism" as if the West were the measure of moderation. Yet the paradox is that Islamic extremists long for a garden where all is moderation and temperance, while we in the modern West are driven by the need to constantly act, contend, achieve, overcome, transform, and revolutionize—in other words, we are driven by compulsions that assume any number of extreme manifestations. What philosophy has traditionally claimed about happiness as the goal of all human action and aspiration is at best only a half-truth. We in the West may hanker for happiness, as long as it eludes us, but somewhere deep inside of us the prospect of happiness—like that of Eden—fills us with dread. This spiritual restlessness is the source of many virtues, as well as many vices, and the least one can say about the modern era that swept away Dante's medieval world order without surrendering its unquiet heart is that it has rendered our spiritual restlessness far more virulent—and far more destructive—in nature, as we will see in what follows.

~ 14 ~

Men Not Destroyers

IN DANTE'S «PARADISO»—AND BY EXTENSION, IN HIS medieval Christian world—ecstasy still had a form, a fixed center around which the intensified motions of love revolved. Nowadays there is no such "still point of the turning world," only an endless pullulating of frenetic impulses. Indeed, in the present age the world no longer turns but jiggles, lurches, plunges, and surges. The times are indeed vertiginous, and the only way we would ever find a still point is if we created one, or better planted one, in their very midst.

In the previous chapter I suggested that Dante's breathless journey in *Paradiso* could be seen as emblematic of the Christian prehistory of modern Western restlessness. Here I propose to look more directly, call it more diagnostically, at this modern spiritual condition and to emphasize its pathology rather than its freedom-seeking energies. Certainly one could say that our congenital Western restlessness is both the consequence and the cause of the loss of those basic structures that once used to direct and regulate the course of human action. Capitalism, for example, has been the most powerful force of social, political, economic, and cultural destabilization the world has ever known, especially in its recent drive to globalize, and in the process deregulate, the international economy. In *The Communist Manifesto* Marx and Engels presciently spoke of how capitalism, by virtue of its self-propelled dynamism, was bound to promote "constant revolutionizing of production, uninterrupted disturbance of all social conditions, everlasting uncertainty and agitation" (Engels and Marx, 68). There is hardly a society anywhere in the world that has not been convulsed by the process described by Marx and Engels—a process that got under way in earnest *after* they wrote the *Manifesto*—and there is no telling what further catastrophic disruptions it may yet hold in store for humankind. Yet while capitalism is a certifiable cause of world upheaval and homelessness, it can also be understood as the profane consequence or socioeconomic correlative of Western spiritual restlessness. At the very least one could say that capitalism opened a whole new stage on which that restlessness could "act out," rather than "work through," its neurosis.

As the defining spiritual condition of our late and perhaps even terminal modernity, the restlessness in question could be characterized as a whirlwind wherein those of us who are swept up in its turbulence are at once driven and aimless. This is a paradoxical condition, to be sure. To be both driven and aimless means that the impulses that set us into motion may have proximate goals but no ultimate aim, unless the perpetuation of aimless motion can be considered an aim in itself. In what follows I will attempt to probe this condition as lucidly as possible and in the process come to a fuller understanding of the spiritual nihilism of the modern era. I will also, in the latter part of this chapter, offer my perspective on the cultural phenomenon that goes by the name *modernism*, which I see mostly as a symptom of, rather than antidote to, the condition in question.

The reader who has made it this far in this book will have noticed that, in general, I tend to favor revelation over demonstration, embodied figures over analytical concepts, and the discernment of poets over the disquisitions of philosophers. That is why this is a book about gardens and not a book about the ethics of care. That is also why, when it comes to the present chapter, I feel that the first order of business is to seek out an emblem, or revelatory figure, for the aimless drivenness of our age. It so happens that I find such an emblem in what some people might consider an unlikely place: in the dusty archives of a by now antiquated—or apparently antiquated—literature. A certain epic that is half a millennium old, despite its age, "knows" the errant passions of the modern era as deeply and essentially as any testament that came after it. I mean Ludovico Ariosto's *Orlando Furioso*, which was composed in the first decades of the sixteenth century and which still today preserves its almost magical powers of insight when it comes to what I would call the behavioral disorder of our times, as well as the covert passions that provoke a good deal of that disorder.

There are very few epics of the modern era, and *Orlando Furioso* is one of them. While the poem ostensibly looks back to a bygone age of chivalry and Christian heroism, it also looks forward to the great upheavals associated with modernity (the invention of gunpowder, the geopolitics of the modern state, the triumph of relativity, and the loss of certainty, to mention just a few). Certainly Ariosto's knights— whether they are Christian or Saracen—are far more modern in spirit than Dante's pilgrim. Whereas the latter seeks the beatitude of heaven in a vertical ascent through the celestial spheres, the former wander the earth laterally in search of action and distraction. In the world of the *Furioso*, desire is a principle of motion, just as it is in Dante's *Comedy*, yet here desire does not have a master plan, nor does it have a final destination. It merely desires more of its own dynamism, more of its own intoxication, more of its own circulating energies. That is why Ariosto's laterally dispersed knights are archetypically modern in a way that Dante's heaven-bound pilgrim is not.

The story of the *Furioso* ostensibly revolves around Charlemagne's war against the Saracens, but the action is forever deviating from the central "plot" as the poem follows the knights along countless errant byways, which intersect for the most part randomly and converge only temporarily if at all. It is difficult to know in what part of the forest or continent the fighting is taking place, or for how long, as the scene of action constantly shifts, sometimes in midcourse. It is a tumultuous world of digressive compulsions, where the knights constantly go astray as they court adventure, pursue elusive erotic objects, and strive to measure up to their rivals. Orlando, the most formidable knight of the Christian army, is so distracted by his love for the Saracen princess

Angelica that he temporarily goes mad, absenting himself from the war for an indefinite amount of time. That madness is in fact the true center—or anticenter—of the poem as a whole. It is like a black hole that devours whatever comes near it.

What do we, five hundred years later, have to learn from these erratic knights? And what does it all have to do with gardens?

There are two very different kinds of gardens in the *Orlando Furioso*, yet both are equally inimical to the demand for action that spurs on the knights. The first is on the island of Alcina and is altogether typical of the enchanted gardens that so captivated the medieval and Renaissance imagination. These are fantasy gardens where the hero (usually a knight) succumbs to the bewitching charms of the resident sorceress and gets trapped in her magical garden world: "This was the abode of youths and maidens, here where soft April, presenting a serene and merry face, seemed constantly to smile. By a spring, some there were who sang in sweet, melodious voice; in the shade of a tree or a cliff others played and danced and indulged in honest fun. Another had gone apart, and was communing with his true love" (Ariosto, 58–59).

As in other enchanted gardens, things are not what they seem on Alcina's island. All is false semblance and appeals to the native desire for illusion that lurks in us all. The gems are not real gems, the plants are not real plants, and the beautiful Alcina herself, so irresistible to the knights she lures into her garden, is eventually revealed to Ruggiero (the epic's main male hero) for what she really is: an ugly and loathsome hag.

Alcina's garden is neither created nor cultivated by human labor. It is created by magic, and therefore it is ultimately sterile. Indeed, the garden is made up of Alcina's former, now disillusioned lovers, who have been transformed by her into the fauna and flora of the place. It is sterile in another sense as well, for as it ensnares and immobilizes the male hero, it removes him from the theater of action on whose stage he presumably finds his productive purpose in life. The classical precedents for the emasculating and even dehumanizing powers of the enchanted garden are the island of Circe in Homer's *Odyssey*, where Odysseus's men are transformed into swine, and the city of Carthage in Virgil's *Aeneid*, where Aeneas, seduced by the blandishments of the queen and a life of leisure, is derailed from his mission to found the future city of Rome. The male heroes who have been thus arrested by a feminine power are in need of rescue, for the story must move forward, cities must be founded, enemies must be fought, in short the hero's purposeful drive must overcome the paralysis of the garden's spell. If reality can have a Medusa effect on those who look too directly and intently on its horrors, the enchanted garden can have a Circe effect, as it were, on those who fall under its fantastical spells, causing them to lose all touch with reality.

But there is a subtle yet crucial difference between traditional heroes like Odysseus or Aeneas and Ariosto's knights. The latter, as I have remarked, are distinctly modern in character, and that means that their wanderings are not guided by a higher personal or historical purpose. One cannot even say that their actions are misdirected, for this would imply that there exists a proper direction or orientation for those actions, whereas in the world of the *Furioso* the actors are fundamentally aimless and without issue, precisely because their action does not have a final destination but feeds on its need for ever-new challenges and exploits. Remaining in motion (wherever that motion may lead) becomes an end in itself. This does not mean that battles are not engaged, that prowess is not demonstrated, that victories are not achieved. It means that there is no fixed center to the poem's agglutination of episodes, no discernible progress toward a redemptive goal, hence no greater underlying purpose to all the digressive commotion that makes the *Furioso* such a delight to read. The knights' craving for action is at bottom a craving for distraction, what Blaise Pascal called *divertissement*, without which the modern male (according to Pascal) quickly succumbs to melancholy. That craving for diversion arises from the pointlessness of their mode of being—the pointlessness of being knights in a postchivalric world, men of action in an age when action has lost its normative or underlying meaning.

This is why Alcina's garden is more than just a trap that temporarily immobilizes the poem's heroes. By the same token, Orlando's madness is not simply a momentary derailing of the hero's military mission but a revelation of the neurotic condition of the times. If the war's true appeal for Ariosto's protagonists is that it offers them endless opportunities for adventure and escapades, then Alcina's enchanted garden is where their motivating passions flower in their truest colors. Alcina is the escapade of all escapades. Her garden remains a source of irresistible fascination. As it lures the knights into its vortex of illusion, it reveals their covert desire for distraction, delusion, and self-dispossession, even at the cost of losing their humanity and becoming plants. Alcina Island is the era's oceanic fantasy: a place where the desire for irreality translates into reality through self-deception. It is not by chance that over the centuries Ariosto's readers, like the poem's knights, have been captivated by Alcina's realm. Remove her enchanted garden from the *Furioso* and you take away the heterotopia around which so much of the reader's desire, as well as the epic's aimless action, gravitates.

The other garden in Ariosto's epic is strangely contiguous with Alcina's island, if not geographically then at least narratively and symbolically. When the valiant but easily distracted Ruggiero finally succeeds in triumphing over Alcina and freeing the knights who have been trapped in her garden, the latter, upon their release, come to Logistilla's realm. If Alcina's island is a false Eden based on illusion, Logistilla's garden is the "real thing," so to speak. Here there are no incantations, no false jewels or flora, no deception. The verdure is "perpetual," as is the "beauty of the eternal flowers." All is peace, benevolence, and leisure, yet astonishingly enough this earthly paradise offers little attraction for Ruggiero and the other liberated knights— not because they hanker after a heavenly paradise, à la Dante, but because they simply do not know what to do with themselves there. After a day or two in this sedate environment, the knights leave Logistilla's garden of their own accord to rejoin a war that offers risks, dangers, intrigues, and rewards. Nor does Ariosto's poem linger very long there either. The poem that sings of "ladies, knights, arms, loves, manners and brave enterprises" comes to Logistilla's garden to die, for the poem's element is the whirlwind of history, the enticements of illusion, the propulsion of desire, the relentless pursuit of moving targets.

It should be obvious by now that the restlessness under description is a highly gendered affair. In the *Furioso* the enclosed garden is the feminine domain par excellence. The fact that it poses a threat of male sterility tells us all we need to know about the lack of traditional male ideals when it comes to making history by other means than self-affirmation through contest, conflict, and conquest. One of the striking things about Ariosto's poem is that it enlists various women on both sides of the war between the Christians and Saracens. These women, often disguised as male knights, show considerable prowess in their confrontations with male enemies. Yet when the action comes close to pitting one woman against another in battle, the poem shrinks from staging such a duel. We can make of this what we will. I make of it the following: that by refusing to pit woman against woman, Ariosto reminds us that women, if given the chance, would make history differently from men. Or better, they *do* make history differently from men, though it is the men who have defined the rules of engagement. This is confirmed in part by the fact that the heroic efforts of Bradamante, the main female heroine of the *Furioso*, come to fruition in marriage and the founding of a family line with Ruggiero.

In his classic study *The Earthly Paradise and the Renaissance Epic*, A. Bartlett Giamatti notes how remarkable it is that Ariosto's knights depart from Logistilla's idyllic garden promptly and willingly. For Giamatti, this shows that the earthly paradise, which had long stood as the image of human happiness in its perfect state, had already lost its traditional appeal in the early modern imagination. Throughout the present study I have tried to show that we can detect an aversion to Eden as far back as Eve, who engineers an escape from the garden, or as far back as Homer's *Odyssey*, where Odysseus longs for Ithaca in the midst of Kalypso's earthly paradise. When Dante's pilgrim enters

Eden at the top of the mountain of Purgatory, he feigns enchantment, but in truth he too is in a hurry to get out of its serene and somniferous environment (he actually falls asleep in the River Lethe). In sum, our impatience with Eden runs deeper than the modern imagination; it runs perhaps as deep as human nature itself, which fulfills its potential only there where its intrinsic care gets activated rather than sedated.

The modern differential in Ariosto's knights is not so much their aversion to Eden as their existential boredom. Boredom indicates a certain deficiency or blockage of care. In a creature created by Cura, boredom can bring about the conditions for desperation and lead to a constant search for diversion, a constant "turning away" from oneself. Giamatti is right to claim that Alcina's dream world is finally far more enticing to Ariosto's knights than Logistilla's earthly paradise, precisely because Alcina diverts them from their boredom while Logistilla's garden offers no such palliatives. In the latter realm they can neither escape from their pointlessness nor find an outlet for their self-alienation. Not so with Alcina's garden. Even after the knights have been freed from its snare, Alcina's garden continues to exert a hold on them—they never really overcome the temptation to fall under its spell again—while Logistilla's Eden holds no lure for them whatsoever. The same could be said of our own terminal modernity. We are so profoundly bored these days that the serenity of Eden has hardly any claims on our imagination, while Alcina's garden of illusion becomes more and more surreal and all of us seek out its potentially lethal charms without even leaving our homes.

I am in no way lamenting or denouncing the aversion to Eden that we find so subtly portrayed in Ariosto's epic. On the contrary, the knights do well to take their leave of Logistilla's realm. Although one appears as the false likeness of the other, in truth both Alcina's garden of illusion and Logistilla's Edenic garden are characterized by a kind of sterile stasis (as opposed to the fertile stasis of humanly cultivated gardens). Both gardens are traps of sorts, for in gardens where cultivation has no role, where care is out of place or superfluous, and where there is no need to "labour to become beautiful," as Yeats put it, human beings remain without issue. The question here is not whether the knights should remain in Logistilla's realm—they should not—but what they do with themselves once they leave it.

The neurotic or obsessive character of these knights is revealed by the fact that, once they depart Logistilla's Eden, they do not follow in the footsteps of Adam and Eve, who set out to cultivate the earth and turn it into a mortal home for themselves; they simply revert to their prior ways, seeking out the tumult of war and the diversions of desire under the impetus of passions they do not, or cannot, bring under control. Their aimless condition more often than not leads to destructive behavior. (A creature of care is more likely to destroy what he fails to care for than to leave it alone.) The destructive behavior in question is acted out most dramatically by the formidable Orlando, who in the central cantos of the *Furioso* loses his mind after his love for Angelica turns into an explosive jealous fury. His loss of self-control merely brings to an extreme the congenital self-dispossession of most of the other knights.

From our point of view, it is significant that Orlando's loss of reason expresses itself in mindless acts of devastating what others have carefully cultivated. In effect Orlando goes on a rampage, like a malfunctioning machine of war, and lays waste to the farmers' fields, the well-husbanded countryside, the quiet forests and rivers of an otherwise serene landscape. He directs his rage particularly against gardeners and shepherds, assaulting flocks of sheep with his bare hands and using these domestic animals to batter the helpless shepherds. This is not the kind of hero one needs in one's midst if one is a cultivator of the earth, yet Orlando is exactly the kind of hero that the age of which he is a harbinger sends forth.

Orlando's fury, which creates a nihilistic vortex at the center of Ariosto's poem, is a figure for the forces of destruction we unleash upon the earth when restlessness reaches a pathological degree of agitation and when there is such disorder in our desires that care gives way to carnage. Again, it is not the knights' restive disposition per se that is the problem. The unquiet heart, after all, is what got us out of Eden and put us on the path to self-realization. The problem is that after taking leave of Logistilla's garden, Ariosto's knights move on to ravage the earth rather than to seed or cultivate it. Herein lies their quintessential and even contemporary modernity, for this is precisely the spiritual condition of the age today: driven and aimless, we are under the compulsion of an unmastered will to destroy whatever lies in our way, even though we have no idea where the way leads or what its end point may be. Whatever the way leads *through*—our landscapes, our heritage, our legacies, our institutions, all that humankind has carefully cultivated over time, and that means first and foremost the earth itself—risks destruction as we rush headlong into a future of which we are not the architects but for which we bear full responsibility. What that future will be most in need of, if human culture on earth is not only to survive but also to thrive, is what we are most determined to obliterate as we plunge into its abyss.

To say that the frenzy of the modern era is fundamentally aimless does not mean that we fail to set goals for ourselves. On the contrary, there is no end of goals when it comes to our endless activity, just as there is no end of desirable objects when it comes to our cupidity. The setting of goals is one of the ways we dissimulate our aimlessness. It's a question once again of deception, as well as self-deception. Be it in its colonialist, capitalist, or communist rhetoric, during the modern era the West has invariably proclaimed some social or moral good that guides its actions and defines its aspirations. But we know from the art, literature, and intellectual history of the nineteenth and twentieth centuries that the putative moral good—be it of colonialism, capitalism, or communism—was more often than not a mask, a lie, or at best an illusion, behind which lurked another intention. When it comes to the moral good of either party (Christian or Saracen, capitalist or communist), we find ourselves once more in Alcina's garden of *falsa sembianza*. Moral ideals in the modern era remain for the most part fictions we pretend to believe in, whether we are aware of our pretense or not, and this holds true for the assault on nature that is presently unearthing the earth and unworlding the world in the name of eliminating poverty and suffering. We let loose Orlando in the guise of Christ, and with a look of grave concern for human suffering he devastates the land.

The unmasking of society's self-serving fictions, as well as the destruction of its false idols, has been the principal task of the artists, poets, and philosophers of the modern era. Many of them, situating themselves on society's margins, saw it as their calling to challenge the bad faith of the age. Like Ruggiero in *Orlando Furioso*, they took it upon themselves to break the deadly spell of Alcina's deceptions. To the degree that these artists and thinkers were successful, we could call them liberators. But can we also call them gardeners, cultivators of the good? In other words, did they do more than expose insidious lies? Did they do more than deal blows to bourgeois complacency? Did they do more than register their dissent, or at least withhold their consent? These are questions that can engaged only on a case-by-case basis. In general, however, I am prepared to say that while I consider myself an heir to the cultural history of modernity, I believe that modernism, for lack of a better term, has been mostly a story of combating and denouncing history, rather than cultivating, in sheltered places, counterforces to history's deleterious forces.

The American critic Wallace Fowlie once wrote that the modern quest for spiritual freedom inevitably entails "some propagation of destructive violence." As he put it: "In order to discover what is the center of themselves, the saint has to destroy the world of evil, and the poet has to destroy the world of specious good" (quoted in Trilling, 66). Certainly the post-Nietzschean age has expended most of its spiritual energies in trying to destroy what it took to be the specious good. Its protagonists (be they artists, thinkers, or revolutionaries) have typically identified the specious good with bourgeois society in its political, social, economic, and ideological guises. Yet identification of the enemy was not the most crucial element in this story. Crucial to modernism was the attack, the assault, and the occasion to propagate cultural violence in the name of spiritual liberation. As Flaubert put it in one of his letters, "Effaroucher, épouvanter le bourgeois; épater le bourgeois. Terrifie le bourgeois par tes extravagances" (Savage, frighten the bourgeois; shock the bourgeois. Terrify the bourgeois with your extravagance). Or in a slightly different vein, F. T. Marinetti in *The Futurist Manifesto*: "Courage, audacity, and revolt will be essential elements of our poetry. . . . We intend to exalt aggressive action, a feverish insomnia, the racer's stride, the mortal leap, the punch and the slap" (Marinetti, 49).

We are entitled to ask at this point how much spiritual freedom was really gained by modernism's cultural war against freedom's putative oppressors. Not much, it seems, despite the creative achievements of its relentless attacks. More often than not, the thrill and intoxication of spiritual militancy itself were what this war was really all about. Intoxication—or the unbounded craving for "more life," as Lionel Trilling once called it—was too often both the means and the end of this supposed quest for spiritual freedom, which more often than not was merely a lie that served to justify the propagation of destructive violence. For all their noble efforts (and they were to a large extent noble), the avatars of modernism craved an ever-greater intensification of life rather than its creative reordering or serenification, if I may evoke with that word the vocation of the Garden School of Epicurus.

What many of the warrior poets of the age failed to appreciate sufficiently was that history's redemption is not the only alternative to history's hell and that destroying false idols is only a first step on the path to rehumanization. One of the tragic aspects of their war was its excessive promiscuity with the nihilism against which it took its stand. The risk of an aggravated cultural militancy is that it partakes of, or employs, the same forces of disfiguration it presumes to counteract. To a certain degree this was unavoidable. After all, our destructive and creative powers arise from the same basic source. The vandal's hammer is the same as the sculptor's; and every gardener knows that cultivation involves a lot of brute destruction, pruning, and cutting back to the ground. Destruction can be liberating, inebriating, creative, and even beautiful; and certainly clearing the ground is a precondition for the productive work of cultivation. Yet much of what we call modernism, in its militant activism, did not take the next step: it did not commit itself to the work of cultivation. In short, it ignored what I would call the gardener's activism—the painstaking, compensatory work of fostering the saving power of human culture. As a result, modernism found its objective correlative in the wasteland rather than the garden. ("The wasteland grows," warned Nietzsche: "woe to him who harbors wastelands within.")

In this regard the fragments that bring Ezra Pound's wild and at times hysterical *Cantos* to a conclusion offer one of modernism's most honest confessions of failure:

> M'amour, m'amour
>   what do I love and
>   where are you?
> That I lost my center
>   fighting the world?
> The dreams clash
>   and are shattered—
> and that I tried to make a paradiso
>   terrestre.
>
>   (Pound, *Cantos* 802)

Pound's failure to make an earthly paradise (to redeem history as a whole) was a historical, not personal, failure. It tells us more about the age than about the artist. That is why it would be pointless and misguided to presume to pass judgment on the cultural militancy of the twentieth century here. That modernism lost its center fighting the world was no doubt a "destiny" that unfolded, at least to some extent, independently of human agency.

Yet it is precisely where history takes on the character of destiny that the role of human agency is both humbled and liberated. We do not ask of artists, thinkers, and visionaries that they turn the wasteland into an earthly paradise or that they shatter against the inevitable. In such times, it is enough to undertake the task of creating or preserving gardens in the midst of the wasteland, whatever forms they may take (and they take many, as we have seen throughout this book). In Italo Calvino's *Invisible Cities*, Marco Polo gives voice to such an imperative in his very last words to the emperor Kubla Khan. "There are two ways to escape suffering from the inferno where we live every day, that we form by being together," says Polo. The first is "to accept the inferno and become such a part of it that you can no longer see it." The second "is risky and demands constant vigilance and apprehension: seek and learn to recognize who and what, in the midst of the inferno, are not inferno, then make them endure, give them space" (*Invisible Cities*, 165). This is the vigilance and apprehension of a gardener who knows what it takes to get things to grow, who knows what the odds are when it comes to planting a garden in the midst of the wasteland, giving space to the human in the midst of the inferno. That is why today more than ever we need to "cultivate our garden," for the alternatives identified by Pound in the very last, fragmentary verse of his *Cantos* are as stark and real as they ever were: "to be men not destroyers."

❧ 15 ❧

The Paradox of the Age

EZRA POUND WROTE: "I LOST MY CENTER FIGHTING THE world.... I tried to make a paradiso terrestre." What is the connection between these two failures? And what would we do with that earthly paradise had Pound been able to "make" one after all? The critic Lionel Trilling wrote back in 1964 that there is nothing that we moderns recoil from as much as the idea of Eden:

> How far from our imagination is the idea of "peace" as the crown of spiritual struggle! The idea of "bliss" is even further removed. The two words propose to us a state of virtual passivity which is the negation of the "more life" that we crave.... We dread Eden, and of all Christian concepts there is none which we understand so well as the *felix culpa* and the "fortunate fall"; not, of course, for the reason on which these Christian paradoxes were based, but because by means of the sin and the fall we managed to get ourselves expelled from that dreadful place. (Trilling 66)

"We" here presumably refers to those of us who share in late modernity's craving for "more life," a craving that makes us impatient with the stasis and contentment of Eden. Upon further review we shall see that things are not as clear cut as that, yet there is little doubt that in the modern era stillness, repose, beauty, and harmony with the cosmic order no longer define, even in a hypothetical way, the ultimate end point of human desire. Desire now desires more of itself, more of its own restlessness.

"Peace as the crown of spiritual struggle"—that could stand as a motto for Epicureanism. Trilling is right that we are very far from such an ethos today. From the point of view of Epicureanism, we live in a mode of extreme ingratitude. For the ingrate, nothing is ever enough. "It is the ungratefulness in the soul that renders the creature endlessly lickerish of embellishments in diet," wrote Epicurus. We are endlessly lickerish of many things these days: wealth, power, life, sex—in short, we want more of everything that promises to perpetuate the cycle of unending consumption. We would prolong our life forever if we could. Soon the citizen will insist not on the right to die but on the right not to die—on the right, that is, to use all the technological and medical means available to demortalize an existence that, lacking in gratitude, is unable to find fulfillment.

One of the paradoxes of the present age is that our craving for more life is precisely what is driving us to re-Edenize the earth, to turn it into a consumerist paradise where everything is given spontaneously, without labor, suffering, or husbandry. This is the paradox that Trilling perhaps failed to appreciate some forty years ago—that "a state of virtual passivity" is *not* necessarily the negation of the "more life" that we crave. Rather, our craving inevitably creates the expectation of an Edenic condition in which the sole higher purpose, if not obligation, of the citizen is to enjoy the fruits of the earth in an increasingly infantilized state of sheer receptivity. At times it seems as if all the forces of modern technology, the global economy, medical research, and telecommunications and information media are conspiring to bring about such a condition. Like Pound we are trying to "make" a *paradiso terrestre*, forgetting that at bottom our restless humanity is not at home in Eden. The craving for more life engenders from its own dynamism the myth that there is a place where all desires are gratified, all pain is abolished, the curse of Adam is overcome, and human beings have no other responsibility than to be unfettered consumers of goods, entertainment, information, and pleasures. That is an impoverishing myth indeed, and if we ever succeed in turning it into reality (which we are fast doing), we will bring to an end the human phenomenon. The paradox of the age is that we are profoundly conflicted when it comes to Eden. On the one hand we dread it, on the other hand we chase after it.

One of the perverse consequences of this paradox is that the path back to Eden is littered with ruins, corpses, and destruction. Our attempts to re-create Eden amount to an assault on creation. That is the danger of the era. Precisely because our frenzy is fundamentally aimless while remaining driven, we set ourselves goals whose main purpose is to keep the frenzy going until it consummates itself in sloth. If at present we are seeking to render the totality of the earth's resources endlessly available, endlessly usable, endlessly disposable, it is because endless consumption is the proximate goal of a production without end. Or better, consumption is what justifies the frenzy of production, which in turn justifies consumption, the entire cycle serving more to keep us busy than to satisfy our real needs. Martin Heidegger describes this syndrome with great acuity in his otherwise portentous and abstract prose:

> The consumption of all material, including the raw material "man," for the unconditional possibility of the production of everything, is determined in a concealed way by the complete emptiness in which beings, the material of what is real, are suspended. This emptiness has to be filled up. But since the emptiness of Being can never be filled up by the fullness of beings, especially when this emptiness can never be experienced as such, the only way to escape it is incessantly to arrange beings in the constant possibility of being ordered as the form of guaranteeing aimless activity. (*The End of Philosophy*, 106–7)

There is nothing objectionable about consumption per se, which is directly related to the biological rhythms of human labor. It's when consumption enables or necessitates hyperactive production that it signals a distinct pathology. If Heidegger is right, then the goal of creating an earthly paradise on earth is not so much the teleological *end* that guides our activity as the fiction that sponsors our *blind demand for endless activity*—a demand that arises from our unacknowledged suffering from, and denial of, the emptiness of Being. If one understands boredom as fundamentally related to that emptiness, then the attempt to escape from the emptiness of Being could be seen as another symptom of our boredom. Or perhaps boredom is the consequence of our inability to experience that emptiness in a genuine way. Be that as it may, the endless productivity mandated by endless consumption, and the endless consumption mandated by endless productivity, becomes in the present age the only way to "escape"—but not to fill—that emptiness.

The more we succeed in turning the earth into an inexhaustible inventory for human consumption, the more we abandon the postlapsarian vocation of care that turned human beings into cultivators of the mortal earth, as well as cultivators of our mortal modes of being on the earth. I have insisted throughout this study that human happiness is a cultivated rather than a consumer good, that it is a question of fulfillment more than of gratification. Neither consumption nor productivity fulfills. Only caretaking does. And since we cannot destroy our way back to Eden, our craving for more life ends up militating against life itself.

When I say that the will of the present age to put all the fruits of the earth, as well as all the fruits of world culture, at the disposal of human consumption is a blind drive, I mean that its dominant impulse is to perpetuate its own dynamism rather than to fulfill an end. Unlike the gardener, who "wants eleven hundred years to test, learn to know, and appreciate fully what is his" (Čapek), we are not projected enough into the future these days to fulfill an end, or to accomplish a purpose, over time. Our action does not so much bear fruit as devour fruit. Thus we find ourselves in the paradoxical situation of seeking to re-create Eden by ravaging the garden itself—the garden of the biosphere on the one hand and the garden of human culture on the other.

Surely it is not by chance that a number of dark science-fiction visions of the future revolve around this paradox. The various *Star Trek* television series are replete with scenarios of an Edenic garden world in the midst of a destroyed wasteland. Likewise in the movie *Aeon Flux*, human beings have destroyed their world; those who have survived the catastrophe live in an eerily idyllic garden environment, except that all the women are infertile. Such garden worlds are not merely the sinister fictions of movies. They are taking shape before our eyes through the increasing artificialization of our habitats. Is there anything quite as depthless as the flower beds that deck the entrances of corporate high-rise buildings in our cities? In these raised, granite-bordered ovals and rectangles, the flowers are always in their prime. Neither strife nor decay is visible, nor the mark of Cura, as a full bed of pansies is replaced overnight by one of full-blown petunias. Here the sublime artifice of Versailles has become the paltry ornamentalization of decorative "landscaping." Here the "perpetual spring" of Eden indeed seems to reign, but it is as arid and worldless as the forced air and artificially regulated environments inside the offices and hotel towers. As we "cute up" the habitat, the gardens become more perfect, yet the gardener recedes further from the scene, to the point of disappearing altogether. These formulaic gardens that are cropping up overnight in our midst are not sustained by personal dedication but are mechanically maintained by anonymous agents. In short, the specious garden world of *Aeon Flux* is already upon us. Soon there will be no getting away from it.

The most compelling version of this sci-fi vision of the future—for our purposes—comes to us from one of the heroes of this book: Karol Čapek, the Czech writer whose garden ethics I discussed in chapter 3. Outside of the Czech Republic, Čapek is best known for his play *R.U.R.* As relevant in its theme today as it was when it was first performed in 1920, this play hypothesizes a future age when technology develops the means to deliver humanity from Adam's curse. In Čapek's scenario, well-intentioned scientists, politicians, and social engineers mass produce a race of "robots" (the word was first coined by Čapek).

These biological but manufactured humanoids are apparently devoid of human needs and passions. They are created to service the needs of "real" human beings: to perform their labor, staff their militaries, and relieve them of their worldly burdens. Early in the play, the idealistic leader of the robot enterprise, Domin, tells Helena, his wife-to-be, "The subjugation of man by man and the enslavement of man by matter will cease. . . . No longer will man need to destroy his soul doing work he hates. . . . Everything will be done by living machines. People will do only what they enjoy. They will live only to perfect themselves" (21). Domin's lofty vision is reminiscent of Marx's ideal of a fully realized communist state where factories would presumably run on their own, where fields would plant and harvest themselves, thanks to a magical technology that dispenses with the need for human labor, leaving people free to fulfill their creative inner potential.

The problem with such ideals—and they come in many versions—is that they fail to appreciate the degree to which human potential is bound up with the condition from which the proponents of these ideals seek liberation. To liberate people from care is to deny them self-realization. The rest of Čapek's play suggests as much. Alquist, the only person who later will survive the annihilation of humanity by the insurgent robots, answers Domin: "Domin, Domin! What you're saying sounds too much like paradise. Domin, there was something good in the act of serving, something great in humility. Oh, Harry, there was some kind of virtue in work and fatigue" (21). Domin is not deaf to Alquist's appeal, yet his conviction and exaltation are irrepressible as he replies:

> There probably was. But we can't exactly compensate for everything that's lost when we recreate the world from Adam. O Adam, Adam! no longer will you have to earn your bread by the sweat of your brow; you will return to Paradise, where you were nourished by the hand of God. You will be free and supreme; you will have no other task, no other work, no other cares than to perfect your own being. You will be the master of creation. (21)

Thanks to a fantastically enhanced technology, Domin's project for human liberation on Earth gets realized, yet not exactly along the lines he envisioned. As the robots relieve people of their responsibilities, there comes plenty of "enjoyment" but precious little self-perfection, to say nothing of the fact that self-perfection (unlike self-cultivation) is an altogether narcissistic and sterile goal. Thus the enjoyment of the newly liberated human race in *R.U.R.* is not of the redeemed paradisiacal variety—a *delectatio* that never lets you down, according to the church fathers—but rather of the decadent, emasculating, and fruitless sort.

As he ceases to make an effort, the new Adam ceases to reproduce:

HELENA [*softly*]: Why have women stopped having babies?

ALQUIST: Because it's not necessary. Because we're in paradise, understand?

HELENA: I don't understand.

ALQUIST: Because human labor has become unnecessary, because suffering has become unnecessary, because man needs nothing, nothing, nothing but to enjoy—Oh, cursèd paradise, this. [*He jumps up.*] Helena, there is nothing more terrible than giving people paradise on earth! Why have women stopped giving birth? . . . People don't even stretch out their hands for food anymore; it's stuffed right into their mouths for them so that they don't even have to get up. . . . And you expect women to have children by such men? Helena, to men who are superfluous women will not bear children! (35)

Perhaps this is what happens to persons who "have no other task, no other work, no other cares than to perfect your own being." Instead of becoming "masters of creation," they become superfluous. And to human beings who become superfluous even robots will react with contempt. The latter, discovering that they are superior in every respect to their masters, embark upon a campaign of extermination, sparing—for some inexplicable reason—only Alquist.

Alquist lives long enough in the holocaust's aftermath to witness the first stirring of human emotions in a pair of robots named Helena and Primus. He is astonished to observe that Primus and Helena (the latter named after Domin's wife) actually love each other and are willing to give up their lives for one another. It is this readiness for sacrifice that confirms their incipient humanity. The play ends with Alquist sending the pair into the wilderness, the way God sent Adam and Eve forth from the garden: "Go, Adam. Go, Eve—be a wife to Primus. Be a husband to Helena, Primus" (84). It is only by sending the pair back into the wilderness, where they will have to cultivate their way to survival, that the prospect of a regenerate humanity is kept open at the end of the play.

It would be a mistake to say that Čapek's *R.U.R.* champions the value of work and suffering over against leisure and enjoyment. A gardener does not exalt the work ethic. He does not espouse the cause of labor. He espouses the cause of what he cultivates. That is why, in *The Gardener's Year*, on the first day of May, Čapek writes: "I do not want to sing the praises of the holiday of labour. . . . If one does a job one ought to do it because one likes it, or because one knows it, or finally because one has to live by it; but to sew boots on principle, work on principle, and for the virtue of it, means to do a job which is not worth much" (41–43). The gardener is not a laborer, regardless of how much real labor cultivation entails. On the first of May he is not going to celebrate Labor Day itself, but, he muses, "If it doesn't rain, I shall certainly celebrate by sitting on my heels and saying: 'Wait a moment, I will give you a bit of humus, and I will cut this shoot; and you would like to go deeper into the ground, wouldn't you?' And the little alyssum will say 'Yes,' and I shall put it deeper into the soil. For this is my soil, sprinkled with my own sweat and blood, and that literally; for when one cuts a twig, or a shoot, almost always one cuts a finger, and that also is only a twig or a shoot" (41). The gardener, in short, is not committed to work, and even less to "productivity." He is committed to the welfare of what he nourishes to life in his garden.

This self-extension of the gardener into care is an altogether different ethic from the one that drives the present age to crave more life and to escape what Heidegger calls the emptiness of Being through a jacked-up productivity. The gardener does not rampage his way to a false Eden but watches over his plot with patience, for "no revolution will hasten the time of germination, or allow the lilac to flower before May; so the [gardener] becomes wise and submits to laws and customs" (42). Nothing is further from the gardener's mind, nothing motivates him less, than self-perfection, the value of work, or the virtue of his deeds. He is altogether handed over to his garden. That is why he says:

> As for you, Campanula Alpina, I will make you a deeper bed. Work! Even this messing with the soil you may call work, for I tell you it strains your back and knees; you are not doing this work because work is beautiful, or because it ennobles, or because it is healthy, but you do it so that a campanula will flower and a saxifrage will grow into a cushion. If you wish to celebrate anything, you should not celebrate this work of yours, but the campanula or saxifrage for which you are doing it. (42)

EPILOGUE

IN MALCOLM LOWRY'S GREAT NOVEL «UNDER THE VOL-
cano», there is a garden scene that brings together many of the strands
of this book and opens the way for a closing word on my theme. The
novel revolves around the figure of Geoffrey Firmin, the so-called British consul to the Mexican city of Cuernavaca, who wastes away in a
mindless, almost demonic alcoholism. The story takes place in a single
day and deals with the Consul's failure to rise to the occasion of his
wife's sudden, unexpected return after a year of estrangement. She reap-
pears one morning almost miraculously, after having filed for a divorce,
to offer the Consul one last chance to save their marriage and begin a
vita nuova in another place. For the Consul it amounts to an offer of
personal salvation, for he is damned without her, yet his "other wife"—
the bottle—will, by the end of the day, win out over Yvonne. Indeed,
it will win out over both of them, for late in the night of that same day,
Yvonne, abandoned, will die in a violent accident in the forest, and the
Consul, having sought out the infernal sanctuary of a low-life cantina,
will be shot by a band of Mexican fascists. His dead body will be thrown
into the *barranca*, or gorge, that cuts through the city of Cuernavaca.

The Consul's house is situated near the edge of this *barranca*,
which has several associations with the chasms of Dante's Inferno.
The house has a lush garden in which the Consul has taken to hiding
bottles of liquor. On the morning of his wife's return, in a mild panic

he seeks out a bottle of tequila there. Reflective of his state of soul as well as the condition of his marriage, the garden is overgrown and turning wild. In its neglect it stands in stark contrast to the adjacent, well-tended garden of his neighbor Mr. Quincey. Quincey, a retired American, observes the Consul drinking stealthily from the bottle of tequila he has retrieved from the underbrush. A tense conversation ensues across the fence:

> "By the way, I saw one of those little garter snakes just a moment ago," the Consul broke out.
>
> Mr. Quincey coughed or snorted but said nothing.
>
> "And it made me think . . . Do you know, Quincey, I've often wondered whether there isn't more in the old legend of the Garden of Eden, and so on, than meets the eye. What if Adam wasn't really banished from the place at all? That is, in the sense we used to understand it. . . . What if his punishment really consisted," the Consul continued with warmth, "in his having to *go on living there*, alone, of course—suffering, unseen, cut off from God. . . . And of course the real *reason* for that punishment—his being forced to go on living in the garden, I mean—might well have been that the poor fellow, who knows, secretly loathed the place! Simply hated it, and had done so all along. *And that the Old Man found this out.*" (137–38)

Lowry no doubt was aware that church fathers traditionally figured the sacrament of marriage as a "foretaste" of the restored Garden of Eden. Of course outside of Eden, on our mortal earth, marriage is a different kind of garden altogether—one that, if it is to thrive, requires a quotient of daily care and long-term commitment. In this regard the Consul is a failed gardener—a failed husband (it is not for nothing that the word husband is etymologically associated with building, dwelling, and cultivating, or that husbandry, in all its various associations, is the core theme of *Under the Volcano*, whose dedication reads "To Margerie, my wife"). Thus in his comment to Quincey about Adam's secret loathing of Eden, the Consul would seem to be expressing—in an oblique way—the deeply conflicted guilt he feels about his marriage, which his alcoholism has ravaged almost beyond repair.

The Consul's thoughts voiced to Quincey in the garden—the revision of the Eden story he articulates there—are crucial to understanding the novel as a whole, for *Under the Volcano* shows, in almost allegorical fashion, that the fall from Eden is a continuous, ongoing event. It shows that long after the original sin, we continue with active will to repeat our expulsion and tumble into our self-chosen inferno. History is a more or less endless fall into the *barranca*.

While the novel was published in 1947, its action takes place on a single day in the year 1938, when history found itself on the verge of a second world war. The timing gives an ominous horizon of reference to the Consul's alcoholism. It makes of his neglected, semi-wild garden a figure of the times. By the same token, it suggests that there is something deceptive about his neighbor's garden, which is no less open to the garter snake than the Consul's. In its well-groomed and meticulous appearance, Quincey's garden offers a false image of the age—an age that, like the Consul, is in the grip of destructive and self-intoxicating passions. For all his sanctimonious disapproval of the Consul's alcoholism, Mr. Quincey also belongs to an age that has lost its sobriety. His name, which recalls the English opium eater Thomas De Quincy, suggests as much.

On the other side of the Consul's garden—away from Mr. Quincey's—there is yet another garden: a public garden still under construction. Peering onto its grounds from a distance, the Consul sees a warning sign in Spanish:

LE GUSTA ESTE JARDIN?

QUE ES SUYO?

¡EVITE QUE SUS HIJOS LO DESTRUYAN! (133)

These Spanish words—which the Consul mistranslates in his mind to mean "You like this garden? Why is it yours? We evict those who destroy!"—recur periodically throughout Lowry's novel; they are in fact its very last words. *Under the Volcano* is a tragedy—one of the few genuine tragedies of the modern canon—about both an individual's and a civilization's "eviction" from a garden neither of them can help destroying, even though it belongs to them. If the Consul is right, this garden is nothing other than the terrestrial world of nature itself. It is the postlapsarian garden of the mortal earth where, for better or worse, we make our human home.

And what if the Consul is right? What if Eden in fact is still all around us? What if we never left it after all, the only difference being that God withdrew from the picture, leaving us alone with our own discontents? In that case we can either, in God's absence, keep the garden or destroy it. If the Consul is right, then the sign he sees in the public garden near his house contains a dire warning indeed. *Le gusta este jardín que es suyo?* Do you love this garden that belongs to you? If so, make sure you and your children don't destroy it: *evite que sus hijos lo destruyan!* It is a piercing question and an uncompromising injunction, for human beings have made it abundantly clear how mindlessly they can turn against the earth, precisely because it is home to our mortality. And yet the *jardín* is ours. Its mortal Eden lies on the edge of a yawning gorge, which awaits those individuals and societies that let their self-destructive drives get the better of their caretaking efforts. Time and again we have, like the Consul, taken the plunge.

The Consul suggests to Mr. Quincey that perhaps Adam secretly loathed the garden and that God punished him by leaving him there "alone," "unseen," "cut off from God." I have suggested—and Genesis invites that speculation—that it is far more likely that Eve was the one who secretly loathed the place and that it was the primal wife, rather than the husband, who found a way to get us expelled, putting humanity on the path to maturity. In the final analysis Eve is the mother of the story. Whether she actually got us out of Eden or whether she merely got God out of Eden, the result is effectively the same. In either case we were handed over to our self-responsibility; in either case we were left in a garden we were called on to keep; and we're still there, in *este jardín*.

From *The Decameron*, Giovanni Boccaccio

From the Introduction to the Third Day

After this, they were shown into a walled garden alongside the palace, and since it seemed at first glance to be a thing of wondrous beauty, they began to explore it in detail. The garden was surrounded and criss-crossed by paths of unusual width, all as straight as arrows and overhung by pergolas of vines, which showed every sign of yielding an abundant crop of grapes later in the year. The vines were all in flower, drenching the garden with their aroma, which, mingled with that of many other fragrant plants and herbs, gave them the feeling that they were in the midst of all the spices ever grown in the East. The paths along the edges of the garden were almost entirely hemmed in by white and red roses and jasmine, so that not only in the morning but even when the sun was at its apex one could walk in pleasant, sweet-smelling shade, without ever being touched by the sun's rays. It would take a long time to describe how numerous and varied were the shrubs growing there, or how neatly they were set out: but all the ones that have aught to commend them and flourish in our climate were represented in full measure. In the central part of the garden (not the least, but by far the most admirable of its features), there was a lawn of exceedingly fine grass, of so deep a green as to almost seem black, dotted all over with possibly a thousand different kinds of gaily-colored flowers, and surrounded by a line of flourishing, bright green orange- and lemon-trees, which, with their mature and unripe fruit and lingering shreds of blossom, offered agreeable shade to the eyes and a delightful aroma to the nostrils. In the middle of this lawn there stood a fountain of pure white marble, covered with marvelous bas-reliefs. From a figure standing on a column in the center of the fountain, a jet of water, whether natural or artificial I know not, but sufficiently powerful to drive a mill with ease, gushed high into the sky before cascading downwards and falling with a delectable plash into the crystal-clear pool below. And from this pool, which was lapping the rim of the fountain, the water passed through a hidden culvert and then emerged into finely constructed artificial channels surrounding the lawn on all sides. Thence it flowed along similar channels through almost the whole of the beautiful garden, eventually gathering at a single place from which it issued forth from the garden and descended towards the plain as a pure clear stream, furnishing ample power to two separate mills on its downward course, to the no small advantage of the owner of the palace.

The sight of this garden, and the perfection of its arrangement, with its shrubs, its streamlets, and the fountain from which they originated, gave so much pleasure to each of the ladies and the three young men that they all began to maintain that if Paradise were constructed on earth, it was inconceivable that it could take any other form, nor could they imagine any way in which the garden's beauty could possibly be enhanced. And as they wandered contentedly through it, making magnificent garlands for themselves from the leaves of the various trees, their ears constantly filled with the sound of some twenty different kinds of birds, all singing as though they were vying with one another, they became aware of yet another delightful feature, which, being so overwhelmed by the others, they had so far failed to notice. For they found that the garden was liberally stocked with as many as a hundred different varieties of perfectly charming animals, to which they all starting drawing each other's attention. Here were some rabbits emerging from a warren, over there hares were running, elsewhere they could observe some deer lying on the ground, whilst in yet another place young fawns were grazing. And apart from these, they saw numerous harmless creatures of many kinds, roaming about at leisure as though they were quite tame, all of which added greatly to their already considerable delight.

When, however, they had wandered about the garden for some little time, sampling its various attractions, they instructed the servants to arrange the tables round the fountain, and then they sang half-a-dozen canzonets and danced several dances, after which, at the queen's command, they all sat down to breakfast. Choice and dainty dishes, exquisitely prepared, were set before them in unhurried succession, and when they rose from the table, merrier than when they had started, they turned once more to music, songs and dancing. Eventually, however, as the hottest part of the day was approaching, the queen decided that those who felt so inclined should take their siesta. Some of them accordingly retired, but the rest were so overwhelmed by the beauty of their surroundings that they remained where they were and whiled away their time in reading romances or playing chess or throwing dice whilst the others slept.

But a little after nones, they all went and refreshed their faces in cool water before assembling, at the queen's request, on the lawn near the fountain, where, having seated themselves in the customary manner, they began to await their turn to tell a story on the topic the queen had proposed. The first of their number to whom she entrusted this office was Filostrato, who began as follows:

III.1
Masetto of Lamporecchio pretends to be dumb, and becomes a gardener at a convent, where all the nuns vie with one another to take him off to bed with them.

Fairest ladies, there are a great many men and women who are so dense as to be firmly convinced that when a girl takes the white veil and dons the black cowl, she ceases to be a woman or to experience feminine longings, as though the very act of making her a nun had caused her to turn into stone. And if they should happen to hear of anything to suggest that their conviction is ill-founded, they become quite distressed, as though some enormous and diabolical evil had been perpetrated against Nature. It never enters their heads for a moment, possibly because they have no wish to face facts, that they themselves are continually dissatisfied even though they enjoy full liberty to do as they please, or that idleness and solitude are such powerful stimulants. Again, there are likewise many people who are firmly convinced that digging and hoeing and coarse food and hardy living remove all lustful desires from those who work on the land, and greatly impair their intelligence and powers of perception. But, since the queen has bidden me to speak, I would like to tell you a little tale, relevant to the topic she has prescribed, which will show you quite clearly that all these people are sadly mistaken in their convictions.

⚘

In this rural region of ours, there was and still is a nunnery, greatly renowned for its holiness, which I shall refrain from naming for fear of doing the slightest harm to its reputation. At this convent, not long ago, at a time when it housed no more than eight nuns and an abbess, all of them young, there was a worthy little man whose job it was to look after a very beautiful garden of theirs. And one day, being dissatisfied with his remuneration, he settled up with the nuns' steward and returned to his native village of Lamporecchio.

On his return he was warmly welcomed by several of the villagers, among them a young labourer, a big, strong fellow called Masetto, who, considering that he was of peasant stock, possessed a remarkably handsome physique and agreeable features. Since the good man, whose name was Nuto, had been away from the village for some little time, Masetto wanted to know where he had been, and when he learned that Nuto had been living at a convent, he questioned him about his duties there.

"I tended a fine, big garden of theirs," Nuto replied, "in addition to which, I sometimes used to go and collect firewood, or I would fetch water and do various other little jobs of that sort. But the nuns gave me such paltry wage that it was barely sufficient to pay for my shoe-leather. Besides, they are all young and they seem to me to have the devil in them, because whatever you do, it is impossible to please them. Sometimes, in fact, I would be working in the garden when one of them would order me to do one thing, another would tell me to do something else, and yet another would snatch the very hoe from my hands, and tell me I was doing things the wrong way. They used to pester me to such an extent that occasionally I would down tools and march straight out of the garden. So that eventually, what with one thing and another, I decided I'd had enough of the place and came away altogether. Just as I was leaving, their steward asked me whether I knew of anyone who could take the job on, and I promised to send somebody along, provided I could find the right man, but you won't catch me sending him anybody, not unless God has provided the fellow with the strength and patience of an ox."

As he listened, Masetto experienced such a longing to go and stay with these nuns that his whole body tingled with excitement, for it was clear from what he had heard that he should be able to achieve what he had in mind. Realizing, however, that he would get nowhere by revealing his intentions to Nuto, he replied:

"How right you were to come away from the place! What sort of a life can any man lead when he's surrounded by a lot of women? He might as well be living with a pack of devils. Why, six time out of seven they don't even know their own minds."

But when they had finished talking, Masetto began to consider what steps he ought to take so that he could go and stay with them. Knowing himself to be perfectly capable of carrying out the duties mentioned by Nuto, he had no worries about losing the job on that particular score, but he was afraid lest he should be turned down because of his youth and his unusually attractive appearance. And so, having rejected a number of other possible expedients, he eventually thought to himself: "The convent is a long way off, and there's nobody there who knows me. If I can pretend to be dumb, they'll take me on for sure." Clinging firmly to this conjecture, he therefore dressed himself in pauper's rags and slung an axe over his shoulder, and without telling anyone where he was going, he set out for the convent. On his arrival, he wandered into the courtyard, where as luck would have it he came across the steward, and with the aid of gestures such as dumb people use, he conveyed the impression that he was begging for something to eat, in return for which he would attend to any wood-chopping that needed to be done.

The steward gladly provided him with something to eat, after which he presented him with a pile of logs that Nuto had been unable to chop. Being very powerful, Masetto made short work of the whole consignment, and then the steward, who was on his way to the wood, took Masetto with him and got him to fell some timber. He then provided Masetto with an ass, and gave him to understand by the use of sign-language that he was to take the timber back to the convent.

The fellow carried out his instructions so efficiently that the steward retained his services for a few more days, getting him to tackle various jobs that needed to be done about the place. One day, the Abbess herself happened to catch sight of him, and she asked the steward who he was.

"The man is a poor deaf-mute, ma'am, who came here one day begging for alms," said the steward. "I saw to it that he was well fed, and set him to work on various tasks that needed to be done. If he turns out to be good at gardening, and wants to stay, I reckon we would do well out of it, because we certainly need a gardener, and this is a strong fellow who will always do as he's told. Besides, you wouldn't need to worry about his giving any cheek to these young ladies of yours."

"I do believe you're right," said the Abbess. "Find out whether he knows what to do, and make every effort to hold on to him. Provide him with a pair of shoes and an old hood, wheedle him, pay him a few compliments, and give him plenty to eat."

The steward agreed to carry out her instructions, but Masetto was not far away, pretending to sweep the courtyard, and he had overheard their whole conversation. "Once you put me inside that garden of yours," he said to himself, gleefully, "I'll tend it better than it's ever been tended before."

Now, when the steward had discovered what an excellent gardener he was, he gestured to Masetto, asking him whether he would like to stay there, and the latter made signs to indicate that he was willing to do whatever the steward wanted. The steward therefore took him on to the staff, ordered him to look after the garden, and showed him what he was to do, after which he went away in order to attend to the other affairs of the convent, leaving him there by himself. Gradually, as the days passed and Masetto worked steadily away, the nuns started teasing and annoying him, which is the way people frequently behave with deaf-mutes, and they came out with the foulest language imaginable, thinking that he was unable to hear them. Moreover, the Abbess, who was possibly under the impression that he had lost his tail as well as his tongue, took little or no notice of all this.

Now one day, when Masetto happened to be taking a rest after a spell of strenuous work, he was approached by two very young nuns who were out walking in the garden. Since he gave them the impression that he was asleep, they began to stare at him, and the bolder of the two said to her companion:

"If I could be sure that you would keep it a secret, I would tell you about an idea that has often crossed my mind, and one that might well work out to our mutual benefit."

"Do tell me," replied the other. "You can be quite certain that I shan't talk about it to anyone."

The bold one began to speak more plainly.

"I wonder," she said, "whether you have ever considered what a strict life we have to lead, and how the only men who ever dare set foot in this place are the steward, who is elderly, and this dumb gardener of ours. Yet I have often heard it said, by several of the ladies who have come to visit us, that all other pleasures in the world are mere trifles by comparison with the one experienced by a woman when she goes with a man. I have thus been thinking, since I have nobody else to hand, that I would like to discover with the aid of this dumb fellow whether they are telling the truth. As it happens, there couldn't be a better man for the purpose, because even if he wanted to let the cat out of the bag, he wouldn't be able to. He wouldn't even know how to explain, for you can see for yourself what a mentally retarded, dim-witted hulk of a youth the fellow is. I would be glad to know what you think of the idea."

"Dear me!" said the other. "Don't you realize that we have promised God to preserve our virginity?"

"Pah!" she said. "We are constantly making Him promises that we never keep! What does it matter if we fail to keep this one? He can always find other girls to preserve their virginity for Him."

"But what if we become pregnant?" said her companion. "What's going to happen then?"

"You're beginning to worry about things before they've even happened. We can cross that bridge if and when we come to it. There'll be scores of different ways to keep it a secret, provided we control our own tongues."

"Very well, then," said the other, who was already more eager than the first to discover what sort of stuff a man was made of. "How do we set about it?"

"As you see," she replied, "it is getting on for nones, and I expect all our companions are asleep. Let's make sure there's nobody else in the garden. And then, if the coast is clear, all we have to do is to take him by the hand and steer him across to that hut over there, where he shelters from the rain. Then one of us can go inside with him while the other keeps watch. He's such a born idiot that he'll do whatever we suggest."

Masetto heard the whole of this conversation, and since he was quite willing to obey, the only thing he was waiting for now was for one of them to come and fetch him. The two nuns had a good look round, and having made certain that they could not be observed, the one who had done all the talking went over to Masetto and woke him up, whereupon he sprang instantly to his feet. She then took him by the hand, making alluring gestures to which he responded with big, broad, imbecilic grins, and led him into the hut, where Masetto needed very little coaxing to do her bidding. Having got what she wanted, she loyally made way for her companion, and Masetto, continuing to act the simpleton, did as he was asked. Before the time came for them to leave, they had each made repeated trials of the dumb fellow's riding ability, and agreed that it was every bit as pleasant an experience as they had been led to believe, indeed more so. And from then on, whenever the opportunity arose, they whiled away many a pleasant hour in the dumb fellow's arms.

One day, however, a companion of theirs happened to look out from the window of her cell, saw the goings-on, and drew the attention of two others to what was afoot. Having talked the matter over between themselves, they at first decided to report the pair to the Abbess. But then they changed their minds, and by common agreement with the other two, they took up shares in Masetto's holding. And because of various indiscretions, these five were subsequently joined by the remaining three, one after the other.

Finally, the Abbess, who was still unaware of all this, was taking a stroll one very hot day in the garden, all by herself, when she came across Masetto stretched out fast asleep in the shade of an almond-tree. Too much riding by night had left him with very little strength for the day's labours, and so there he lay, with his clothes ruffled up in front by the wind, leaving him all exposed. Finding herself alone, the lady stood with her eyes riveted to this spectacle, and she was seized by the same craving to which her young charges had already succumbed. So, having roused Masetto, she led him away to her room, where she kept him for several days, thus provoking bitter complaints from the nuns over the fact that the handyman had suspended work in the garden. Before sending him back to his own quarters, she repeatedly savoured the one pleasure for which she had always reserved her most fierce disapproval, and from then on she demanded regular supplementary allocations, amounting to considerably more than her fair share.

Eventually, Masetto, being unable to cope with all their demands, decided that by continuing to be dumb any longer he might do himself some serious injury. And so one night, when he was with the Abbess, he untied his tongue and began to talk.

"I have always been given to understand, ma'am," he said, "that whereas a single cock is quite sufficient for ten hens, ten men are hard put to satisfy one woman, and yet here am I with nine of them on my plate. I can't endure it any longer, not at any price, and as a matter of fact I've been on the go so much that I'm no longer capable of delivering the goods. So you'll either have to bid me farewell or come to some sort of an arrangement."

When she heard him speak, the lady was utterly amazed, for she had always believed him to be dumb.

"What is all this?" she said. "I thought you were supposed to be dumb."

"That's right, ma'am, I was," said Masetto, "but I wasn't born dumb. It was owing to an illness that I lost the power of speech, and, praise be to God, I've recovered it this very night."

The lady believed him implicitly, and asked him what he had meant when he had talked about having nine on his plate. Masetto explained how things stood, and when the Abbess heard, she realized that every single one of the nuns possessed sharper wits than her own. Being of a tactful disposition, she decided there and then that rather than allow Masetto to go away and spread tales concerning the convent, she would come to some arrangement with her nuns in regard to the matter.

Their old steward had died a few days previously. And so, with Masetto's consent, they unanimously decided, now that they all knew what the others had been doing, to persuade the people living in the neighbourhood that after a prolonged period of speechlessness, his ability to talk had been miraculously restored by the nuns' prayers and the virtues of the saint after whom the convent was named, and they appointed him their new steward. They divided up his various functions among themselves in such a way that he was able to do them all justice. And although he fathered quite a number of nunlets and monklets, it was all arranged so discreetly that nothing leaked out until after the death of the Abbess, by which time Masetto was getting on in years and simply wanted to retire to his village on a fat pension. Once his wishes became known, they were readily granted.

Thus it was that Masetto, now an elderly and prosperous father who was spared the bother of feeding his children and the expense of their upbringing, returned to the place from which he had set out with an axe on his shoulder, having had the sense to employ his youth to good advantage. And this, he maintained, was the way that Christ treated anyone who set a pair of horns on His crown.

From *Mr. Palomar*, Italo Calvino

The Sand Garden

A little courtyard covered with a white sand, thick-grained, almost gravel, raked in straight, parallel furrows or in concentric circles, around five irregular groups of stones or low boulders. This is one of the most famous monuments of Japanese civilization, the garden of rocks and sand of the Ryoanji of Kyoto, the image typical of that contemplation of the absolute to be achieved with the simplest means and without recourse to concepts capable of verbal expression, according to the teaching of the Zen monks, the most spiritual of Buddhist sects.

The rectangular enclosure of colorless sand is flanked on three sides by walls surmounted by tiles, beyond which is the green of trees. On the fourth side there is a wooden platform, of steps, where the public can file or linger and sit down. "If our inner gaze remains absorbed in the viewing of this garden," explains the pamphlet offered visitors, in Japanese and in English, signed by the abbot of the temple, "we will feel divested of the relativity of our individual ego, whereas the sense of the absolute I will fill us with serene wonder purifying our clouded minds."

Mr. Palomar is prepared to accept this advice on faith, and he sits on the steps, observes the rocks one by one, follows the undulations of the white sane, allows the indefinable harmony that link the elements of the picture gradually to pervade him.

Or rather, he tries to imagine all these things as they would be felt by someone who could concentrate on looking at the Zen garden in solitude and silence. Because—we had forgotten to say—Mr. Palomar is crammed on the platform in the midst of hundred of visitors, who jostle him on every side; camera-lenses and movie-cameras force their way past the elbows, knees, ears of the crowd, to frame the rock and sand from every angle, illuminated by natural light or by flashbulbs. Swarms of feet in wool socks step over him (shoes, as always in Japan, are left at the entrance); numerous offspring are thrust to the front row by pedagogical parents; clumps of uniformed students shove one another, eager only to conclude as quickly as possible this school outing to the famous monument; earnest visitors nodding their heads rhythmically check and make sure that everything written in the guidebook corresponds to reality and that everything seen in reality is also mentioned in the guide.

"We can view the garden as a group of mountainous islands in a great ocean, or as mountain tops rising above a sea of clouds. We can see it as a picture framed by the ancient mud walls, or we can forget the frame as we sense the truth of this sea stretching out boundlessly."

These "instructions for use" are contained in the leaflet, and to Mr. Palomar they seem perfectly plausible and immediately applicable, without effort, provided one is really sure of having a personality to shed, of looking at the world from inside an ego that can be dissolved, to become only a gaze. But it is precisely this outset that demands an effort of supplementary imagination, very difficult to muster when one's ego is glued into a solid crowd looking through a thousand eyes and walking on its thousand feet along the established itinerary of the tourist visit.

Must the conclusion be that the Zen mental techniques for achieving extreme humility, detachment from all possessiveness and pride, require as their necessary background aristocratic privilege, and assume an individualism with so much space and so much time around it, the horizons of a solitude free of anguish?

But this conclusion, which leads to the familiar lament over a paradise lost in the spread of mass civilization, sounds too facile for Mr. Palomar. He prefers to take a more difficult path, to try to grasp what the Zen garden can give him, looking at it in the only situation in which it can be looked at today, craning his neck among other necks.

What does he see? He sees the human race in the era of great numbers, which extends in a crowd, leveled but still made up of distinct individualities like the sea of grains of sand that submerges the surface of the world. . . . He sees that the world, nevertheless, continues to turn the boulder-back of its nature indifferent to the fate of mankind, its hard substance that cannot be reduced to human assimilation. . . . He sees the forms in which the assembled human sand tends to arrange itself along lines of movement, patterns that combine regularity and fluidity like the rectilinear or circular tracks of a rake. . . . And between mankind-sand and world-boulder there is a sense of possible harmony, as if between two non-homogeneous harmonies: that of the non-human in a balance of forces that seems not to correspond to any pattern, and that of human structures, which aspires to the rationality of a geometrical or musical composition, never definitive. . . .

APPENDIX 3

"The Garden," Andrew Marvell

How vainly men themselves amaze
To win the palm, the oak, or bays;
And their uncessant labors see
Crowned from some single herb or tree,
Whose short and narrow-vergèd shade
Does prudently their toils upbraid;
While all the flowers and trees do close
To weave the garlands of repose.

Fair Quiet, have I found thee here,
And Innocence, thy sister dear!
Mistaken long, I sought you then
In busy companies of men:
Your sacred plants, if here below,
Only among the plants will grow;
Society is all but rude,
To this delicious solitude.

No white nor red was ever seen
So amorous as this lovely green;
Fond lovers, cruel as their flame,
Cut in these trees their mistress' name.

Little, alas, they know or heed,
How far these beauties hers exceed!
Fair trees! Wheresoe'er your barks I wound
No name shall but your own be found.

When we have run our passion's heat,
Love hither makes his best retreat:
The gods who mortal beauty chase,
Still in a tree did end their race.
Apollo hunted Daphne so,
Only that she might laurel grow,
And Pan did after Syrinx speed,
Not as a nymph, but for a reed.

What wondrous life is this I lead!
Ripe apples drop about my head;
The luscious clusters of the vine
Upon my mouth do crush their wine;
The nectarine and curious peach
Into my hands themselves do reach;
Stumbling on melons as I pass,
Insnared with flowers, I fall on grass.

Meanwhile the mind, from pleasure less,
Withdraws into its happiness:
The mind, that ocean where each kind
Does straight its own resemblance find;
Yet it creates, transcending these,
Far other worlds, and other seas;
Annihilating all that's made
To a green thought in a green shade.

Here at the fountain's sliding foot,
Or at some fruit-tree's mossy root,

Casting the body's vest aside,
My soul into the boughs does glide:
There like a bird it sits and sings,
Then whets and combs its silver wings;
And, till prepared for longer flight,
Waves in its plumes the various light.

Such was that happy garden-state,
While man there walked without a mate:
After a place so pure and sweet,
What other help could yet be meet!
But 'twas beyond a mortal's share
To wander solitary there:
Two paradises 'twere in one
To live in Paradise alone.

How well the skillful gard'ner drew
Of flowers and herbs this dial new;
Where from above the milder sun
Does through a fragrant zodiac run;
And, as it works, th' industrious bee
Computes its time as well as we.
How could such sweet and wholesome hours
Be reckoned but with herbs and flowers!

APPENDIX 4

A Note on Islamic Carpet Gardens

THE QUR'AN'S REPEATED EVOCATIONS OF EDEN'S FOUN-
tains, its streams, its delicious shade, its abundance of fruit, and its
atmosphere of perfect tranquillity are the basis of the extraordinary
garden art of the Islamic world. The traditional *chahar-bagh* structure
of the Islamic garden (from the Persian *chahar*, meaning four, and
bagh, meaning garden) consists of a symbolic central fountain from
which flow four streams at geometrical angles. The fourfold structure
was used by Persian garden makers long before the Persians were
converted to Islam, yet when Islamic architects took over the *chahar-
bagh* and made it the basis of their garden designs, they refounded its
symbolism upon the Qur'an, in particular by associating its fourfold
streams with the four rivers of Eden mentioned by the Prophet. Islamic gardens offer themselves to the eye as intimations, or symbolic
prefigurations, of the gardens of Paradise that await the faithful after
death.

While the fourfold design of the Islamic garden is remarkably constant and reiterative, it may take different material forms. "Here in this
carpet lives an ever-lovely spring," begins a sixteenth-century Sufi
poem. Some of the most beautiful Islamic gardens are in fact woven
into carpets. The famous "Aberconway" carpet, for example, with
its repeating geometric pattern of the *chahar-bagh*, is an eighteenth-
century Persian wonder on the order of the Hanging Gardens of

Babylon. No photographic image of it can convey its sensuous texture or the way its dyes inflect the light, variegating its reflection off the carpet's surface. Here every square or rectangular plot contains a species of tree or fruit watered by four streams that flow from a central fountain toward the four quadrants of the universe. Within the embroidered borders that define the garden's enclosure, all is order, harmony, and cosmic unity. Garden carpets, as this genre of art is called, show that gardens need not be made of stone, water, and plants. They can grow in vegetable-dyed wool and lie on a floor. And since in traditional Muslim households it was customary to sit on the floor, it was not around but *in* the carpet's garden that one was seated, symbolically speaking. Through the carpet's tapestry a piece of the earthly paradise was brought into the interior of the house, infusing the domestic space with the delight and serenity promised to the righteous by God.

That the relation between carpets and gardens is a fluid one is proven by the so-called Carpet Garden built by the prince of Wales at Highgrove in Gloucestershire. This is an outdoor garden whose design and colors are loosely based on two Anatolian tribal carpets owned by the prince. The Highgrove Carpet Garden (conceived by Prince Charles himself and initially designed for the Chelsea Flower Show of 2001 by Michael Miller) creatively translates the garden motifs of the Anatolian carpets into a "real" garden, and not the other way around. To judge by the images in Emma Clark's splendid book *The Art of the Islamic Garden*, the result is one of the most exquisite little gardens in England.

It seems that the Islamic art of garden carpets owed its initial inspiration, at least in part, to the spectacular "Winter Carpet" of the Sassanian king Chrosroses I (sixth century AD), whose winter capital, Ctesiphon, was located on the Tigris River south of Baghdad. Although it depicted scenes of spring, it was called the Winter Carpet because it was used for festivities held inside the palace during the winter season, when it was too cold to hold them in outdoor gardens. A contemporary source described its material as consisting of "silk, gold and silver, and precious stones. On it was represented a beautiful pleasure ground with brooks and interlacing paths, with trees and flowers of springtime" (173). When Muslim Arab invaders sacked Ctesiphon in AD 637, they cut the carpet into pieces and apportioned them, not so much for its precious materials but because they deemed that its splendor did not, as required by Islam, acknowledge its source in God. In short, it did not properly symbolize the transcendent power behind the visible world. By the time Persian masters began weaving stylized depictions of the gardens of Paradise into their carpets in the tenth century AD, this prime directive of the Islam religion—that all things beautiful declare their debt to God—had been incorporated into the Islamic art of garden carpets, which was to flourish for centuries to come.

Symbolism is everything in Islamic garden art. One of the basic tenets of Islam is that the visible world is a "sign" of its Creator. Everything in the world, however small or grand, is a sign, including the words of the Qur'an (the Arabic word for "sign," *aya*, is also the word for a verse of the Qur'an). Likewise all the beautiful forms that Islamic art and architecture bring into being are to be seen as signs; indeed they are especially charged signs, since their purpose is to signify the infinite wisdom of the Creator. In that respect, garden carpets are on the same symbolic order as "real" gardens, insofar as both are visible manifestations of an otherwise hidden essence. The fountain and streams may be literal or they may be merely figurative, that is to say they may flow with "real" water (as in the case of the Generalife gardens of the Alhambra Palace in Granada) or they may be merely represented by formal lines (as in the case of garden carpets, for example). But this distinction is secondary, for at the primary level both types of gardens point beyond themselves to a transcendent order of being. The fountain, for instance, symbolizes various spiritual or metaphysical principles (unity, life-giving power, grace, divine source, etc.), just as the fourfold design stands for various cosmological or formal principles (the four rivers of Eden, the four elements, the four seasons, the four cardinal directions, the four quadrants of the universe). As

Titus Burckhardt, one of the great Western scholars of Islamic art, phrased it: "The object of art is the beauty of form, whereas the object of contemplation is beauty beyond form" (Burckhardt, 197). In Islam the religious purpose of the former is to enable or inspire the latter.

Islamic culture contains some of the most beautiful forms that have arisen in the history of art, beginning with its calligraphy, yet nowhere does the outward beauty of form draw attention to its inner spiritual referent more intensely than in the calm geometric harmonies of the Islamic garden. This is due to the fact that the Islamic garden stands in a direct signifying relationship to the true, as yet still invisible home-land of the faithful: the gardens of Paradise where the faithful will, after their death, dwell in the full presence of God. The Arabic word *al-jannah* means both "garden" and "concealment," suggesting that there is indeed a secret "garden of the heart," as the mystical Sufi tradition affirms, where the true rewards of Paradise, invisible to us here on earth, find their ultimate realization. The Islamic garden (be it figured in a carpet or embodied in stone, water, and plants) invites the believer to look beyond the repose and harmony of its outward form to the otherworldly repose of the spirit, or better, to see *in* the gardens wrought by human art intimations of the perfect spiritual repose of the afterlife. Thus we owe the afterlife a debt of gratitude, regardless of whether it exists or not.

NOTES

SINCE THIS BOOK RANGES WIDELY IN ITS TOPICS AND CULTURAL references, the secondary works cited here represent only a small portion of the relevant bibliography. For the most part I cite articles and books that were directly useful to me or that I feel might be useful for the reader to consult. In some cases I use the notes as an occasion to expand upon or provide more information about select themes or issues. Unless otherwise indicated, all translations in the chapters as well as the notes are mine.

The seed for this book goes back to 2002, when Thomas Padon from the American Federation of Arts solicited an essay from me on gardens in the Western imagination. My essay was subsequently published in the catalog book for a traveling exhibition of garden photographs by an international group of contemporary artists. The book, edited by Padon, was published in 2004 under the title *Contemporary Photography and the Garden: Deceits and Fantasies*. My essay (pp. 146–57) signals several of the themes that I treat here in a more expansive manner. In addition to my contribution and some of the most extraordinary garden photographs I have ever seen, *Contemporary Photography and the Garden* contains a fine introduction on the theme of gardens and culture by Thomas Padon (10–25), as well as two short but highly suggestive essays: Shirin Neshat's "Gardens as Metaphors" (136–38) and Ronald Jones's "The Promise of a Garden" (138–45).

Chapter One: The Vocation of Care

There is considerable obscurity surrounding the origins and concept of Elysium. Succinctly put, "Elysium, or the Isles of the Blest, situated at the ends of the earth, appears in Homer (*Odyssey* 4.561–69) and Hesiod (*Op.* 167–73) as the place to which certain favoured heroes, exempted from death, are translated by the gods. Elysium appears to be a survival of Minoan religion; when a later age concerned itself with the fate of the blessed dead, Elysium was transferred to the nether regions, in conformity with Greek ideas and the Homeric picture" (Hornblower and Spawforth, *Oxford Classical Dictionary*, 23). For a general discussion of immorality and Greek religion, see Erwin Rohde, *Psyche*; Walter Burkert, *Greek Religion*; and Jasper Griffin, *Homer on Death and Life*. For a history of the afterlife in the Western tradition, including a discussion of Dante and the Roman Elysium, see Jeffrey Burton Russell, *A History of Heaven: The Singing Silence*. On the mortality of Achilles, see Graham Zanker, *The Heart of Achilles: Characterization and Personal Ethics in the "Iliad."*

Dante's Limbo, described in *Inferno* 4, is intensely reminiscent of the Elysian Fields in Virgil's underworld (see *Aeneid*, bk. 6). On Dante's Limbo, see Amilcare A. Iannucci, "Limbo: The Emptiness of Time." On the differences between Dante's Paradise and the Greco-Roman Elysium, see Jeffrey T. Schnapp, " 'Sì pïa l'ombra d'Anchise si porse': *Paradiso* 15.25."

On the figure of Kalypso, see chapter 5 of Bruce Louden's *The Odyssey: Structure, Narration, and Meaning*; and the first two chapters of Simon Goldhill, *The Poet's Voice: Essays on Poetics and Greek Literature*, 1–166.

The fable of Cura, as I cite it here, comes from the Macquarrie and Robinson English translation of Heidegger's *Being and Time* (242n5), where Heidegger references the fable in his discussion of the so-called inner unity of Dasein's being, which he defines precisely as *Sorge* or Care. The fable has come down to us from the late Roman mythographer Hyginus. For the Latin original, see the Teubner edition of *Hygini Fabulae*; the only translation of Hyginus available in English is Mary Grant's *The Myths of Hyginus*.

While I am sympathetic in principle to the so-called ethics of care, my reflections on gardens in this book are not particularly indebted to this movement, which originated in psychology and feminist theory. The foundations of the movement's ethical theory can be traced back in part to Emmanuel Lévinas's metaphysical ethics (for which see *Totality and Infinity*.) Some of the major contributions in this domain include Carol Gilligan, *In a Different Voice: Psychological Theory and Women's Development*; Selma Sevenhuijsen, *Citizenship and the Ethics of Care*; Virginia Held, *The Ethics of Care: Personal, Political, Global*; Ruth E. Groenhout, *Connected Lives: Human Nature and the Ethics of Care* and *Theological Echoes in an Ethic of Care*. Recently the ethics of care has been applied to ecological theory; see Sherilyn MacGregor, *Beyond Mothering Earth: Ecological Citizenship and the Politics of Care*, and Robert C. Fuller, *Ecology of Care: An Interdisciplinary Analysis of the Self and Moral Obligation*.

In Italy, Adriana Cavarero and the feminist philosophical community called Diotima propose their own, distinctive, and (to me) very compelling version of an ethics of care. Diotima was formed in 1983 at the University of Verona. Its philosophical underpinnings are based largely on the political philosophy of Hannah Arendt and, to a lesser extent, the feminism of Luce Irigaray and the theoretical and political debate of the women's movement. The Diotima group still holds an annual seminar from which books are published. The first of these collections was published in 1987 under the title *Il pensiero della differenza sessuale*, to which Adriana Cavarero contributed a seminal essay, "Per una teoria della differenza sessuale." In my view Cavarero (who subsequently distanced herself from the group) is one of the most interesting philosophers writing today. See her *Nonostante Platone* (*In Spite of Plato*); *Corpo in figure* (*Stately Bodies*); *Tu che mi guardi, tu che mi racconti* (*Relating Narratives*); and most recently *A più voci: Filosofia dell'espressione vocale* (*For More Than One Voice*). Other thinkers associated with Diotima include Wanda Tommasi, Chiara Zamboni, Anna Maria Piussi, and Giannina Longobardi. For an excellent anthology of critical essays in English, see Graziella Parati and Rebecca J. West, eds., *Italian Feminist Theory and Practice: Equality and Sexual Difference*, esp. Lucia Re's essay "Diotima's Dilemmas: Authorship, Authority, Authoritarianism," 50–74.

The scholarly literature on Eden in the Bible and in later literature is vast and voluminous. Most directly useful to me was A. Barlett Giamatti's 1966 study *The Earthly Paradise and the Renaissance Epic*. Some more recent studies of note include James E. Miller, *The Western Paradise: Greek and Hebrew Traditions*; Paul Morris and Deborah Sawyer, eds., *A Walk in the Garden: Biblical, Iconographical, and Literary Images of Eden*; and Martin Herbst, *God's Womb: The Garden of Eden, Innocence and Beyond*.

I use the term *felix culpa* in a somewhat different sense from the Catholic tradition. The term was coined by St. Augustine (or perhaps St. Ambrose) in an Easter hymn—the Exsultet—on the fall from innocence of Adam and Eve: "O certe necessarium Adame peccatum, quod Christi morte deletum est! O felix culpa quae talem et tantum meruit habere redemptorem!" (O truly necessary sin of Adam, which Christ's death has blotted out! O happy fault, that merited such and so great redeemer!). The fall was fortunate in that it permitted humankind to be redeemed through the Christ. This hymn is still a part of the Catholic liturgy on Holy Saturday. For a poetic articulation, see Milton's *Paradise Lost*, book XII:

> O goodness infinite, goodness immense!
> That all this good of evil shall produce,
> And evil turn to good; more wonderful
> Than that which by creation first brought forth
> Light out of darkness! Full of doubt I stand,
> Whether I should repent me now of sin
> By mee done and occasiond, or rejoyce
> Much more, that much more good thereof shall spring.

(469–76)

For Hannah Arendt's theory of the *vita activa* in its three aspects of labor, work, and action, see her *The Human Condition*. The secondary literature on Arendt in of course vast. The following represents only a tiny selection of useful studies and collections: Dana Villa, ed., *The Cambridge Companion Guide to Hannah Arendt*; Malcolm Bull, "The Social and the Political"; James W. Bernauer, ed., *Amor Mundi: Explorations in the Faith and Thought of Hannah Arendt*; and Maurizio Passerin d'Entrèves, *The Political Philosophy of Hannah Arendt* (esp. 64–100 on her philosophy of action). See also chapter 4 of Linda M. G. Zerilli's *Feminism and the Abyss of Freedom*.

When Dante speaks of Italy as "the garden of the empire," he means the center and legitimate seat of the monarchy willed by Providence. The quotation comes from his invective against Italy in the *Purgatorio* 6: "Ch'avete tu e 'l tuo padre sofferto / Per cupidigia di costà distretti,/ Che 'l giardino dello 'mperio sia diserto?" (6.103–5).

The translations from Dante's *Paradise* are by Allen Mandelbaum in *Paradiso*. For the quotations from Homer's *Odyssey*, I have used Richmond Lattimore's translation. Quotations from the Bible, in this chapter and others, are from the New Oxford Annotated Bible.

Chapter Two: Eve

The expulsion scene of Giusto de' Menabuoi (ca. 1320–91) is in the Chapel of S. Giovanni Battista in Padua. Masaccio's is in the Brancacci Chapel in Florence (1424–28). Michelangelo's is in the Sistine Chapel (1508–12). Albrecht Dürer's woodcut *Small Passion* (1510) is now in the British Museum. In addition to these works, one should mention the extraordinary majolica floor of Leonardi Chiaiese in the Chiesa Monumentale di San Michele at Anacapri. This beautiful representation of Eden (ca. 1761) depicts an angel casting Adam and Eve out of the garden with an outstretched arm. It is in fact difficult to identify with certainty which of the two human figures is Adam and which is Eve, since both look either like effeminate men or masculine women; both are dressed in exactly the same clothing, and neither seems to have pronounced female breasts. The figure on the left is more muscular but also has longer hair. The figure on the right, with arms in the air, is already in motion toward the exit, while the figure of the left looks more forlorn, in a gesture of supplication. From the point of view presented in this chapter, the spirit of Eve is captured by the figure to the right, who seems to be moving toward a new future in eagerness and anticipation, although the neutral viewer will be more naturally inclined to identify that figure as Adam because of the shorter hair.

Both of the Wilner poems cited in this chapter come from her collection *The Girl with Bees in Her Hair*.

Stendhal's definition of beauty as "a promise of happiness" appears twice in his writings: "La beauté n'est jamais, ce me semble, qu'une promesse de bonheur," *Rome, Naples et Florence*, 45–46, and "La beauté n'est jamais que la promesse de bonheur," *De l'amour*, chap. 17, 74n1 (*Love*, 66n1).

Wallace Stevens's "Sunday Morning" originally appeared in the journal *Poetry* in 1913 and was revised for inclusion in his 1923 volume *Harmonium*. For excellent introductions to the poetry of Wallace Stevens, see Joseph Hillis Miller's chapter on Stevens in *Poets of Reality: Six Twentieth-Century*

Writers and Harold Bloom's *Wallace Stevens: The Poems of Our Climate*, both of which discuss this poem.

The translation of Pablo Neruda's poem "Oda a la jardinera" is from *Selected Poems*, 252–53. For a good introduction to Pablo Neruda and his poetry, see Manuel Durán and Margery Safir, *Earth Tones: The Poetry of Pablo Neruda*.

Chapter Three: The Human Gardener

The quotations from *The Gardener's Year* are from the 2002 reprint of the Modern Library 1931 translation by M. and R. Weatherall. The book has recently been retranslated by Geoffrey Newsome for Claridge Press. The illustrations that accompany the Modern Library text are by Čapek's brother Josef. Čapek is best known in the English-speaking world for his early science fiction and for having coined the word *robot* along with his brother. Most of the criticism of Karel Čapek's literary works and political life is in Czech. An essential study in English is the Ivan Klíma's *Karel Čapek: Life and Work*. Among other works in English, see William Harkins's 1962 biography *Karel Čapek* and chapter 4 of Peter Swirski's *From Lowbrow to Nobrow*. For a comparison of Čapek with Anton Chekhov (with whom he had much in common), see Peter Z. Schubert's *The Narratives of Čapek and Cexov: A Typological Comparison of the Authors' Worldviews*. Specifically on his politics, see B. R. Bradbrook's *Karel Čapek: In Pursuit of Truth, Tolerance, and Trust*.

Montmorillonite is a clay mineral discovered in 1847 in Montmorillon, France, from which it takes its name. In 2003 researchers Jack W. Szostak, Martin M. Hanczyc, and Shelly M. Fujikawa from the Howard Hughes Medical Institute and Massachusetts General Hospital published findings in *Science* that Montmorillonite may have acted as a catalyst in the formation of the first living cells ("Experimental Models of Primitive Cellular Compartments: Encapsulation, Growth, and Division," October 23, 2003).

The primitive bacteria that contributed to the formation of the Earth's atmosphere as we know it today is known as *cyanobacteria*, or "blue-green algae." During the Arachean and Proterozoic eras (3.8 billion to 543 million years ago) these bacteria increased oxygen in the atmosphere from around

1 percent to 20 percent, making it hospitable for life. On this aspect of cyano-bacteria, see James F. Kasting and Janet L. Siefert, "Life and the Evolution of Earth's Atmosphere," *Science*, May 10, 2002. Cyanobacteria are important for plant life in general because they are one of only a few organisms that can produce organic nitrogen (obtained by plants from the soil) from atmo-spheric nitrogen. Cyanobacteria are also the chloroplasts that produces food for plants from photosynthesis.

Chapter Four: Homeless Gardens

The quotation from Rilke's letter to Salomé (August 8, 1903) is from *Rainer Maria Rilke and Lou Andreas-Salomé: The Correspondence*, 70.

William S. Merwin's affirmation about gardening's arising prior to agri-culture comes from a personal conversation between Merwin and me in the year 2004.

Pietro Laureano's *Giardini di pietra* has not yet been published in English. The translations here are my own.

For some historical examples of community gardens, see Sir Ebenezer Howard, *To-morrow: A Peaceful Path to Real Reform*; John Esten, *Hampton Gardens: A 350-Year Legacy*; and Peter Clark, ed., *The European City and Green Space: London, Stockholm, Helsinki, and St. Petersburg, 1850–2000*. For more on contemporary community gardens and urban gardening in general, see Peter L. Wilson and Bill Weinberg, eds., *Avant-Gardening: Ecological Struggle in the City and the World*; Laura J. Lawson, *City Bountiful: A Century of Community Gardening in America*; Mary Jane Pool, *Gardens in the City: New York in Bloom*; Anne-Mie Devolder, ed., *The Public Garden: The Enclo-sure and Disclosure of the Public Garden*; Malve von Hassell, *The Struggle for Eden: Community Gardens in New York City*.

For an extended discussion of biophilia, a term coined by Erich Fromm in his book *The Heart of Man*, see Edward O. Wilson's *Biophilia* and, more recently, Stephen R. Kellert and Edward O. Wilson, eds., *The Biophilia Hy-pothesis*.

T. S. Eliot speaks of "the still point of the turning world" in the "Burnt Norton" section of his *Four Quartets*, which invokes the memory of a rose garden.

The citations from Rudolf Borchardt's *The Passionate Gardener* is from Henry Martin's translation of *Leidenschaftliche Gärtner*.

Chapter Five: *"Mon jardin à moi"*

It was not until after I had written this chapter that my research assistant David Lummus and I made a concerted effort to track down information about the creation of Kingscote Gardens and the architect responsible for the design. Our initial inquiries led nowhere, thus reconfirming what I affirm in the second paragraph of the chapter: "Few people, in fact, when you ask them about it, are aware of its existence, and in the various volumes about the history and architecture of Stanford in the university bookstore there is no mention of it. It is almost as if it didn't exist." The story of Kingscote Gardens is largely unknown, if not lost in obscurity. Every so often in the past ninety years an article has appeared in the student newspaper titled "What Is Kingscote Gardens?" or something to that effect.

What we were able to determine with certainty is that Kingscote was, until quite recently, one of the few pieces of land on the central Stanford campus that are not under the direct control of the university. In 1915 Sarah Howard, widow of Stanford political science professor Burt Estes Howard, approached then president Ray Lyman Wilbur about the construction of an apartment building for visiting professors. The enterprise would, she said, provide needed housing for the growing university and would provide financial security for her daughter, who had just graduated from college. President Wilbur endorsed the project and subsequently leased four acres of an oak grove at the heart of the Stanford campus to Mrs. Howard. By fall 1917 the apartment building and gardens were built and the first residents moved in. After the death of Sarah Howard and her daughter, the management of the property and its profits went to the Howard Holding Company, which employed a manager and gardener for the property. The original eighty-year lease to the Howard family expired in the mid-1990s, and control of both the gardens and the apartments has reverted to Stanford. Information on the architect and landscape designer is—for the time being—unavailable. The Howard family estate, which may have information on the topic, has opted not to cooperate with the Stanford University records and archives offices on the matter.

For historical discussions of gardens as art, see Margherita Azzi Visentini, ed., *L'arte dei giardini: Scritti teorici e pratici dal XIV al XIX secolo*; Penelope Hill, *Contemporary History of Garden Design: European Gardens between Art and Architecture* (trans. of *Jardins d'aujour'hui en Europe*); Mark Laird, *The Formal Garden: Traditions of Art and Nature;* Filippo Pizzoni, *The Garden: A History in Landscape and Art* (trans. of *Giardino, arte e storia*); Tom Turner, *Garden History: Philosophy and Design*, 2000 BC–2000 AD. For early discussions of gardens as art, see Marie Luise Schroeter Gothein, *A History of Garden Art* (trans. of 1913 *Geschichte der Gartenkunst*); Christian Cajus Lorenz Hirschfeld, *Theory of Garden Art* (trans by Linda B. Parshall of 1779–85 original *Theorie der Gartenkunst*). For more theoretical discussions of gardens as art, see Michel Conan, *Essais de poetique des jardins*; John Ernest Grant White, *Garden Art and Architecture*; Mara Miller, *The Garden as an Art*; Simon Pugh, *Garden, Nature, Language*; Massimo Venturi Ferriolo, *Giardino e filosofia*; John Dixon Hunt, ed., *The Italian Garden: Art, Design, and Culture*; John Dixon Hunt, *Greater Perfections: The Practice of Garden Theory*; Germain Bazin, *Paradeisos: The Art of the Garden* (trans. of *Paradeisos, ou, L'art du jardin*); William Howard Adams, *Roberto Burle Marx: The Unnatural Art of the Garden*; Stephanie Ross, *What Gardens Mean*; the excellent collection of essays in Baldan Zenoni-Politeo and Pietrogrande, eds., *Il giardino e la memoria del mondo*; and the whimsical but fascinating little book by Arie Graafland, *Versailles and the Mechanics of Power: The Subjugation of Circe*.

The lyric "The Jewel Stairs' Grievance" is by the Chinese poet Li Po (AD 701–62), whom Ezra Pound identifies as Rihaku. "Rihaku" is the English transliteration of the Japanese rendition of his name. Because of the sources that he used, Pound followed this circuitous route in rendering many proper names in his *Cathay*. Pound adds the following note to the poem: "Jewel Stairs, therefore a palace. Grievance, therefore there is something to complain of. Clear autumn, therefore he has no excuse on account of weather. Also, she has come early, for the dew has not merely whitened the stairs, but has soaked her stockings. The poem is especially prized because she utters no direct reproach" (*Selected Poems*, 131).

The translation of Campana's poem "Autumnal Garden" (which I do not quote in its entirety) is by George Kay, in the *Penguin Book of Italian Verse*. I have versified Kay's prose translation.

For a philosophical meditation on human gardens with special emphasis on gardens as the place of epiphany, see David E. Cooper's thoughtful book *A Philosophy of Gardens*.

Chapter Six: Academos

For a comprehensive treatment of the history of higher education in the West, see Edward J. Power's two studies *Main Currents in the History of Education* and *Legacy of Learning: A History of Western Education*; also Roy Lowe, *History of Education: Major Themes* (4 vols.).

Scholars have argued about whether Plato's Academy was actually a fully institutionalized school during his own lifetime and about what actually went on there, but it is evident from the secondary literature mentioned below that the Academy consolidated its institutional status in the generation after Plato's death. Most scholars concede that during his lifetime the Academy was (minimally speaking) an open area where people could listen to and converse with Plato. Because we do not know very much about the political agenda of the Academy, many scholars have claimed that Plato had no intention to influence Athenian politics through his "school" at the Academy. Yet despite this long-standing scholarly debate about the practical or political goals of his pedagogical endeavors, most scholars agree that Plato must have intended to have *some* kind of direct influence on the politics of the Hellenic world. P. A. Brunt, in his essay on the Academy and Plato's politics (cited below), challenges this consensus, although he admits that those who would have come to hear Plato and participate in the activities of the Academy were likely to have been of the landed aristocratic and educated caste—in other words, potential future statesmen. Josiah Ober, in chapter 4 of his book on dissent in democratic Athens (also cited below), argues that Plato's philosophy was "an alternative politics" with a "political agenda" (165). We know for certain that Isocrates—Plato's contemporary—was directly involved in using "philosophy" for political ends. He had his own school that competed with Plato's, and he even had a four-year plan for learning to be a politician. At the end of the *Euthydemus*, Socrates describes Isocrates and his kind in these terms:

These are the persons, Crito, whom Prodicus describes as occupying the no-man's-land between the philosopher and the statesman.

They think that they are the wisest of men, and that they not only are but also seem to be so in the eyes of a great many, so that no one else keeps them from enjoying universal esteem except the followers of philosophy. . . . They regard themselves as very wise, and reasonably so, since they think they are not only pretty well up in philosophy but also in politics. Yes, their conceit of wisdom is quite natural because they think they have as much of each as they need; and, keeping clear of both risk and conflict, they reap the fruits of wisdom. (305c–e)

(My thanks to James Collins in the Classics Department at Stanford for pointing out these references.)

The bibliography that surrounds Plato in general and Plato's educational aims and politics in particular is enormous. Here I cite only a small fraction of what has been written on the subject. For a comprehensive reconstruction of Plato as a man, philosopher, and teacher see volumes 4–5 of W. K. C. Guthrie's *A History of Greek Philosophy*. For Plato's political philosophy see Malcolm Schofield's *Plato: Political Philosophy*; P. A. Brunt's "Plato's Academy and Politics"; and more recently, chapter 4 of Josiah Ober's *Political Dissent in Democratic Athens: Intellectual Critics of Popular Rule*. For the Academy as a place and school, see the first section of chapter 1 ("The Physical Structure of the Academy") of John Dillon, *The Heirs of Plato: A Study of the Old Academy (347–274 BC)*, 2–15; Harold F. Cherniss, *The Riddle of the Early Academy*; and R. M. Dancy, *Two Studies in the Early Academy*. On Plato's theories of education see Samuel Scolnicov's *Plato's Metaphysics of Education*. On the "rhetoric of usefulness" in Plato and Aristotle, see Andrea Nightingale, *Spectacles of Truth in Classical Greek Philosophy: Theoria in Its Cultural Context*, 191–97.

One of the most extensive discussions of Plato's analogy in the *Phaedrus* between education and the sowing of seeds is to be found in Kenneth M. Sayre's *Plato's Literary Garden*. Sayre reinterprets Plato's style of philosophizing in his open-ended dialogues as the instantiation of his concept of so-called gardens of literature. For another comprehensive study of the *Phaedrus*, see G. R. F. Ferrari, *Listening to the Cicadas: A Study of Plato's "Phaedrus."* For Jacques Derrida's by now classic deconstruction of Plato's distinction between speech and writing in the *Phaedrus*, see "Plato's Pharmacy," in *Dissemination*, 61–172.

Plato's remark in *The Republic* about the need for the philosopher to shelter himself behind a wall is considered by many scholars to be an allusion to the Academy, which was indeed walled. The remark occurs in 6.496d.

For more on the Persian word *pairideiẓa* and Persian gardens in general, see Mehdi Khonsari, M. Reza Moghtader, and Minouch Yavari, eds., *The Persian Garden: Echoes of Paradise*.

For an excellent discussion of Plato's analogy of the gardens of Adonis, see 166–68 of Andrea Nightingale's *Genres in Dialogue: Plato and the Construct of Philosophy*; also Jack Winkler's chapter "The Laughter of the Oppressed: Demeter and the Gardens of Adonis," in *The Constraints of Desire*, 188–209.

Chapter Seven: The Garden School of Epicurus

Apart from Lucretius, whose *De rerum natura* is a systematic apology for Epicurean doctrine, most of what is known about Epicurus and Epicureanism comes to us from hostile witnesses, such as the Stoics, Skeptics, Platonists, and Christians. One of our main sources is Cicero (see *About the Ends of Goods and Evils* and *On the Nature of the Gods*). See also Sextus Empiricus (*Against the Physicians*), Diogenes Laertius (*Lives of Eminent Philosophers*), and Plutarch (*Against Colotes*). The very few original writings of Epicurus that survive include three letters (to Herodotus, to Pythocles, and to Menoeceus), a group of quotations known as the *Principal Doctrines*, and another known as the *Vatican Sayings*. Two main Epicurean sources exist: Lucretius and Philodemus, whose works were discovered at Herculaneum in the early nineteenth century in carbonized papyri and are still being edited and published to this day by the scholars of the international Philodemus Project in Naples, under the direction of David Blank, Richard Janko, and Dirk Obbink.

For an excellent, mostly sympathetic study of Epicurus that reconstructs his thought from the fragments as a coherent whole, see N. W. De Witt, *Epicurus and His Philosophy*. This is the book that I have relied on most in my reconstruction of Epicurus's doctrine. English quotes from Epicurus's extant writings in my chapter come from De Witt's book.

For Epicurean thought in the longer history of Hellenistic philosophy, see A. A. Long and D. N. Sedley, *The Hellenistic Philosophers*, vol. 1. For the original texts in translation, see the second volume of that work. See also Diskin Clay's collection of critical essays *Paradosis and Survival: Three*

Chapters in the Epicurean Philosophy. On *ataraxia* see James Warren, *Epicurus and Democritean Ethics: An Archaeology of Ataraxia*. On the concept of *parresia* see Tim O'Keefe, *Epicurus on Freedom*. On the influence of Epicurean thought in Augustan literature, see David Armstrong et al., eds., *Vergil, Philodemus, and the Augustans*. For the afterlife of Epicurean philosophy see Howard Jones, *The Epicurean Tradition*, and the last chapter of De Witt. For Thomas Jefferson's self-avowed Epicureanism, see his 1819 letter to William Short in volume 15 of *The Writings of Thomas Jefferson*, pp. 219-23.

For Foucault's views on ancient ethics and its *culture de soi*, see the second and third volumes of his *History of Sexuality*: *The Use of Pleasure* and, above all, *The Care of the Self*.

For a philosophy of gratitude that is not necessarily Epicurean but is germane nonetheless, see Paul Ricoeur's *The Course of Recognition* (translated from the French *Parcours de la reconnaissance*).

Chapter Eight: Boccaccio's Garden Stories

Giuseppe Mazzotta's book *The World at Play in Boccaccio's "Decameron"* remains the best commentary on Boccaccio's masterpiece, in my view. See also the study by Marilyn Migiel, *A Rhetoric of the "Decameron."* On Boccaccio's so-called Naturalism, see Aldo D. Scaglione, *Nature and Love in the Middle Ages*, and the more recent study by Gregory Stone, *The Ethics of Nature in the Middle Ages: On Boccaccio's Poetaphysics*. For a very interesting interpretation of the philosophical implications of Boccaccio's art of storytelling, see Richard F. Kuhns, *The "Decameron" and the Philosophy of Storytelling: Author as Midwife and Pimp*. On the presence of gardens in Boccaccio's literary corpus, see Maria Elisa Raja, *Le muse in giardino: Il paesaggio ameno nelle opere di Giovanni Boccaccio*. For a short note and bibliography of Italian literary gardens in general, see Bruno Basile's excellent entry "Giardino" in *Luoghi della letteratura italiana*, 213–21, as well as his book-length study *L'elisio effimero: Scrittori in giardino*. See also Franco Ferrucci's remarkable study *Il giardino simbolico: Modelli letterari e autobiografia dell'opera*.

The garden environment in which the *brigata* tells its stories is "marginal" with respect to Florence, in much the same way that literature is marginal to social reality. For an extensive treatment of Boccaccio's vision of the marginality of literature in the *Decameron*, see Mazzotta, *World at Play*, 46–74.

Edith Wharton's *Italian Villas and Their Gardens*, which was published in 1904, is still an enchanting and profoundly insightful book, in my view. See also John C. Shepherd, *Italian Gardens of the Renaissance*, from 1925, and Claudia Lazzaro's fine book *The Italian Renaissance Garden*, which deals mostly with the Villa Lante near Rome. More recently, see Günter Mader's *Italienische Gärten*.

On the Masetto story in particular, see Mazzotta, *World at Play*, 110–15, and Migiel, *Rhetoric of the "Decameron,"* 71–76.

On the relationship between the *Novellino* and the *Decameron* see Mazzotta, *World at Play*, 264, and Migiel, *Rhetoric of the "Decameron,"* 33–35.

By using term *civil humanism* instead of *civic humanism* I seek to highlight the importance for Boccaccio of individual human relations over political relations. His civil humanism, as seen in the *Decameron*, was more an ethics of sociality than was the politically determined civic humanism of his Florentine heirs Coluccio Salutati and Leonardo Bruni.

The narrative movement of the *Decameron* is interpreted by most critics as upward. I am convinced, however, that an attentive reading of the stories of Day 10 would show that in almost every case the virtues which these stories presumably exalt are suspended over an abyss of irony. Upon closer inspection there is hardly a protagonist in Day 10 whose virtue is not undercut by his or her all-too-human failings or, what is worse, by self-deception. In Boccaccio's universe, literature is the best antidote to this kind of self-deception, though clearly the odds are greatly against it, as is evident precisely from the lack of irony with which most critics read Day 10.

Chapter Nine: Monastic, Republican, and Princely Gardens

On monastic cloister gardens see Mick Hales, *Monastic Gardens*; Veronique Rouchon Mouilleron, *Cloisters of Europe: Gardens of Prayer*; and Anne Jennings, *Medieval Gardens*. Also on the cloister garden, see Terry Comito's "Sacred Space and the Image of Paradise," which is the second chapter of his excellent book *The Idea of the Garden in the Renaissance*, 25–50.

The line from Wordsworth is from "Lines Written in Early Spring" in *Poems*, 43–44.

Bruni's *Dialogi ad Petrum Paulum Histrum* can be found in its Latin original, with facing Italian translation, in *Opere letterarie e politiche*, 73–144. English translations in this chapter are mine.

For a history of Italian humanism see Ronald G. Witt's *In the Footsteps of the Ancients: The Origins of Humanism from Lovato to Bruni* (on Bruni, see 392–442).

The term *civic humanism* (*Bürger Humanismus*) was coined in 1928 by Hans Baron in his commentary in *Leonardo Bruni: Humanistisch-philosophische Scriften*. He further elaborates and expounds his idea of civic humanism in his groundbreaking book *The Crisis of the Early Italian Renaissance*. The volume of essays *In Search of Florentine Civic Humanism: Essays on the Transition from Medieval to Modern Thought* collects his thoughts on the issue. More recently, see the volume of critical essays, most of them excellent, edited by James Hankins, *Renaissance Civic Humanism*.

On the contemporary heirs of civic humanism, see Adrian Oldfield, *Citizenship and Community: Civic Republicanism and the Modern World*; J. G. A. Pocock, "Civic Humanism and Its Role in Anglo-American Thought," in *Politics, Language, and Time: Essays on Political Thought and History*, 80–103; and Quentin Skinner's "The Republican Idea of Political Liberty," in *Machiavelli and Republicanism*, ed. Gisela Bock, Quentin Skinner, and Maurizio Viroli.

On Castiglione and the court of Urbino during the sixteenth century, see the collection of critical essays edited by Robert W. Hanning and David Rosand, *Castiglione: The Ideal and the Real in Renaissance Culture*; especially germane is Thomas M. Greene's article "*Il Cortegiano* and the Choice of a Game," 1–16.

The passage from Ficino is from the 1576 Basel edition of his *Opera omnia*, reprinted in 1959 by the Bottega d'Erasmo, 2/1:1129–30. The English translation in this chapter is mine, in collaboration with David Lummus. On Ficino, see Konrad Eisenbichler and Olga Zorzi Pugliese, eds., *Ficino and Renaissance Neoplatonism*; Michael J. B. Allen and Valery Rees, eds., *Marsilio Ficino: His Theology, His Philosophy, His Legacy*. See also Comito's excellent discussion in *Idea of the Garden in the Renaissance*, 76–87. On the Platonic Academy of Careggi, see Arnaldo della Torre, *Studi dell'Accademia platonica di Firenze*. On Lorenzo de' Medici and fifteenth-century Florence, see Patrizia Salvadori, *Dominio e patronato: Lorenzo dei Medici e la Toscana nel Quattrocento*, and Frank W. Kent, *Lorenzo de' Medici and the Art of Magnificence*. On Renaissance Platonism see Christine Raffini, *Marsilio Ficino, Pietro Bembo, Baldasarre Castiglione: Philosophical, Aesthetic, and Political Approaches in Renaissance Platonism*.

Lorenzo de Medici's "Canzone di Bacco" is from his *Canti carnescialeschi*. The poem is included in *The Penguin Book of Italian Verse*, ed. and trans. Kay (142–43).

Chapter Ten: A Note on Versailles

The literature on Versailles is as sprawling and humbling as the grounds themselves. I found helpful Allen Weiss's *Mirrors of Infinity: The French Formal Garden and Seventeenth-Century Metaphysics* (especially "Versailles: Versions of the Sun, the Fearful Difference," 52–77) and chapters 2–3 of his *Unnatural Horizons: Paradox and Contradiction in Landscape Architecture*, 44–83. Arie Graafland has an intriguing discussion of Versailles' "mechanics of power" in his book *Versailles* (72–147). For a general overview of the architecture of the garden and palace, see Jean-Marie Pérouse de Montclos, *Versailles*. For the cultural context of the construction of Versailles, see Ian H. Thompson, *The Sun King's Garden: Louis XIV, André Le Nôtre, and the Creation of the Gardens of Versailles*. On Nicolas Fouquet and his gardens at Vaux-le-Vicomte, see Michael Brix, *The Baroque Landscape: André Le Nôtre and Vaux-le-Vicomte*; Jean-Marie Pérouse de Montclos, *Vaux le Vicomte*; and "Vaux-le-Vicomte: Anamorphosis Abscondita," in Allen Weiss's *Mirrors of Infinity*, 32–51.

Chapter Eleven: On the Lost Art of Seeing

On Rilke's doctrine that the earth is destined to become "invisible," see my *The Dominion of the Dead*, 44–51.

For an intensive investigation of the "dry landscape gardens" of Japan, and one that includes speculative reflections on the presence of rocks in Zen gardens, see the book by the French scholar Francois Berthier, *Reading Zen in the Rocks: The Japanese Dry Landscape Garden*. Marc Peter Keane is the author and coauthor of several excellent books on Japanese gardens, including *Japanese Garden Design*; *The Art of Setting Stones: And Other Writings from the Japanese Garden*; and, along with David Scott and Sian Evans, *Simply Zen: Interior Japanese Gardens*. Some other studies (among so many in the secondary literature) include Wybe Kuitert, *Themes, Scenes, and Taste in the History of Japanese Garden Art*; Norris Brock Johnson, "Mountain, Temple, and the Design of Movement: Thirteenth-Century Japanese Zen Buddhist

Landscapes," in *Landscape Design and the Experience of Motion*, ed. Michel Conan, 157–85; and Christopher McIntosh, *Gardens of the Gods: Myth, Magic, and Meaning*, 18–34.

For a general overview of Andrew Marvell's life and poetry, see Robert Wilcher, *Andrew Marvell*; for a more detailed discussion of nature in Marvell's poetry, see John Rogers, *The Matter of Revolution: Science, Poetry, and Politics in the Age of Milton*, 39–102.

The quotation from Descartes' *Discourse on Method* is from the Donald A. Cress translation published by Hackett, 6.33.

Chapter Twelve: Sympathetic Miracles

T. S. Eliot proposes the notion of the "objective correlative" quite casually in a short essay on *Hamlet* (1919), in which he claims that the play fails to find the proper objective correlative for Hamlet's state of mind, hence that it must be considered to some extent a failed work of art. The full quote reads: "The only way of expressing emotion in the form of art is by finding an 'objective correlative'; in other words, a set of objects, a situation, a chain of events which shall be the formula of that *particular* emotion; such that when the external facts, which must terminate in sensory experience, are given, the emotion is immediately evoked" (*Selected Prose*, 48). Eliot's concept has been much discussed and much attacked in the decades after it was first articulated. Although I argue against it in this chapter, I believe it is still an ingenious and in many cases valid one.

The version of the O'Grady poem I cite in this chapter is slightly different from the one found in his collected poems *The Road Taken*. The original version was first printed privately as a kind of folio in 1978, along with a handful of other poems, where its title was not "Pillow Talk" but rather "Prologue," for it was in fact the prologue poem to a series called *The Wandering Suras* (now called *The Wandering Celt*). I prefer the earlier version and I hope O'Grady will forgive me for that.

Chapter Thirteen: The Paradise Divide: Islam and Christianity

The Hebrew Bible alludes to a coming messianic age of world peace, when lion and lamb will rest together and the peoples of Assyria, Egypt, and Israel will come together to worship the one true God, yet there is no mention of paradise or Eden as a place of the afterlife. See the entries for "Paradise" (by Tigay and Bamberger) and "Garden of Eden" (S. Sperling) in the *Encyclopaedia Judaica*. On the concept of paradise in Christianity and Judaism, see Gerard P. Luttikhuizen, ed., *Paradise Interpreted: Representations of Biblical Paradise in Judaism and Christianity*. For a comparative study of Jewish and Christian beliefs regarding the afterlife, see Richard Bauckham, *The Fate of the Dead: Studies on Jewish and Christian Apocalypses*. On the afterlife as conceived in Judaism, see José Costa, *L'au delà et la résurrection dans la littérature rabbinique*, and Klaas Spronk, *Beatific Afterlife in Ancient Israel and in the Ancient Near East*; Joseph S. Park, *Conceptions of Afterlife in Jewish Inscriptions: With Special Reference to Pauline Literature*; Emile Puech, *La croyance des Esséniens en la vie future: Immoralité, résurrection, vie éternelle?*; Neil Gillman, *The Death of Death: Resurrection and Immortality in Jewish Thought*; Simcha Paull Raphael, *Jewish View on the Afterlife*; Casey Deryl Elledge, *Life after Death in Early Judaism: The Evidence of Josephus*. On paradise in Islam, see the second chapter of Edward Hotaling's *Islam without Illusions: Its Past, Its Present, and Its Challenge for the Future*, 15–26; Andrew Rippin, *Muslims: Their Religious Beliefs and Practices*, 25–27; David Waines, *An Introduction to Islam*, 129–30. There are also a number of good studies of the Islamic afterlife and eschatology, such as Bashiruddin Mahmud Ahmad, *Mechanics of the Doomsday and Life after Death: The Ultimate Fate of the Universe as Seen through the Holy Quran*; Everett K. Rowson, *A Muslim Philosopher on the Soul and Its Fate: Al-`Amiri's Kitab al-Amad `ala l-abad*. See also premodern poet-philosopher Al-Ghazali, *The Precious Pearl: A Translation from the Arabic* (trans. Jane Idleman Smith). For a general view of the afterlife in all three Western religious traditions, see Hiroshi Obayashi, ed., *Death and Afterlife: Perspectives of World Religions*, 67–142. For more references to the earthly paradise, see the note to chapter 2 on Eden.

On the question of what happens to women in the Islamic paradise, there is some ambiguity. Most of the rewards described by the Qur'an are intended for men, yet the Qur'an does mention, albeit in very few passages, that women also go to paradise (most unambiguously in 9:72: "God has promised the men and women who believe in Him gardens watered by running streams"; more vaguely, "Enter Paradise, you and your spouses, in all delight" [43:70]). What kinds of rewards await the women are not specified. What is certain is that the women who do go to paradise—either through their own merit or as their husband's spouse—are *not* the virginal concubines who surround the men in Eden.

The literature on the gardens of the Islamic world is as vast as it is excellent. The following proved particularly helpful to me: Jonas B. Lehrman, *Earthly Paradise: Garden and Courtyard in Islam*; the fine collection of essays in *The Islamic Garden*, edited by Elisabeth B. Macdougall and Richard Ettinghausen; *Persian Gardens and Garden Pavilions*, by Donald Newton Wilber, esp. chapter 1, "Persian Gardens and Paradise," 3–22; Titus Burckhardt, *Art of Islam: Language and Meaning*; also McIntosh, *Gardens of the Gods*, 35–45.

For my discussion of carpet gardens in appendix 4, I benefited greatly from Emma Clark's *The Art of the Islamic Garden*, esp. 23–36, 171–88. On carpet gardens in India, see Daniel Walker, *Flowers Underfoot: Indian Carpet Gardens of the Mughal Era*.

On Dante's representation of Paradise in the *Comedy*, see Rachel Jacoff, "Shadowy Prefaces," in *The Cambridge Companion to Dante*, 208–25; John Freccero, "Introduction to the *Paradiso*," in *Dante: The Poetics of Conversion*, 209–20; Joan Ferrante, "Words and Images in the *Paradiso*" in *Dante, Petrarch, Boccaccio: Studies in the Italian Trecento in Honor of Charles S. Singleton*, 115–32; and Jeffrey Schnapp, *The Transfiguration of History at the Center of Dante's Paradise*.

Chapter Fourteen: Men Not Destroyers

On Marx's view of capitalism's upheavals, see Miranda Joseph, *Against the Romance of Community*, and N. Scott Arnold, *Marx's Radical Critique of Capitalist Society: A Reconstruction and Critical Evaluation*. For the disruptive effects of consumerism and consumption, see *Cities of Europe: Changing Contexts, Local Arrangements, and the Challenge to Urban Cohesion*, edited by Yuri Kazepov; *The Consumer Society and the Postmodern City* by David B. Clarke; *Consumption in an Age of Information*, edited by Sande Cohen and R. L. Rutsky; *A High Price for Abundant Living: The Story of Capitalism* by Henry Rempel; and Edmond Préteceille's *Capitalism, Consumption, and Needs*. On consumption and the modern self, see Clive Hamilton's *Growth Fetish*; Roger A. Salerno, *Landscapes of Abandonment: Capitalism, Modernity, and Estrangement*; and John Xiros Cooper, *Modernism and the Culture of Market Society*. On the future of capitalism see Victor D. Lippit, *Capitalism*; Michel Vakaloulis, *Le capitalisme post-moderne: Éléments pour une critique sociologique*; and Phillip Brown and Hugh Lauder, *Capitalism and Social Progress: The Future of Society in a Global Economy*.

On Ariosto's *Orlando Furioso* in general, see Alberti Ascoli's excellent study *Ariosto's Bitter Harmony: Crisis and Evasion in the Italian Renaissance*; for Ascoli's extended reflections on the episode of Alcina and Logistilla in particular, see 122–257. For another view of the Renaissance epic in its cultural and literary context, see David Quint, *Origin and Originality in Renaissance Literature*, esp. 81–92 on Ariosto. On the theme of wandering and restlessness in Ariosto, see chapter 1 of Patricia Parker's *Inescapable Romance: Studies in the Poetics of a Mode*, 16–54; and chapters 2–4 of Deanna Shemek's *Ladies Errant: Wayward Women and Social Order in Early Modern Italy*, 45–157. On the gardens of the *Furioso*, see Eduardo Saccone's essay "Wood, Garden, 'locus amoenus' in Ariosto's *Orlando Furioso*."

On Pascal's crucial notion of diversion, see Kurt Stenzel, *Pascals Theorie des Divertissement*, and Laurent Thirouin, "Le cycle du divertissement." See also Jean Giono's 1947 novel inspired by Pascal, *Un roi sans divertissement*.

The Fowlie passage is quoted by Lionel Trilling in his essay "The Fate of Pleasure" (*Beyond Culture*, 66).

The Flaubert quote comes from his letter to Eugène Delattre on August 1, 1858, in *Correspondance*, ed. Franklin-Grout, 4:273.

The Marinetti passage comes from the "Founding and Manifesto of Futurism," originally published in *Le Figaro* on February 29, 1909, and translated in *Let's Murder the Moonshine* by R. W. Flint and Arthur A. Coppotelli.

For more on Nietzsche's dictum about wastelands, as well as a discussion of the wasteland as the "objective correlative" of modernism, see my chapter "Wastelands," in *Forests: The Shadow of Civilization*, 148–54.

On Pound's failed endeavor to make an earthly paradise, see two essays in *Paideuma*—Stephen Sicari, "History and Vision in Pound and Dante: A Purgatorial Poetics"; Reed W. Dasenbrock, "Dante's Hell and Pound's Paradiso: 'Tutto spezzato' "—and Matthew Reynolds's essay "Ezra Pound in the Earthly Paradise" in *Dante and the Unorthodox*. One of the best critics of literary modernism in general, and Pound's poetics in particular, is Marjorie Perloff. On Pound, see Perloff's *The Dance of the Intellect: Studies in the*

Poetry of the Pound Tradition and her radio interview with Robert Harrison, "A Conversation with Marjorie Perloff"; on literary modernism in general, see Perloff's *Poetics of Indeterminacy from Rimbaud to Cage* and the essays in *Differentials: Poetry, Poetics, Pedagogy*. Another excellent study of Pound's importance in literary modernism is Hugh Kenner's *The Pound Era*.

Chapter Fifteen: The Paradox of the Age

The quotation from Trilling comes from *Beyond Culture*, 50–76. See A. Bartlett Giamatti's brief invocation of this essay in the conclusion to his *The Earthly Paradise and the Renaissance Epic*, 357–59. For more on Trilling's views of modernity and spiritual militancy, see Dravid Kamalini, *Acculturation of Anti-culture: A Study of Trilling's "Beyond Culture."*

On boredom as the basic mood of modernity, see Heidegger's probing discussion in his *The Fundamental Concepts of Metaphysics: World, Finitude, Solitude*, 78–173. See also two other excellent studies, one by Lars Svendsen, *A Philosophy of Boredom*, and other by Elizabeth S. Goodstein, *Experience without Qualities: Boredom and Modernity*. See also chapter 3 of Miguel de Beistegui, *Thinking with Heidegger: Displacements* ("Boredom: Between Existence and History," 61–82); and Andrew Benjamin, "Boredom and Distraction: The Moods of Modernity," in *Walter Benjamin and History*, 156–70.

My reflections about how our contemporary urban habitat is already undergoing a specious Edenization are inspired in part by my correspondence with Weixing Su, a brilliant young scholar who was my colleague at Stanford University before she left to teach at Peking University in 2006. My remarks about the "careless" overnight flower beds of corporate high-rise buildings are indebted to her comments on an early draft of this chapter.

WORKS CITED

Adams, William Howard. *Roberto Burle Marx: The Unnatural Art of the Garden*. New York: Museum of Modern Art, 1991.

Al-Ghazali. *The Precious Pearl: A Translation from the Arabic*. Translated by Jane Idleman Smith. Missoula, MT: Scholars, 1979.

Allen, Michael J. B., and Valery Rees, eds. *Marsilio Ficino: His Theology, His Philosophy, His Legacy*. Leiden: Brill, 2002.

Anonymous. *Novellino*. Edited by Alberto Conte. Rome: Salerno, 2001.

Arendt, Hannah. *The Human Condition*. 2nd ed. Chicago: University of Chicago Press, 1998.

———. *Men in Dark Times*. New York: Harcourt, Brace, 1968.

Ariosto, Ludovico. *Orlando Furioso*. Translated by Guido Waldman. Oxford: Oxford University Press, 1974.

Armstrong, David, et al., eds. *Vergil, Philodemus, and the Augustans*. Austin: University of Texas Press, 2004.

Arnold, N. Scott. *Marx's Radical Critique of Capitalist Society: A Reconstruction and Critical Evaluation*. New York: Oxford University Press, 1990.

Ascoli, Albert. *Ariosto's Bitter Harmony: Crisis and Evasion in the Italian Renaissance*. Princeton, NJ: Princeton University Press, 1987.

Baldan Zenoni-Politeo, Giuliana, and Antonella Pietrogrande, eds. *Il giardino e la memoria del mondo*. Florence: L. S. Olschki, 2002.

Balmori, Diana, and Morton Margaret. *Transitory Gardens, Uprooted Lives*. New Haven, CT: Yale University Press, 1993.

Baron, Hans. *The Crisis of the Early Italian Renaissance: Civic Humanism and Republican Liberty in an Age of Classicism and Tyranny.* 2 vols. Princeton, NJ: Princeton University Press, 1955.

———. *In Search of Florentine Civic Humanism: Essays on the Transition from Medieval to Modern Thought.* 2 vols. Princeton, NJ: Princeton University Press, 1988.

Bashiruddin Mahmud Ahmad. *Mechanics of the Doomsday and Life after Death: The Ultimate Fate of the Universe as Seen through the Holy Quran.* New Delhi: Kitab Bhavan, 1991.

Basile, Bruno. *L'elisio effimero: Scrittori in giardino.* Bologna: Il Mulino, 1993.

———. *"Giardino."* In Luoghi della letteratura italiana, edited by Gian Mario Anselmi and Gino Ruozzi. Milan: Mondadori, 2003.

Bassani, Giorgio. *The Garden of the Finzi-Continis.* Translated by Jamie McKendrick. New York: Penguin, 2007.

Bauckham, Richard. *The Fate of the Dead: Studies on Jewish and Christian Apocalypses.* Boston: Brill, 1998.

Bazin, Germain. *Paradeisos: The Art of the Garden.* Boston: Little, Brown, 1990.

Benjamin, Andrew. *"Boredom and Distraction: The Models of Modernity."* In *Walter Benjamin and History,* edited by Andrew Benjamin. London: Continuum, 2005.

Bernauer, James W., ed. *Amor Mundi: Explorations in the Faith and Thought of Hannah Arendt.* Boston: M. Nijhoff, 1987.

Berthier, Francois. *Reading Zen in the Rocks: The Japanese Dry Landscape Garden.* Translated by Graham Parkes. Chicago: University of Chicago Press, 2000.

Bloom, Harold. *Wallace Stevens: The Poems of Our Climate.* Ithaca, NY: Cornell University Press, 1977.

Boccaccio, Giovanni. *Decameron.* Translated by G. H. McWilliam. 2nd ed. London: Penguin, 1993.

Borchardt, Rudolf. *The Passionate Gardener.* Translated by Henry Martin. Kingston, NY: McPherson, 2006.

Bradbrook, B. R. *Karel Čapek: In Pursuit of Truth, Tolerance, and Trust.* Brighton, UK: Sussex Academic, 1998.

Brix, Michael. *The Baroque Landscape: André Le Nôtre and Vaux-le-Vicomte.* Translated by Steven Lindberg. New York: Rizzoli, 2004.

Brown, Phillip, and Hugh Lauder. *Capitalism and Social Progress: The Future of Society in a Global Economy*. Basingstoke, UK: Palgrave, 2001.

Bruni, Leonardo. *Humanistisch-philosophische Schriften*. Edited with commentary by Hans Baron. Wiesbaden: M. Sändig, 1969 [orig. Leipzig: Teubner, 1928].

———. *Opere letterarie e politiche*. Edited by Paolo Viti. Turin: UTET, 1996.

Brunt, P. A. *"Plato's Academy and Politics."* In Studies in Greek History and Thought. Oxford: Oxford University Press, 1993.

Bull, Malcolm. "The Social and the Political." *South Atlantic Quarterly* 104, no. 4 (2005): 675–92.

Burckhardt, Titus. *Art of Islam: Language and Meaning*. Translated by J. Peter Hobson. London: World of Islam Festival Publishing, 1976.

Burkert, Walter. *Greek Religion*. Translated by John Raffan. Cambridge, MA: Harvard University Press, 1985.

Calvino, Italo. *Invisible Cities*. Translated by William Weaver. New York: Harcourt Brace Jovanovich, 1974.

———. *Mr. Palomar*. Translated by William Weaver. New York: Harcourt Brace Jovanovich, 1985.

Camus, Albert. *Lyrical and Critical Essays*. Translated by Ellen Conroy Kennedy. New York: Vintage, 1970.

Čapek, Karel. *The Gardener's Year*. Translated by M. and R. Weatherall. Modern Library. New York: Random House, 2002.

———. *R.U.R. (Rossum's Universal Robots)*. Translated by Claudia Novack-Jones. New York: Penguin Books, 2004.

———. *Talks with T. G. Masaryk*. Translated by Dora Round. Edited by Michael Henry Heim. North Haven, CT: Catbird, 1995.

Cavarero, Adriana. *For More Than One Voice: Towards a Philosophy of Vocal Expression*. Translated by Paul Kottman. Stanford, CA: Stanford University Press, 2005.

———. *In Spite of Plato: A Feminist Rewriting of Ancient Philosophy*. Translated by Serena Anderlini-D'Onofrio and Áine O'Healy. New York: Routledge, 1995.

———. *Relating Narratives: Storytelling and Selfhood*. Translated by Paul Kottman. London and New York: Routledge, 2000.

———. *Stately Bodies: Literature, Philosophy, and the Question of Gender*. Translated by Robert de Lucca and Deanna Shemek. Ann Arbor: University of Michigan Press, 2002.

Cherniss, Harold F. *The Riddle of the Early Academy*. New York: Russell and Russell, 1962.

Clark, Emma. *The Art of the Islamic Garden*. Ramsbury, UK: Crowood, 2004.

Clark, Peter, ed. *The European City and Green Space: London, Stockholm, Helsinki, and St. Petersburg, 1850–2000*. Aldershot, UK: Ashgate, 2006.

Clarke, David B. *The Consumer Society and the Postmodern City*. London: Routledge, 2003.

Clay, Diskin. *Paradosis and Survival: Three Chapters in the Epicurean Philosophy*. Ann Arbor: University of Michigan Press, 1998.

Cohen, Sande, and R. L. Rutsky, eds. *Consumption in an Age of Information*. Oxford: Berg, 2005.

Comito, Terry. *The Idea of the Garden in the Renaissance*. New Brunswick, NJ: Rutgers University Press, 1978.

Conan, Michel. *Essais de poetique des jardins*. Florence: L. S. Olschki, 2004.

Coogan, Michael D., ed. *The New Oxford Annotated Bible*. 3rd ed. Oxford: Oxford University Press, 2001.

Cooper, David E. *A Philosophy of Gardens*. Oxford: Oxford University Press, 2006.

Cooper, John Xiros. *Modernism and the Culture of Market Society*. Cambridge: Cambridge University Press, 2004.

Costa, José. *L'au delà et la résurrection dans la littérature rabbinique*. Paris: Peeters, 2004.

Dancy, R. M. *Two Studies in the Early Academy*. Albany: State University of New York Press, 1991.

Dante Alighieri. *The Divine Comedy of Dante Alighieri*, vol. 1, *Inferno*. Translated by Robert M. Durling and Ronald L. Martinez. Oxford: Oxford University Press, 1993.

————. *The Divine Comedy of Dante Alighieri*, vol. 2, *Purgatorio*. Translated by Robert M. Durling and Ronald L. Martinez. Oxford: Oxford University Press, 2004.

————. *Paradiso*. Translated by Allen Mandelbaum. New York: Bantam, 1986.

Dasenbrock, Reed W. "Dante's Hell and Pound's Paradiso: 'Tutto spezzato.'" *Paideuma* 9 (1980): 501–4.

Dawood N. J. *The Koran*. London: Penguin, 1995.

de Beistegui, Miguel. *Thinking with Heidegger: Displacements*. Bloomington: Indiana University Press, 2003.

della Torre, Arnaldo. *Studi dell'Accademia platonica di Firenze*. Florence: Tipografia G. Carnesecchi, 1902.

de Montclos, Jean-Marie Pérouse. *Vaux le Vicomte*. Paris: Editions Scala, 1997.

————. *Versailles*. New York: Abbeville, 1991.

d'Entrèves, Maurizio Passerin. *The Political Philosophy of Hannah Arendt*. London: Routledge, 1993.

Derrida, Jacques. *Dissemination*. Translated by Barbara Johnson. Chicago: Chicago University Press, 1981.

Descartes, René. *Discourse on Method and Meditations on First Philosophy*. Trans. Donald A. Cress. Indianapolis: Hackett, 1998.

Devolder, Anne-Mie, ed. *The Public Garden: The Enclosure and Disclosure of the Public Garden*. Rotterdam: NAi, 2002.

De Witt, N. W. *Epicurus and His Philosophy*. Minneapolis: University of Minnesota Press, 1954.

Dillon, John. *The Heirs of Plato: A Study of the Old Academy (347–247 BC)*. Oxford: Oxford University Press, 2003.

Durán, Manuel, and Margery Safir. *Earth Tones: The Poetry of Pablo Neruda*. Bloomington: Indiana University Press, 1981.

Eisenbichler, Konrad, and Olga Zorzi Pugliese, eds. *Ficino and Renaissance Neoplatonism*. University of Toronto Italian Studies. Ottawa, Canada: Dovehouse Editions Canada, 1986.

Eliot, T. S. *Four Quartets*. London: Faber and Faber, 2001.

————. *Selected Prose of T. S. Eliot*. New York: Farrar and Straus, 1975.

Elledge, Casey Deryl. *Life after Death in Early Judaism: The Evidence of Josephus*. Tübingen: Mohr Siebeck, 2006.

Engels, Frederick, and Karl Marx. *The Communist Manifesto*. Edited by John E. Toews. Boston: Bedford/St. Martin's, 1999.

Esten, John. *Hampton Gardens: A 350-Year Legacy*. New York: Rizzoli, 2004.

Ferrante, Joan. "Words and Images in the Paradiso." In *Dante, Petrarch, Boccaccio: Studies in the Italian Trecento in Honor of Charles S. Singleton*. Edited by Aldo S. Bernardo and Anthony Pellegrini. Binghamton: Center for Medieval and Early Renaissance Studies, State University of New York at Binghamton, 1983.

Ferrari, G. R. F. *Listening to the Cicadas: A Study of Plato's "Phaedrus."* Cambridge: Cambridge University Press, 1987.

Ferriolo, Massimo Venturi. *Giardino e filosofia.* Milan: Guerini e Associati, 1992.

Ferrucci, Franco. *Il giardino simbolico: Modelli letterari e autobiografia dell'opera.* Rome: Bulzoni, 1980.

Ficino, Marsilio. *Opera omnia.* Turin: Bottega d'Erasmo, 1959 (orig. 1576).

Flaubert, Gustave. *Correspondance.* Edited by Caroline Franklin-Grout. 9 vols. Oeuvres complètes de Gustave Flaubert. Paris: L. Conard, 1926–33.

Foucault, Michel. *The History of Sexuality,* vol. 2, *The Use of Pleasure.* Translated by Robert Hurley. New York: Pantheon, 1985.

————. *The History of Sexuality,* vol. 3, *The Care of the Self.* Translated by Robert Hurley. New York: Pantheon, 1986.

Freccero, John. "Introduction to the *Paradiso.*" In *Dante: The Poetics of Conversion,* edited by Rachel Jacoff. Cambridge, MA: Harvard University Press, 1986.

Fromm, Erich. *The Heart of Man: Its Genius for Good and Evil.* New York: Harper and Row, 1964.

Fuller, Robert C. *Ecology of Care: An Interdisciplinary Analysis of the Self and Moral Obligation.* Louisville, KY: Westminister John Knox Press, 1992.

Giamatti, A. Barlett. *The Earthly Paradise and the Renaissance Epic.* Princeton, NJ: Princeton University Press, 1966.

Gilligan, Carol. *In a Different Voice: Psychological Theory and Women's Development.* Cambridge, MA: Harvard University Press, 1993.

Gillman, Neil. *The Death of Death: Resurrection and Immortality in Jewish Thought.* Woodstock, VT: Jewish Lights, 1997

Giono, Jean. *Un roi sans divertissement.* Montréal: Gallimard, 1948.

Goldhill, Simon. *The Poet's Voice: Essays on Poetics and Greek Literature.* Cambridge: Cambridge University Press, 1991.

Goodstein, Elizabeth S. *Experience without Qualities: Boredom and Modernity.* Stanford, CA: Stanford University Press, 2004.

Gothein, Marie Luise Schroeter. *A History of Garden Art.* Edited by Walter P. Wright. Translated by Laura Archer-Hind. 2 vols. New York: Hacker Art Books, 1966.

Graafland, Arie. *Versailles and the Mechanics of Power: The Subjugation of Circe.* Translated by John Kirk Patrick. Rotterdam: Ø1Ø Publishers, 2003.

Griffin, Jasper. *Homer on Death and Life*. Oxford: Clarendon, 1980.

Groenhout, Ruth E. *Connected Lives: Human Nature and the Ethics of Care.* Lanham, MD: Rowman and Littlefield, 2004.

———. *Theological Echoes in an Ethic of Care.* Notre Dame, IN: Erasmus Institute, 2003.

Guthrie, W. K. C. *A History of Greek Philosophy.* 6 vols. Cambridge: Cambridge University Press, 1962–81.

Hales, Mick. *Monastic Gardens.* New York: Stewart, Tabori and Chang, 2000.

Hamilton, Cilve. *Growth Fetish.* London: Pluto, 2004.

Hanczyc, Martin M., Shelly M. Fujikawa, and Jack W. Szostak,. "Experimental Models of Primitive Cellular Compartments: Encapsulation, Growth, and Division." Science 302, no. 5645 (24 October 2003): 618–22.

Hankins, James, ed. *Renaissance Civic Humanism.* Cambridge: Cambridge University Press, 2000.

Hanning, Robert W., and David Rosand, eds. *Castiglione: The Ideal and the Real in Renaissance Culture.* New Haven, CT: Yale University Press, 1983.

Harkins, William. *Karel Čapek.* New York: Columbia University Press, 1962.

Harrison, Robert. *The Dominion of the Dead.* Chicago: University of Chicago Press, 2003.

———. *Forests: The Shadow of Civilization.* Chicago: University of Chicago Press, 1992.

Hazzard, Shirley. *The Evening of the Holiday.* New York: Picador, 1966.

Heidegger, Martin. *Being and Time.* Translated by John Macquarrie and Edward Robinson. New York: Harper, 1962.

———. *The End of Philosophy.* Translated by Joan Stambaugh. Chicago: University of Chicago Press, 1973.

———. *The Fundamental Concepts of Metaphysics: World, Finitude, Solitude.* Translated by William McNeill and Nicholas Walker. Bloomington: Indiana University Press, 1995.

Held, Virginia. *The Ethics of Care: Personal, Political, Global.* Oxford: Oxford University Press, 2006.

Herbst, Martin. *God's Womb: The Garden of Eden, Innocence and Beyond.* Bethlehem, NH: Menachem, 2003.

Hill, Penelope. *Contemporary History of Garden Design: European Gardens between Art and Architecture*. Basel: Birkhäuser, 2004.

Hirschfeld, Christian Cajus Lorenz. *Theory of Garden Art*. Edited and translated by Linda B. Parshall. Philadelphia: University of Pennsylvania Press, 2001.

Homer. *The Iliad*. Translated by Richard Lattimore. New York: Harper Perennial, 1965.

————. *The Odyssey*. Translated by Richard Lattimore. Chicago: University of Chicago Press, 1951.

Hornblower, Simon, and Antony Spawforth, eds. *The Oxford Classical Dictionary*. 3rd ed. Oxford: Oxford University Press, 1996.

Hotaling, Edward. *Islam without Illusions: Its Past, Its Present, and Its Challenge for the Future*. Syracuse, NY: Syracuse University Press, 2003.

Howard, Ebenezer. *To-morrow: A Peaceful Path to Real Reform*. London: Routledge, 2003 (orig. London: Swann Sonnenschein, 1898).

Hunt, John Dixon. *Greater Perfections: The Practice of Garden Theory*. Philadelphia: University of Pennsylvania Press, 2000.

————, ed. *The Italian Garden: Art, Design, and Culture*. Cambridge: Cambridge University Press, 1996.

Hyginus. *Hygini Fabulae*. Edited by Peter K. Marshall. Stuttgart: Teubner, 1993.

————. *The Myths of Hyginus*. Translated by Mary Grant. Humanistic Studies 34. Lawrence: University of Kansas Publications, 1960.

Iannucci, Amilcare A. "Limbo: The Emptiness of Time." *Studi Danteschi* 72 (1979–80): 69–128.

Jacoff, Rachel. "Shadowy Prefaces." In *The Cambridge Companion to Dante*, edited by Rachel Jacoff. Cambridge: Cambridge University Press, 1993.

Jefferson, Thomas. *The Writings of Thomas Jefferson*. Vol. 15. N.p.: Thomas Jefferson Memorial Association, 1904.

Jennings, Anne. *Medieval Gardens*. London: English Heritage, 2004.

Johnson, Norris Brock. "Mountain, Temple, and the Design of Movement: Thirteenth-Century Japanese Zen Buddhist Landscapes." In *Landscape Design and the Experience of Motion*, edited by Michel Conan. Washington, DC: Dumbarton Oaks Research Library and Collection, 2003.

Jones, Howard. *The Epicurean Tradition*. London: Routledge, 1989.

Joseph, Miranda. *Against the Romance of Community*. Minneapolis: University of Minnesota Press, 2002.

Kamalini, Dravid. *Acculturation of Anti-culture: A Study of Trilling's "Beyond Culture."* New Delhi: Associated Publishing House, 1989.

Kasting, James F., and Janet L. Siefert. "Life and the Evolution of Earth's Atmosphere." *Science* 296, no. 5570 (10 May 2002): 1066–68.

Kay, George, ed. and trans. *The Penguin Book of Italian Verse*. Baltimore: Penguin, 1966.

Kazepov, Yuri, ed. *Cities of Europe: Changing Contexts, Local Arrangements, and the Challenge to Urban Cohesion*. Malden, MA: Blackwell, 2004.

Keane, Marc Peter. *The Art of Setting Stones: And Other Writings from the Japanese Garden*. Berkeley, CA: Stone Bridge, 2002.

———. *Japanese Garden Design*. Rutland, VT: C. E. Tuttle, 1996.

Keane, Marc Peter, with David Scott and Sian Evans. *Simply Zen: Interior Japanese Gardens*. San Francisco: Soma, 1999.

Kellert, Stephen R., and Edward O. Wilson, eds. *The Biophilia Hypothesis*. Washington, DC: Island, 1993.

Kenner, Hugh. *The Pound Era*. Berkeley: University of California Press, 1973.

Kent, Frank W. *Lorenzo de' Medici and the Art of Magnificence*. Baltimore: Johns Hopkins University Press, 2004.

Khansari, Mehdi, M. Reza Moghtader, and Minouch Yavari, eds. *The Persian Garden: Echoes of Paradise*. Washington, DC: Mage, 1998.

Klima, Ivan. *Karel Čapek: Life and Work*. Translated by Norma Comrada. North Haven, CT: Catbird, 2002.

Kuhns, Richard F. *The "Decameron" and the Philosophy of Storytelling: Author as Midwife and Pimp*. New York: Columbia University Press, 2005.

Kuitert, Wybe. *Themes, Scenes, and Taste in the History of Japanese Garden Art*. Amsterdam: J. C. Gieben, 1988.

Laird, Mark. *The Formal Garden: Traditions of Art and Nature*. New York: Thames and Hudson, 1992.

Lane, Patrick. *What the Stones Remember*. Boston: Trumpeter, 2005.

Laureano, Pietro. *Giardini di pietra: I sassi di Matera e la civiltà mediterranea*. Turin: Bollati Boringhieri, 1993.

Lawson, Laura J. *City Bountiful: A Century of Community Gardening in America*. Berkeley: University of California Press, 2005.

Lazzaro, Claudia. *The Italian Renaissance Garden: From the Conventions of Planting, Design, and Ornament to the Grand Gardens of Sixteenth-century Central Italy.* Photographs by Ralph Lieberman. New Haven, CT: Yale University Press, 1990.

Lehrman, Jonas B. *Earthly Paradise: Garden and Courtyard in Islam.* Berkeley: University of California Press, 1980.

Lévinas, Emmanuel. *Totality and Infinity: An Essay on Exteriority.* Translated by Alphonso Lingis. Pittsburgh: Duquesne University Press, 1969.

Lippit, Victor D. *Capitalism.* London: Routledge, 2005.

Long, A. A., and D. N. Sedley. *The Hellenistic Philosophers.* 2 vols. Cambridge: Cambridge University Press, 1987.

Louden, Bruce. *The Odyssey: Structure, Narration, and Meaning.* Baltimore: Johns Hopkins University Press, 1999.

Lowe, Roy. *History of Education: Major Themes.* 4 vols. London: Routledge/Falmer, 2000.

Lowrie, Malcolm. *Under the Volcano.* New York: Harper and Row, 1984.

Luttikhuizen, Gerard P., ed. *Paradise Interpreted: Representations of Biblical Paradise in Judaism and Christianity.* Leiden: Brill, 1999.

Macdougall, Elisabeth B., and Richard Ettinghausen, eds. *The Islamic Garden.* Washington, DC: Dumbarton Oaks, 1976.

MacGregor, Sherilyn. *Beyond Mothering Earth: Ecological Citizenship and the Politics of Care.* Vancouver: University of British Columbia Press, 2006.

Mader, Günter, and Laila Neubert-Mader. *Italienische Gärten.* Stuttgart: Deutsche Verlag-Anstalt, 1987.

Marinetti, F. T. *Let's Murder the Moonshine: Selected Writings.* Edited by R. W. Flint. Translated by R. W. Flint and Arthur A. Coppotelli. Los Angeles: Sun and Moon Classics, 1991.

Mazzotta, Giuseppe. *The World at Play in Boccaccio's "Decameron."* Princeton, NJ: Princeton University Press, 1986.

McIntosh, Christopher. *Gardens of the Gods: Myth, Magic, and Meaning.* London: I. B. Tauris, 2005.

Migiel, Marilyn. *A Rhetoric of the "Decameron."* Toronto: University of Toronto Press, 2003.

Miller, James E. *The Western Paradise: Greek and Hebrew Traditions.* San Francisco: International Scholars, 1996.

Miller, Joseph Hillis. *Poets of Reality: Six Twentieth-Century Writers.* Cambridge: Belknap/Harvard University Press, 1965.

Miller, Mara. *The Garden as Art.* Albany: State University of New York Press, 1993.

Milton, John. *Paradise Lost.* Edited by John Leonard. London: Penguin, 2003.

Montale, Eugenio. *Selected Poems.* New York: New Directions, 1965.

Morris, Paul, and Deborah Sawyer, eds. *A Walk in the Garden: Biblical, Iconographical, and Literary Images of Eden.* Sheffield, UK: JSOT Press, 1992.

Mouilleron, Veronique Rouchon. *Cloisters of Europe: Gardens of Prayer.* Translated by Deke Dusinberre. New York: Viking Studio, 2001.

Neruda, Pablo. *Selected Poems.* Translated by Ben Belitt. New York: Grove, 1961.

Nightingale, Andrea. *Genres in Dialogue: Plato and the Construct of Philosophy.* Cambridge: Cambridge University Press, 1996.

———. *Spectacles of Truth in Classical Greek Philosophy: Theoria in Its Cultural Context.* Cambridge: Cambridge University Press, 2004.

Obayashi, Hiroshi, ed. *Death and Afterlife: Perspectives of World Religions.* New York: Greenwood, 1992.

Ober, Josiah. *Political Dissent in Democratic Athens: Intellectual Critics of Popular Rule.* Princeton, NJ: Princeton University Press, 1998.

O'Grady, Desmond. *The Road Taken: Poems, 1956–1996.* Salzburg: University of Salzburg Press, 1996.

O'Keefe, Tim. *Epicurus on Freedom.* Cambridge: Cambridge University Press, 2005.

Oldfield, Adrian. *Citizenship and Community: Civic Republicanism and the Modern World.* London: Routledge, 1990.

Padon, Thomas. *Contemporary Photography and the Garden: Deceits and Fantasies.* New York: Harry N. Abrams and American Federation of Arts, 2004.

Pagnol, Marcel. *The Water of the Hills: Jean de Florette and Manon of the Springs.* Translated by W. E. van Heyningen. San Francisco: North Point, 1988.

Parati, Graziella, and Rebecca J. West, eds. *Italian Feminist Theory and Practice: Equality and Sexual Difference.* Madison, NJ: Fairleigh Dickinson University Press, 2002.

Park, Joseph S. *Conceptions of Afterlife in Jewish Inscriptions: With Special Reference to Pauline Literature.* Tübingen: Mohr Siebeck, 2000.

Parker, Patricia. *Inescapable Romance: Studies in the Poetics of a Mode.* Princeton, NJ: Princeton University Press, 1979.

Perloff, Marjorie. "A Conversation with Marjorie Perloff about the Poetry and Politics of Ezra Pound." Interview by Robert Harrison. *Entitled Opinions (about Life and Literature),* aired on KZSU-FM, Stanford, CA, 5 November 2005. Available at http://www.stanford.edu/dept/fren-ital/opinions/shows/eo10011.mp3 (accessed April 11, 2007).

———. *The Dance of the Intellect: Studies in the Poetry of the Pound Tradition.* Cambridge: Cambridge University Press, 1985.

———. *Differentials: Poetry, Poetics, Pedagogy.* Tuscaloosa: University of Alabama Press, 2004.

———. *The Poetics of Indeterminacy from Rimbaud to Cage.* Princeton, NJ: Princeton University Press, 1981.

Pizzoni, Filippo. *The Garden: A History in Landscape and Art.* New York: Rizzoli International, 1999.

Plato. *Complete Works.* Edited by John M. Cooper. Indianapolis: Hackett, 1997.

———. *Phaedrus and Letters VII and VIII.* Translated by Walter Hamilton. New York: Penguin, 1986.

Pocock, J. G. A. "Civic Humanism and Its Role in Anglo-American Thought." In *Politics, Language, and Time: Essays on Political Thought and History.* New York: Atheneum, 1971.

Pool, Mary Jane. *Gardens in the City: New York in Bloom.* New York: Harry N. Abrams, 1999.

Pound, Ezra. *The Cantos of Ezra Pound.* New York: New Directions, 1983.

———. *Selected Poems.* London: Faber and Faber, 1978.

Power, Edward J. *Legacy of Learning: A History of Western Education.* Albany: State University of New York Press, 1991.

———. *Main Currents in the History of Education.* New York: McGraw-Hill, 1970.

Préteceille, Edmond. *Capitalism, Consumption, and Needs.* Translated by Sarah Matthews. Oxford: Blackwell, 1985.

Puech, Emile. *La croyance des Esséniens en la vie future: Immoralité, résurrection, vie éternelle? Histoire d'une croyance dans la le judaïsme ancien.* Paris: Libr. Lecoffre, 1993.

Pugh, Simon. *Garden, Nature, Language*. Manchester, UK: Manchester University Press, 1988.

Quint, David. *Origin and Originality in Renaissance Literature*. New Haven, CT: Yale University Press, 1983.

Raffini, Christine. *Marsilio Ficino, Pietro Bembo, Baldasarre Castiglione: Philosophical, Aesthetic, and Political Approaches in Renaissance Platonism*. New York: P. Lang, 1998.

Raja, Maria Elisa. *Le muse in giardino: Il paesaggio ameno nelle opere di Giovanni Boccaccio*. Alessandria, Italy: Edizioni dell'Orso, 2003.

Raphael, Simcha Paull. *Jewish View on the Afterlife*. Northvale, NJ: J. Aronson, 1994.

Re, Lucia. "Diotima's Dilemmas: Authorship, Authority, Authoritarianism." In *Italian Feminist Theory and Practice: Equality and Sexual Difference*, edited by Graziella Parati and Rebecca J. West, 50–74. Madison, NJ: Fairleigh Dickinson University Press, 2002.

Rempel, Henry. *A High Price for Abundant Living: The Story of Capitalism*. Waterloo, ON: Herald, 2003.

Reynolds, Matthew. "Ezra Pound in the Earthly Paradise." In *Dante and the Unorthodox: The Aesthetics of Transgression*, edited by James Miller, 316–66. Waterloo, ON: Wilfrid Laurier University Press, 2005.

Ricoeur, Paul. *The Course of Recognition*. Translated by David Pellauer. Cambridge, MA: Harvard University Press, 2005.

Rilke, Rainer Maria. *Translations from the Poetry of Rainer Maria Rilke*. Translated by Hester Norton. New York: W. W. Norton, 1938.

Rilke, Rainer Maria, and Lou Andreas-Salomé. *Rainer Maria Rilke and Lou Andreas-Salomé: The Correspondence*. Translated by Edward Snow and Michael Winkler. New York: W. W. Norton, 2006.

Rippin, Andrew. *Muslims: Their Religious Beliefs and Practices*. 2nd ed. London: Routledge, 2001.

Rogers, John. *The Matter of Revolution: Science, Poetry, and Politics in the Age of Milton*. Ithaca, NY: Cornell University Press, 1996.

Rohde, Erwin. *Psyche: The Cult of Souls and Belief in Immortality among the Greeks*. Translated by W. B. Hills. 2 vols. New York: Harper and Row, 1966.

Ross, Stephanie. *What Gardens Mean*. Chicago: University of Chicago Press, 1998.

Rowson, Everett K. and Abu al-Hasan Muhammad ibn Yusuf Amiri. *A Muslim Philosopher on the Soul and Its Fate: Al-Amiri's Kitab al-Amad ala l-abad.* New Haven, CT: American Oriental Society, 1988.

Russell, Jeffrey Burton. *A History of Heaven: The Singing Silence.* Princeton, NJ: Princeton University Press, 1997.

Saccone, Eduardo. "Wood, Garden, 'locus amoenus' in Ariosto's *Orlando Furioso.*" *MLN* 12, no. 1 (January 1997): 1–20.

Salerno, Roger A. *Landscapes of Abandonment: Capitalism, Modernity, and Estrangement.* Albany: State University of New York Press, 2003.

Salvadori, Patrizia. *Dominio e patronato: Lorenzo dei Medici e la Toscana nel Quattrocento.* Rome: Edizioni di Storia e Letteratura, 2000.

Sayre, Kenneth M. *Plato's Literary Garden.* Notre Dame, IN: Notre Dame University Press, 1995.

Scaglione, Aldo D. *Nature and Love in the Middle Ages.* Berkeley: University of California Press, 1963.

Schnapp, Jeffrey T. "'Si pïa l'ombra d'Anchise si porse': *Paradiso* 15.25." In *The Poetry of Allusion: Virgil and Ovid in Dante's "Commedia,"* edited by Rachel Jacoff and Jeffrey T. Schnapp. Stanford, CA: Stanford University Press, 1991.

———. *The Transfiguration of History at the Center of Dante's Paradise.* Princeton, NJ: Princeton University Press, 1986.

Schofield, Malcolm. *Plato: Political Philosophy.* Oxford: Oxford University Press, 2006.

Schubert, Peter Z. *The Narratives of Čapek and Cexov: A Typological Comparison of the Authors' Worldviews.* Bethesda, MD: International Scholars, 1997.

Schurmann, Reiner. *Heidegger on Being and Acting: From Principle to Anarchy.* Bloomington: Indiana University Press, 1990.

Scolnicov, Samuel. *Plato's Metaphysics of Education.* London: Routledge, 1988.

Sevenhuijsen, Selma. *Citizenship and the Ethics of Care: Feminist Considerations on Justice, Morality, and Politics.* New York: Routledge, 1998.

Shemek, Deanna. *Ladies Errant: Wayward Women and Social Order in Early Modern Italy.* Durham, NC: Duke University Press, 1998.

Shepherd, John C. *Italian Gardens of the Renaissance.* Princeton, NJ: Princeton Architectural Press, 1986.

Sicari, Stephen. "History and Vision in Pound and Dante: A Purgatorial Poetics." *Paideuma* 19 (Spring-Fall 1990): 9–35.

Skinner, Quentin. "The Republican Idea of Political Liberty." In *Machiavelli and Republicanism*, edited by Gisela Bock, Quentin Skinner, and Maurizio Viroli. Cambridge: Cambridge University Press, 1990.

Sperling, S. "Garden of Eden." In *Encyclopaedia Judaica*, ed. Michael Berenbaum and Fred Skonik, 7:388–89. 22 vols. 2nd ed. Detroit: Macmillan Reference USA, 2007.

Spronk, Klaas. *Beatific Afterlife in Ancient Israel and in the Ancient Near East.* Kevelaer, Germany: Butzon and Bercker, 1986.

Stendhal. *De l'amour.* Paris: Champion, 1926.

———. *Love.* Translated by Gilbert and Suzanne Sale. London: Penguin, 1957.

———. *Rome, Naples et Florence.* Paris: Champion, 1919.

Stenzel, Kurt. "Pascals Theorie des Divertissement." PhD diss., Ludwig-Maximilians-Universität, Munich, 1965.

Stevens, Wallace. *The Collected Poems.* New York: Vintage, 1990.

Stone, Gregory. *The Ethics of Nature in the Middle Ages: On Boccaccio's Poetaphysics.* New York: St. Martin's, 1998.

Svendsen, Lars. *A Philosophy of Boredom.* Translated by John Irons. London: Reaktion, 2005.

Swirski, Peter. *From Lowbrow to Nobrow.* Montréal: McGill-Queen's University Press, 2005.

Thirouin, Laurent. "Le cycle du divertissement." *Studi Francesi* 143, no. 2 (May-August 2004): 260–72.

Thompson, Ian H. *The Sun King's Garden: Louis XIV, André Le Nôtre, and the Creation of the Gardens of Versailles.* London: Bloomsbury, 2006.

Thoreau, Henry David. *Walden and Civil Disobedience.* New York: W. W. Norton, 1966.

Tigay, Jeffrey, and Bernard Bamberger. "Paradise." In *Encyclopaedia Judaica*, ed. Michael Berenbaum and Fred Skonik, 15:623–29. 22 vols. 2nd ed. Detroit: Macmillan Reference USA, 2007.

Tournier, Michel. *Gemini.* Translated by Anne Carter. Garden City, NY: Doubleday, 1981.

Trilling, Lionel. *Beyond Culture: Essays on Literature and Learning.* Uniform ed. New York: Harcourt Brace Jovanovich, 1978.

Tsao, Hsueh Sueh-Chin, and Ngo Kao. *The Dream of Red Mansions.* Translated by Hsien-Yi Yang and Gladys Yang. Boston: Cheng and Tsui, 1996.

Turner, Tom. *Garden History: Philosophy and Design, 2000 BC–2000 AD.* London: Spon, 2005.

Vakaloulis, Michel. *Le capitalisme post-moderne: Eléments pour une critique sociologique.* Paris: P.U.F., 2001.

Vergil. *The Aeneid of Virgil.* New York: Bantam, 1981.

Villa, Dana, ed. *The Cambridge Companion Guide to Hannah Arendt.* Cambridge: Cambridge University Press, 2000.

Visentini, Margherita Azzi, ed. *L'arte dei giardini: Scritti teorici e pratici dal XIV al XIX secolo.* 2 vols. Milan: Il Polifilo, 1999.

von Hassell, Malve. *The Struggle for Eden: Community Gardens in New York City.* Westport, CN: Bergin and Garvey, 2002.

Waines, David. *An Introduction to Islam.* 2nd ed. Cambridge: Cambridge University Press, 2003.

Walker, Daniel. *Flowers Underfoot: Indian Carpet Gardens of the Mughal Era.* New York: Metropolitan Museum of Art, 1997.

Warren, James. *Epicurus and Democritean Ethics: An Archaeology of Ataraxia.* Cambridge: Cambridge University Press, 2002.

Weiss, Allen. *Mirrors of Infinity: The French Formal Garden and Seventeenth-Century Metaphysics.* New York: Princeton Architectural, 1995.

———. *Unnatural Horizons: Paradox and Contradiction in Landscape Architecture.* New York: Princeton Architectural, 1998.

Wharton, Edith. *Italian Villas and Their Gardens.* Illustrated by Maxfield Parrish. New York: Century, 1904.

White, John Ernest Grant. *Garden Art and Architecture.* London: Abelard-Schuman, 1968.

Wilber, Donald Newton. *Persian Gardens and Garden Pavilions.* Washington, DC: Dumbarton Oaks, 1979.

Wilcher, Robert. *Andrew Marvell.* Cambridge: Cambridge University Press, 1985.

Wilner, Eleanor. *The Girl with Bees in Her Hair.* Port Townsend, WA: Copper Canyon, 2004.

Wilson, Edward O. *Biophilia.* Cambridge, MA: Harvard University Press, 1984.

Wilson, Peter L., and Bill Weinberg, eds. *Avant-Gardening: Ecological Struggle in the City and the World.* Broooklyn, NY: Autonomedia, 1999.

Winkler, John J. "The Laughter of the Oppressed: Demeter and the Gardens of Adonis." In *The Constraints of Desire: The Anthropology of Sex and Gender in Ancient Greece*, by John J. Winkler. New York: Routledge, 1990.

Witt, Ronald G. *In the Footsteps of the Ancients: The Origins of Humanism from Lovato to Bruni.* Leiden: Brill, 2000.

Wordsworth, William. *Selected Poetry of William Wordsworth.* Edited by Mark Van Doren. New York: Modern Library, 2001.

Yeats, William Butler. *The Collected Poems of W. B. Yeats.* Edited by Richard J. Finneran. New York: Scribner, 1996.

Zanker, Graham. *The Heart of Achilles: Characterization and Personal Ethics in the "Iliad."* Ann Arbor: University of Michigan Press, 1984.

Zerilli, Linda M. G. *Feminism and the Abyss of Freedom.* Chicago: University of Chicago Press, 2005.

INDEX

Page numbers in italics refer to illustrations.

Eden, Garden of
    carelessness and, 7–8
    in Dante's *Purgatorio*, 11, 21, 55,
        88–89, 144–45, 147, 155–56
    fall from, 8, 11–12, 14–24, 28,
        40–41, 157–58, 203
    Genesis account, 7–8
    lack of borders in, 57
    in Lowry's *Under the Volcano*,
        173–75
    medieval cloisters and, 97
    Qur'an's description of, 137–43, 194
    science-fiction visions and, 167–70
    Western aversion to, 148, 155–56,
        163–65
    Wilner's description of, 15–18
    See also paradises, earthly
education, mission of, 64–65
Elective Affinities (Goethe), 118
Eliot, T. S.
    concept of "objective correlative,"
        126, 214
    Four Quartets, 42, 46
elitism, Plato and, 65–66, 73
Elysium, 2, 3, 4, 11, 200
Empyrium, 11
End of Philosophy, The (Heidegger),
    165–66
Engels, Friedrich, *The Communist
    Manifesto*, 149–50
English landscape gardens, 86, 118
Epic of Gilgamesh, The, 1
Epicurean philosophy, 71–82, 160,
    210–11
    Boccaccio and, 83–85, 93
    concept of happiness in, 72–76,
        79–82, 85–86
    politics and, 72–73
    serenity and, 108, 136, 164
    virtues in, 76–79
    women viewed by, 93

Epicurus
    Garden School of, 72–82
    Little Epitome, 74–75
    Plato and, 71–73
    writings of, 210
Epicurus and His Philosophy (De Witt),
    210
epiekeia, 77
epiphanies, gardens as sites of, 55–56
eros, eroticism, 68–69, 88–90, 145–47
Euthydemus (Plato), 208–9
Eve, 3, 8, 14–24, 40–41
    as creator, 23–24
    initiative of, 15, 19–21, 30, 155
    as progenitor of humanity, 14, 24,
        175
Evening of the Holiday, The (Hazzard),
    126–28

felix culpa, 9, 163, 202
Ficino, Marsilio, 104–8
Flaubert, Gustave, 159–60
Florence
    Carregi Academy garden, 105–6
    humanism in, 97–108
    Medici palace garden, 102
    Rossi villa garden, 97–99, 104
Foucault, Michel, 74
Fouquet, Nicolas, 112
Four Quartets (Eliot), 42, 46
Fowlie, Wallace, 159
French gardens, 86, 109–13
friendship, as Epicurean virtue, 76
future, gardening as investment in,
    37, 118
Futurist Manifesto, The (Marinetti),
    160

"Garden, The" (Marvell), 119, 191–93
Garden of the Finzi-Continis, The (Bas-
    sani), 71

Garden School (Epicurus), 72–82,
160
Gardener's Year, The (Čapek), 25–37,
118, 166, 170–71, 204
gardening
care and, 6–8, 25–37, 129, 156–57,
166, 171
democracy and, 36
destruction and, 160–62
as investment in future, 37, 118
obsessiveness and, 26–28
gardens
academia and, 58, 59–82
agriculture and, 39–40
art and, 41, 56, 109
art of seeing and, 114–24
borders of, 56–57, 60, 67, 155
conviviality and, 45–46, 84
death and, 74–75
in *Decameron*, 84
destruction and, 47
as gateways to other worlds,
54–56
healing power of, 131–34
as human creations, 46–48
impermanence of, 39, 42–43
inward-looking, 97, 108
Islamic, 142, 194–97
lyrical, 52–58
as metaphor, 51, 59, 70, 142–43,
150
in *Orlando Furioso*, 152–54
outward-looking, 97–98, 108
pleasure and, 85–87
as pockets of repose, 42–43, 57–58,
124, 138
power and, 95–96, 102–8, 109–13
secret, 52
states of soul and, 125–34
structure of, 52–53, 95, 117–19
vices cultivated in, 111–13

vulnerability of, 129–31
See also specific names and types
Gemini (Tournier), 120–23, 128–29,
135–36, 147
generosity, as Epicurean virtue, 94
Giamatti, A. Bartlett, *The Earthly
Paradise and the Renaissance
Epic*, 155, 156
Giardini di pietra (Laureano), 40
Gilgamesh epic, 1
giving, cultivation and, 33–34
gluttony, ingratitude and, 79, 82, 160,
163–64
goals, setting, 158–59
Goethe, Johann Wolfgang von, *Elective Affinities*, 118
Gould, Stephen Jay, 33
gratitude, as Epicurean virtue, 78–79,
82, 93

Hades, 2, 3
happiness, Epicurean concept of,
72–76, 79–82, 85–86
Havel, Václav, 35
Hazzard, Shirley, *The Evening of the
Holiday*, 126–28
healing, gardens and, 131–34
Heidegger, Martin, 165–66, 171
Being and Time, 25, 200
Helen of Troy, 2
Hesiod, 200
Highgrove Carpet Garden, Glouces-
tershire, 195
homeless gardens, 41–48
Homer, *Odyssey*, 2, 4–7, 12–13,
152–53, 155, 200
homo, concept of, 6, 10, 25, 28, 33
hope, as Epicurean virtue, 78, 82
Howard, Burt Estes, 206
Howard, Sarah, 206
Hrabal, Bohumil, 35